P9-CEH-743

ADDITIONAL PRAISE FOR *CONSCIOUS LEADERSHIP*

"Developing leaders who know how to do the right thing—to lead with integrity—is of critical importance as the global economy evolves and organizations face new challenges. John Mackey and his co-authors have made an important contribution to the conversation about how to lead."

—**Jeff Wilke**, CEO of Worldwide Consumer, Amazon

"This important book, full of inspiring examples, lays out a path by which leaders can develop themselves so that their companies are not only more sustainably successful, but also become active contributors to a better world."

—**Tony Schwartz**, bestselling author of *The Way We're Working Isn't Working* and CEO of The Energy Project

"John Mackey is a proven innovator and leader. Here he shares insights from evolution and psychology as well as his own experience and that of others in business to set out with clarity and eloquence what it means to lead with love, purpose, and integrity." —**Matt Ridley**, author of *How Innovation Works*

"This is one of the best leadership books I have ever read. It is a manual for creating value and doing the right thing."

—**Ed Freeman**, professor at UVA's Darden School of Business and author of *The Power of And*

"This book clearly integrates both the world of personal growth and the world of business, presenting a path forward that each of us can travel to fulfill our highest purpose. If you want to contribute to the world at the highest level, this is the book to read!"

—**Doug Rauch**, former president of Trader Joe's, founder of Daily Table

"Rarely does a book move me to tears, yet this one did, by holding up a mirror to the kind of leader I most deeply want to be. *Conscious Leadership* is a powerful invitation to shift our mindset from the win/lose games of war to the community-building virtues of love, authenticity, and integrity. It is a book built on the radical idea that business can be a force for bringing more love into the world. Count me in." —**Brian Robertson**, creator of Holacracy

"John Mackey and his co-authors bring a rich assortment of my favorite type of leadership lessons—*experiential* ones, sometimes learned from the school of hard knocks. Especially for anyone who's never heard the phrase 'conscious leadership' before, these pages provide a master class."

—**David Gardner**, co-founder of The Motley Fool

"*Conscious Leadership* brings deep and important insights in business and consciousness. It gives both women and men permission to lean into their feminine and masculine, critical traits of a conscious leader. A must read."

—**Radha Agrawal**, co-founder and CEO of Daybreaker, co-founder of THINX, and bestselling author of *Belong*

"The most important essence of *Conscious Leadership* is how a reader can think about their life and our society filtered through the wisdom represented on these pages. You will finish this book aspiring for greater outcomes for us all."

—**Bob Greifeld**, former CEO of Nasdaq, chairman of Virtu Financial

"In the same way that John Mackey revolutionized grocery shopping, he's taken on leadership—infusing it with decidedly non-corporate yet consummately human notions of love, compassion, and self-development. The result is a Leadership Bible of sorts. Whether you aspire to launch a start up, run a Fortune 100 company, or simply raise conscious children, you *must* read this book."

—**Dan Buettner**, National Geographic fellow, founder of Blue Zones, and multiple *New York Times*–bestselling author

"This book is a revelation and a revolution. It helped me deeply align with my purpose, ask myself the important questions of what kind of leader I want to be, and remind myself that it's okay to constantly evolve."

—**Miki Agrawal**, founder of TUSHY, THINX, and Wild, and author of #1 bestsellers *Disrupt-Her* and *Do Cool Shit*

"Leaders today are called to a faster pace, sharper strategy, and broader responsibilities, but also to greater awareness, humility, and authenticity. *Conscious Leadership* will help you summon the courage to open your heart, dig deeper, and keep growing as a conscious leader."

—**Walter Robb**, principal of Stonewall Robb, former co-CEO of Whole Foods Market

"*Conscious Leadership* is about the presence, energy, and mindset a leader brings to everything he or she does, and how that ripples out to make a difference. This is the kind of leadership the world is calling for, and this book provides a road map for becoming that kind of leader."

—**Alexander McCobin**, CEO of Conscious Capitalism, Inc.

CONSCIOUS LEADERSHIP

CONSCIOUS LEADERSHIP

Elevating Humanity Through Business

JOHN MACKEY
STEVE MCINTOSH
CARTER PHIPPS

PORTFOLIO / PENGUIN

Portfolio / Penguin
An imprint of Penguin Random House LLC
penguinrandomhouse.com

Library of Congress Cataloging-in-Publication Data

Names: Mackey, John, 1954- author. | McIntosh, Steve, author. |
Phipps, Carter, author.
Title: Conscious leadership : elevating humanity through business /
John Mackey, Steve McIntosh, Carter Phipps.
Description: New York : Portfolio, 2020. |
Includes bibliographical references and index.
Identifiers: LCCN 2020023547 (print) | LCCN 2020023548 (ebook) |
ISBN 9780593083628 (hardcover) | ISBN 9780593083635 (ebook)
Subjects: LCSH: Social responsibility of business. | Business ethics. |
Capitalism—Moral and ethical aspects. | Corporations—Moral
and ethical aspects. | Social values.
Classification: LCC HD60 .M286 2020 (print) |
LCC HD60 (ebook) | DDC 658.4/08—dc23
LC record available at https://lccn.loc.gov/2020023547
LC ebook record available at https://lccn.loc.gov/2020023548

ISBN 9780593189214 (international edition)

Printed in the United States of America
1 3 5 7 9 10 8 6 4 2

BOOK DESIGN BY ELLEN CIPRIANO

To all the conscious leaders I have worked with at Whole Foods, especially Walter Robb, Glenda Flanagan, A.C. Gallo, Jim Sud, Jason Buechel, Sonya Gafsi Oblisk, and Keith Manbeck.

—John Mackey

To my beloved wife, Tehya McIntosh, and our two beautiful sons, Ian and Peter. And to the conscious leaders of the future.

—Steve McIntosh

To the many individuals who have taught me—through their courage, wisdom, and insight, as well as their struggles and challenges—the immense value of conscious leadership.

—Carter Phipps

CONTENTS

INTRODUCTION: My Awakening to Conscious Leadership, by John Mackey xi

PART I: VISION & VIRTUE

1. Put Purpose First 3
2. Lead with Love 25
3. Always Act with Integrity 53

PART II: MINDSET & STRATEGY

4. Find Win-Win-Win Solutions 79
5. Innovate and Create Value 101
6. Think Long Term 127

PART III: PEOPLE & CULTURE

7. Constantly Evolve the Team 155
8. Regularly Revitalize 181
9. Continuously Learn and Grow 203

APPENDIX: ON CULTIVATING CULTURAL INTELLIGENCE 229

ACKNOWLEDGMENTS 235

NOTES 237

INDEX 245

INTRODUCTION

My Awakening to Conscious Leadership

John Mackey

AS THE PLANE TOUCHED DOWN in Florida in January of 2001 and I looked out over a world of palm trees and sunshine, I knew my life had come to a crossroads. I wasn't here for a vacation, although I could have used one. I was here at the behest of the Whole Foods Market board of directors. My job and my future were on the line. At a meeting planned for the next day, I was going to be interviewed, along with the other members of the company's executive team, as part of an investigation intended to determine who should lead the company into the future. Would I remain as CEO of the company I had co-founded in 1978 and shepherded for more than two decades? Or would I be asked to step aside and make way for a new leader? The answer was far from clear.

As I disembarked the plane and got my bags, I felt somewhat numb. The prospect of losing so much of my life's work hung heavily over me, and even Florida's sun-drenched beauty couldn't dispel the psychological clouds that darkened my disposition. How had it come to this? Driving away from the airport, I reflected on the series of events that had culminated in this difficult day.

Only a couple of years earlier, the internet boom of the nineties had been in its maximum ascendency. Like many during the era, our team recognized the profound disruptions that were coming to the retail market as a result of the online revolution. It was exciting; it was transformative; it was all happening fast. How could we be part of it? Looking back on those heady days, I can also admit that, like many others, we were a bit caught up in the moment. We drank our own version of the internet Kool-Aid.

At Whole Foods Market, we hatched a plan to get out in front of the dot-com revolution. We had a loyal, growing customer base that was passionate about natural and organic foods. Why wouldn't they also be interested in a natural, organic lifestyle? In fact, the LOHAS market (lifestyles of health and sustainability) was the hot new sector at the time. And we had a direct pipeline to the wants and needs of those influential consumers. So we decided to make a significant online move. We bought a mail order nutritional supplement firm in Boulder, Colorado, named Amrion and launched WholePeople.com. We took on some venture capital to help fund the initiative. We set about selling food, supplements, books, clothing, travel—everything our target market wanted, and all of it available in one place: online.

To focus on this new project, I moved to Boulder to lead Whole People.com. Of course, I still kept one eye on the larger company, but most of my day-to-day attention was on the extraordinary possibilities of this new venture. I'm an entrepreneur at heart, and after many years growing Whole Foods Market into a large national company, it energized me to be back in startup mode.

The saga of WholePeople.com, which ultimately failed, is its own longer story. Our timing was not ideal, the expense of getting the enterprise off the ground proved excessive, and as the dot-com boom turned into the dot-com bust, it became clear that the business was facing dimmer prospects and a much, much longer, more difficult runway than we had anticipated. It simply wasn't going to be the out-of-the-gate success that we had hoped for. Moreover, our shareholders didn't like the internet initiative, and our share price over that period reflected their distaste. As the internet bubble deflated, it became clear to me and my team that it was time to refocus on what already made Whole Foods wonderful.

In late 2000, we sold a majority ownership in WholePeople.com to the lifestyle brand Gaiam, and I returned to Austin, ready to get back to leading our well-established company. What I didn't anticipate was that a coup was afoot. One of my most trusted leaders on our executive team, plus two members of our board of directors, had decided that this was the moment to replace me, and a battle for control was under way. My job and my future were suddenly in doubt. I wasn't in the envious position that some entrepreneurs enjoy these days, with special super-voting shares and de facto control over their company. Despite having co-founded and built Whole Foods from the ground up, I owned a relatively minor percentage of shares. In other words, I served at the pleasure of the board of directors. But I still had supporters on the board, and I was very close to most of the executive team—many of whom had been with the company since its early days. Together we had helped build the company into the natural foods behemoth that it had become. I was shocked by this turn of events but still hoped I could convince the board that I was, in fact, the right person to continue to lead the company into the future.

In Florida, knowing there was not much more I could do to prepare for the fateful meeting the following day, I decided to do what I always do when traveling and take the time to tour our local stores. As I walked the aisles, stocked with an abundance of healthy, natural food, and as I spoke to the team members who were doing incredible work on the ground, the clouds lifted for the first time in weeks. The mission of Whole Foods reawakened for me, in all of its clarity and relevance. *This* was what our company was about—not boardroom battles or dreams of dot-com success. This was the heart of Whole Foods—beautiful stores filled with smiling team members, working hard to support our customers in their quest to eat the healthiest and most delicious natural foods possible. This was what I loved; it was my passion and my calling. This was why I'd been inspired to start the company all those years before. I felt my own purpose renewed. At forty-seven, I was just entering my prime leadership years. There was so much left to do. I deeply wanted to continue to build this amazing company; I only hoped I would have the opportunity to do so.

When I entered the board meeting late that afternoon, I was still very much in an altered state. The transmission of love and purpose that I had received from the Whole Foods team members I encountered was still fresh, and my anxiety about the challenge I faced had completely evaporated. The board asked me many questions, which I answered from my heart. I didn't defend myself or try to prove anything. I just authentically shared my passion and my conviction in the power and potential of Whole Foods, and my commitment to go forward with the company into the new millennium.

The meeting ended and I flew back to Austin, where I awaited the board's decision. But I didn't just wait. A new realization was dawning on me. Whatever the result of their deliberations, it had become apparent that I needed to grow and change. The entire episode was a wake-up call. My leadership style had to evolve. I was called to step up to a much greater degree of care for the company I had co-founded. Part of the debacle I was facing, I realized, was my own fault. I wasn't just facing an external challenge to my leadership—there was an internal challenge to be confronted as well. I had shied away from being the confident and conscious leader the company needed me to be. In fact, my unwillingness to take that necessary growth step had created a leadership vacuum, and I had been all too willing to let others step in and fill that void—people who had the drive to be in charge but not necessarily the right skills, motives, or care. When one doesn't appropriately step up and take the reins of effective conscious leadership, that vacuum is inevitably filled by people who want power, and not always for the right reasons.

If I wanted to continue to lead Whole Foods into its bright future, I needed to grow and evolve as a conscious leader. I had to take a deeper responsibility for this billion-dollar company I had co-created. That didn't mean I had to micromanage everything—not at all. I've always had an entrepreneurial focus and been good at keeping my attention on the big picture. But in some fundamental way, I had to fully embrace the role of CEO in all its responsibility and power, and that also meant putting a healthy, productive team around me that represented an effective complement to my strengths rather than an abdication of responsibility. I had to up my game in all kinds of ways.

Over the next several weeks, I did a lot of soul-searching. I spoke frankly with close friends and mentors; I journaled; I read; I meditated; I engaged in some powerful therapeutic techniques. Through these processes, I came to appreciate even more deeply the transformations I needed to personally undergo. I was at a critical transition point; it was no time for halfway measures. The CEO I had been up through 2000 was finished. It was time to become a deeper, wiser, more confident, and more conscious leader.

In many respects, my own journey of conscious leadership greatly accelerated that day in Florida. I went from riding the momentum of my natural skills and entrepreneurial passion to becoming a truly conscious CEO, capable of effectively leading a multi-billion-dollar public company into the future. We are all born with certain talents and qualities of character, some of which make for effective leadership. I certainly had some innate strengths, but like most people, I definitely had some weaknesses as well. And I found out, like many who have gone before me, that being a *conscious* leader is something quite different. It means embarking upon an intentional journey of development. It means purposefully stepping up to a much higher level of integrity and responsibility. This book was born out of everything I learned walking down that path.

In those dark days of 2000, when it temporarily seemed like I might lose everything, I came upon the recognition of the necessity of my own conscious leadership for Whole Foods. It was almost too late. Thankfully, not quite. Soon I got a call from a board member letting me know that the decision had been made to keep me as CEO. But that wasn't all. They wanted to make a number of changes—in the executive team, the board of directors, and the structure of the organization. *Good,* I thought to myself. *I do, too.*

Since that day, Whole Foods has grown from doing about $1 billion in annual sales to more than $19 billion annually. In large part, it was the team we put in place in 2001 that oversaw that remarkable period of progress. Whole Foods survived and thrived through those years largely because of the decisions we made after my leadership crisis and awakening. They weren't strategic decisions about market share and products. That would all come later. They were decisions about leadership and people—about who was going to shepherd the company we all loved into a bright future, and the kind of leaders we were all going to become in the process.

Out of that dark night came a bright morning. This book is a tribute to that morning light, and my conviction that with the right attitude and approach to leadership, it can shine for all of us.

WHY WE WROTE THIS BOOK

I first articulated my understanding of conscious leadership as part of a larger project: the book *Conscious Capitalism*, which I co-authored with Raj Sisodia and published in 2013. That book helped catalyze a global movement toward changing the way the world thinks about business, and the way business thinks about itself. It showed that capitalism can be a great force for good in the world. I'm proud that the book has become a bestseller; been translated into a dozen languages; become cultural shorthand for an elevated way of doing business; and inspired leaders and entrepreneurs all over the world to uplift their companies, communities, and countries. In fact, in 2019, Business Roundtable—a collective of CEOs from America's largest companies, responsible for more than fifteen million team members and more than $7 trillion in annual revenues—issued a formal statement that would have been unimaginable even a decade earlier. In it, they redefined the purpose of a corporation as being to benefit not just shareholders but all stakeholders, including customers, team members, suppliers, and communities.[1]

As I travel around the world speaking about Conscious Capitalism, I've noticed something interesting. Among all the important themes the book addressed, there has been a consistent favorite among my audiences: conscious leadership. Readers love what we said on that topic, and they want more. *Conscious Leadership* is the long-awaited answer to those many, many requests.

It's also a response to something that has become ever more clear to me in the years since we published *Conscious Capitalism*: the major limiting factor, both in changing the narrative about business and evolving the behavior of business, is that we need tens of thousands more conscious leaders. It's a well-established truth that an organization's potential is constrained by the abilities of its leader. (John Maxwell called this "the law of the lid.") So if our goal is for business to become more conscious, there is no escaping the imperative for leaders to step up to the challenge personally. And more and more leaders are doing just that. Just as I felt compelled to rise up and embrace a deeper responsibility and care for Whole Foods Market, leaders around the world, in every industry, are responding to the same inner calling. You'll hear many of their voices in the pages ahead. They hail from a diversity of sectors—from retail to commercial real estate to manufacturing to healthcare to technology to venture capital. But they echo the same passions and the same commitment to personal growth *and* organizational transformation.

Leadership has always presented challenges, but today, amid our rapidly changing global economy, those challenges are truly monumental. Technology is proving increasingly disruptive, global competition is ever present, generational shifts in the workplace are complicating organizational culture, and changing attitudes about the responsibilities of business are putting more pressure on leaders. The sheer diversity of issues that any CEO must respond to requires the wisdom of Buffett, the assertiveness of Churchill, the creativity of Jobs, the emotional intelligence of Oprah, and the patience of Mandela! No individual perfectly meets these multiple demands, but the best learn an invaluable lesson: that leadership is an ongoing journey of service, not a static position of power. Most important, there is always room for further development.

It isn't easy to become a more conscious leader. It's not enough to simply follow rules or adopt the latest leadership fashions. The term *conscious* implies being more thoughtful, more awake, and more intentional in our embrace of our role and the responsibilities it confers. It's a word one might more readily associate with personal growth, spirituality, or philosophy than with professional development. And that's precisely the point: conscious leadership is first and foremost an inner journey of character development and personal transformation, informed by a powerful understanding of human nature and human culture. It is for this reason that when the time came to write this book, I chose two co-authors whom I've come to respect for their deep knowledge and experience in traversing this terrain.

Steve McIntosh and Carter Phipps are both independent and astute thinkers whose insights and wisdom I've turned to repeatedly in my own endeavors to become more conscious. Steve and Carter cofounded the nonprofit Institute for Cultural Evolution, and I joined the board and help support it financially. Moreover, their writings helped inspire the vision of Conscious Capitalism, and gave me new perspectives on my own inner life and the challenges I faced as a leader. They're well versed in the workings of business, but, more important, they've both delved deeply into the realms of personal and cultural transformation. The three of us share a passion for helping cultural evolution to advance in constructive and dynamic ways, and we all realize that conscious leadership is one of the keys to this kingdom.

To some extent, what conscious leadership means and looks like for each individual will be different. However, in our conversations and interactions with hundreds of men and women, we've uncovered nine distinguishing characteristics and behaviors that unite those leaders whom we recognize as striving to be more conscious. For the purposes of this book, we have organized these into three categories.

Vision & Virtue

Conscious leaders **put purpose first**, guided not only by profit but by a vision for the value they can contribute to the world. They **lead with love**—treating business not as cutthroat competition but as an opportunity to serve and uplift people and communities. And they strive to **always act with integrity**, holding themselves to the highest standards in order to earn the trust of those they lead and those they serve.

Mindset & Strategy

Conscious leaders are determined to **find win-win-win solutions** to every challenge. They **innovate and create value**, and build cultures around them that nurture and liberate the creative spirit. They are not blinkered by short-termism; they **think long term** about the impact of their actions and choices.

People & Culture

Conscious leaders are sensitive to the culture around them and work to **constantly evolve the team**. They recognize how important it is to **regularly revitalize**—renewing their own physical, mental, emotional, and spiritual energy. And they have a commitment to **continually learn and grow**, both personally and professionally.

Our business community—and our world—has never been in greater need of conscious leaders. Indeed, it is not only companies that need conscious leaders, but governments, nonprofits, educational institutions, the military, and more. While the examples in this book are drawn primarily from business, our intention is that the principles and practices we share can be applied in any sector. When leaders become more conscious, the organizations they lead become more conscious, creating an ever-widening circle of purpose-driven cultures and communities. We elevate business through our humanity, and we elevate humanity through business. In this way, everyone wins.

PART I

VISION & VIRTUE

PUT PURPOSE FIRST

> If you love your work, you'll be out there every day trying to do it the best you possibly can, and pretty soon everybody around will catch the passion from you—like a fever.
>
> —SAM WALTON

IT WAS A FINE DAY. Not a cloud in the sky, some witnesses observed. A large crowd had gathered to hear a great orator deliver his remarks on the graveyard of a momentous battle. For a people torn asunder by violence and suffering, the ceremony offered a chance to find some thread of hope among the ghosts of the fallen. How to weave the threads of war into a meaningful tapestry of redemption and renewal? What purpose could be found on the other side of such pain?

As thousands watched, the greatest orator of the day began his remarks. For more than two hours he spoke, recalling the details of battle, placing it in the pantheon of history, and appealing to his audience's emotion and patriotism. By all accounts, he was inspiring, erudite, and powerful. He then turned over the stage to another speaker, and a second address—this one shorter, simpler, plainer. Instead of a few hours, it lasted a few minutes. Afterward, with the audience in reverent silence, its author was concerned that his words had been poorly received. He needn't have worried. The first address of the day would end up an afterthought of history; the second constitutes 272 of the most remembered words ever uttered.

A great purpose—whether for a company or a country—is simple. When Abraham Lincoln looked out on the crowd gathered at Gettysburg on that November day in 1863 and read from the small paper on which was inscribed the Gettysburg Address, he articulated—simply, beautifully, unforgettably—the purpose of the nation, and of the Union. He articulated its mission, its history, and the larger context of its current struggles. As any great purpose can do, it galvanized, energized, and helped unify a troubled, divided people. It showed a way forward and touched upon the higher chords of our common humanity.

Lincoln had many notable strengths as a leader. But perhaps the most exceptional—the one that ultimately guided and empowered his other strengths—was his deep and unyielding commitment to a higher purpose. He used the calamitous fires of the Civil War to hone and refine that purpose into a statement that all Americans could embrace and understand. His renewed articulation of America's founding mandate—a unique nation dedicated to the liberty and equality of all people—has been a wellspring of cultural solidarity and national identity for Americans ever since.

Whether they know it or not, every person and every organization has the potential to embrace, enact, and unify people around a higher purpose. It may not require the oratorical skills of Lincoln or rise to the historical significance of the Gettysburg Address, but it is there. Great leaders and enduring enterprises are built on higher purpose as surely as great buildings are built on solid, sturdy foundations. It might be present at the very beginning; it might be discovered, cultivated, and developed over time. But one way or another, purpose is foundational. For an individual, it provides the direction and motivation to funnel the activities of life into ever more fruitful endeavors. For an organization or institution, a higher purpose provides the shaping context that transforms a collection of individual human beings into an organized, productive, creative, engaged workforce.

The first and foremost job of every conscious leader, as Lincoln knew, is to *connect people to purpose*. A leader's job is to ensure that, amid all the complexity of daily activity, purpose shines brightly—that it remains vital and relevant, a guiding context, both ethically and practically. This entails more than just believing in our organization's higher purpose. A conscious leader embodies it, and lives it out in a way that makes that purpose vivid and exciting. As exemplified by the way in which Lincoln once rallied a nation—simply, humbly, resolutely—conscious leaders infuse their organization's purpose with authenticity and meaning. They make it come alive, in little ways and big ways, every day. Their passion for purpose can become a touchstone for those around them. They demonstrate and embody the "why" of an organization. And they show a reasonable pathway to "how."

A LEADER'S JOURNEY TO PURPOSE

Before there are organizations, there are individuals. Before there was a company called Patagonia, there was a young man named Yvon who cared deeply about climbing and wilderness, and struggled to find the right clothes to match his hobby. In the days before there was a movie studio named Disney, there was a young animator named Walt, hawking his wares in Hollywood, who was passionate about sketching and cartoons. In the nineteenth century, when the environmental movement was barely a thought in the cultural mind, and the Sierra Club was years away from its founding, there was a young explorer and lover of nature named John Muir who collected and cataloged plants in the (then) wilds of Ontario. And long before there was Whole Foods, there was an idealistic twenty-three-year-old man who found an unexpected home and a newfound passion for natural food in a countercultural, vegetarian collective.

For every company purpose statement that adorns the lobby wall or company website, there was once an individual nurturing inner visions and fumbling around with novel ideas and approaches. But how does one discover a higher purpose? How does a future conscious leader take the first step on that journey? Before a leader can put purpose first, they have to discover exactly what that purpose may be. For most, that process begins with some type of passion or curiosity, the natural pursuit of one's life interests. That may be a highly intentional process, or it may seem almost accidental, bouncing from one interest to another with no obvious or discernible path—at least initially. We don't come out of adolescence understanding what makes us tick, and most of us have barely begun finding our purpose. It's not something that comes attached to a college degree or a twenty-first-birthday card. Of course, there are always some who know exactly what they want to do, and why, from an early age—more power to them. But for most future leaders, finding purpose is not so simple—a fumbling, perhaps half-conscious exploration of talents, capacities, values, and curiosities.

"Don't ask kids what they want to do when they grow up. Ask them what they love to do,"[1] Roy Spence, founder of the Purpose Institute, likes to say. Sometimes the best way to start is by simply following our own individual inclinations, with some degree of conviction and commitment. The things we are drawn to really are windows into our souls, and they can lead us down unexpected paths that may surprise us with unforeseen opportunity.

At some point along the journey of self-discovery, a purpose begins to reveal itself. A "true north" begins to appear on one's internal compass. It might be bright and vivid, or it may slowly emerge, frame by frame, over time. But eventually a path, or at least a direction, can be seen. A critical journey has begun. And, for the conscious leader, something else has happened: a dialogue has been initiated between the core passions of their own heart and the intentional activities of their life.

That dialogue, like an engine, will generate the animating energy for the journey of a conscious leader. It may lead us forward on one singular, straightforward path, or it may become the foundation of several distinct, evolving, and overlapping ones. It may even inspire us to take a leap into the unknown, to build something new, make something great, learn something obscure, create something beautiful, or start something that makes the world a better place. A life in pursuit of higher purpose is rarely safe, easy, or predictable. It usually requires venturing out beyond the safe harbors of comfort and security and engaging the world in new ways. It may involve emotional disruption, personal challenges, or other significant developmental hurdles. Most important, there is every chance that the person who arrives at the other end of the journey of purpose will be entirely different from the one who began. Such are the risks and rewards of a life lived in pursuit of purpose. It offers satisfaction, significance, success, and empowerment. But it demands independence, courage, change, development, and sacrifice.

As a purpose begins to come into focus, a new question arises: *How do I best express this purpose in the world?* That is, how does one take the nascent aspirations of the heart and turn them into demonstrable attributes of a life? For some, that question has an obvious answer. If you feel a calling to heal, some form of medicine is likely in your future. If you feel a passion to understand the deeper nature of the physical universe, there are plenty of astrophysics departments that will channel that aspiration. But for others, it's not so simple. The long and winding road taken by many entrepreneurs is testimony to the fact that discovering our purpose and finding a way to express it in the world of business is a journey and not simply a destination. Phil Knight had the inspiration, back in his days at Stanford, to sell inexpensive, quality shoes to running enthusiasts like himself. But he had no idea of the extraordinarily circuitous route that would eventually lead him all around the world before he founded the most successful and inspirational sports brand in history, Nike. Richard Branson was a hippie, a music lover with a passion for business, and he followed his interests and instincts on a very eclectic route through multiple industries—magazines, music, airlines, cola, finance—until he had finally built one of the most successful and purpose-driven collections of companies in the world. In his case, the higher purpose wasn't the specific product or service; it was the act of shaking up the status quo—disrupting entrenched industries and, in so doing, making a difference in people's lives. Having that clear sense of purpose, Branson points out, was hugely significant in his success—much more so than a desire to make money.[2]

Leaders like Knight and Branson are able to take the individual pursuit of a higher purpose and turn it into a collective aspiration. It can become so powerful and so intentional that it draws others into its wake—hundreds, thousands, perhaps even millions. What starts out as a fumbling search for the sweet spot between talent, passion, market opportunity, and a higher calling can evolve into something much greater than any one individual. Lincoln didn't set out at the beginning of his political career to change the direction of the country and put an end to slavery. But over time, his growing commitment became so strong that it roused a nation to a new sense of its destiny. A personal purpose can grow to inspire an entire organization, a movement, a community, even a country. What starts out as one person's search for meaning ends up infused with such collective power and energy that others find their own lives enriched by participating in the journey.

LOVE, DESIGN, AND FURNITURE

When Shawn David Nelson stood on Nasdaq's iconic MarketSite in June of 2018 and rang the opening bell to celebrate his company's IPO, the purpose-driven nature of his online furniture company was clear and unambiguous. Lovesac, as he named his upstart business, sells furniture that is "designed for life," meaning that it is built with sustainable, recyclable materials, and also that it's modular, changeable, and upgradeable. It can adjust as life changes and, in so doing, allow customers to keep their furniture longer, saving millions of tons of waste from the landfill every year and pushing back against the concept of planned obsolescence. Today Nelson is passionate and articulate about the principles that inform his company, but he didn't start Lovesac with that purpose back when he was just a clean-cut Mormon kid making plans in his college dorm in the nineties. Such high-minded concerns were low on the priority list when he spent two obligatory years on his Mormon mission to Taiwan and worked around the clock to get the company off the ground in his early twenties. In those days, he wanted to pursue his entrepreneurial passion, enjoy life, and make the world's biggest beanbag (filled with recycled foam), which he designed in his teens. But something happened on the road to selling thousands of Lovesacs and having a good time doing it. Little by little, Nelson's own deeper reason for running the business began to come into view.

For leaders who are conscious and who care about the world around them, purpose has a way of catching up with them. Even if, at first, it's just a few seeds of interest, over time it will evolve, deepen, and expand. A voracious reader, Nelson came across theorist Victor Papanek's work on ecologically sensitive design. As he considered what it might take to apply those concepts to the design and production of furniture, he read William McDonough and Michael Braungart's *The Upcycle: Beyond Sustainability—Designing for Abundance*. "Human beings don't have a pollution problem, they have a design problem,"[3] the authors write.

Inspired and challenged, Nelson took their words to heart. The young entrepreneur was struck by the idea of building a different kind of furniture company, one that could massively reduce landfill usage and negative waste by-products. Furniture, he discovered, is particularly culpable in our waste stream, accounting for a third of what we put into landfills each year. Could a furniture business help reinvent the supply chain for a more sustainable economy? As Lovesac went through the ups and downs of trying to make it in the ultracompetitive retail furniture industry, Nelson's perspective on his company matured and he honed his sense of purpose. As he found his purpose, his company found its footing. As the company aligned around this renewed vision, it found increasing success.

Today, Lovesac is one of the fastest-growing furniture companies in the country, pioneering a new type of design and infused with a sense of purpose in doing business differently. And the onetime missionary who founded it is on fire with a new sense of mission—upending business as usual in the massive furniture industry.

Purpose is an evolutionary journey. That's true whether we are talking about individuals or companies. But sometimes we need to walk through the wilderness to find a sense of direction. And even when it's found, it must be rediscovered, remembered, reinvented, and renewed. In that sense, purpose is a living thing. In fact, it's not really a "thing" at all, but a process. It's not an object that we "find," but an ongoing discovery that unfolds throughout our lives. For most conscious companies and leaders, purpose will continue to deepen and expand over time.

Experts have even suggested that the mistaken notion that purpose is "out there" waiting to be found is a source of confusion that proves counterproductive for young leaders. Carol Dweck, the Stanford psychology professor and bestselling author of *Mindset*, recently led a research team that concluded that our personal passions and interests almost always need to be developed gradually.[4] While some rare individuals might manage to tap into a deeper purpose that immediately consumes them, for most of us it's something that must be intentionally cultivated. Like the capacity for leadership itself, purpose is not something we are either born with or not. Purpose is a lifelong practice.

PRACTICING PURPOSE: Commune with Your Heroes

Who are your heroes? What quotes remind you of your own purpose? What books have changed your life? Whose stories have moved you to new action? A key part of the pursuit of higher purpose is simply returning to the original sources of your inspiration—for renewal, connection, and communion. Perhaps you have a favorite inspirational handbook to contemplate or a tale of personal breakthrough. Maybe you prefer to meditate on the words of a beloved author or commune with a great historical figure through a book or movie. Some read the Bible, the Koran, or the Bhagavad Gita. Some hang portraits of their heroes in their home or office. We have honored many of our heroes in these pages, including Abraham Lincoln, with whom we began this chapter. One of the leaders we interviewed, who shares our admiration for Lincoln, reads Doris Kearns Goodwin's *Team of Rivals* whenever he feels disconnected from his higher purpose, finding new depths of wisdom in each return. However you commune with your heroes, don't take them for granted. Make it an honored, sacred practice. Elevate its significance in your life. When the going gets rough and the way forward seems murky, the conscious leader finds wisdom in the guidance of those who have walked the path of purpose before.

PURPOSE POWERS PROFITS: THE ENGINE OF CONSCIOUS CAPITALISM

Many people have a hard time relating the idea of a higher or transcendent purpose to a business enterprise. Indeed, the very distinction between for-profits and nonprofits captures the way we tend to think: businesses are seen as dedicated to making a profit for their shareholders (which is all too often interpreted as greed), while purpose-driven organizations by definition don't intend to make money at all. We expect organizations like the Humane Society, the Nature Conservancy, or Doctors Without Borders to be guided by noble aims and altruistic motives rather than the desire to maximize revenue. Purpose and profit, in too many minds, are mutually exclusive—if we choose to serve one, the thinking goes, the other must be abandoned. Over the past few decades, there have been some laudable and important attempts to find a middle ground, such as the creation of new business categories like B Corps and the triple bottom line framework, but this binary attitude still persists, especially in our age of anti-corporate sentiment.

At the heart of Conscious Capitalism is a radical refutation of the negative perceptions of business, and a rejection of the split between purpose and profit. It claims that the two need not be mutually exclusive, that contained in the very heart of the profit-making activity is the potential of realizing a positive purpose and elevating that higher purpose to an ever more important place in the enterprise. In other words, there is the seed of a higher purpose in most business endeavors, and when a leader recognizes that and elevates its importance, the economic and social benefits of that business expand exponentially.

We hear a lot today about transforming business or reforming capitalism, but too often this is something that we are only imposing from the outside—as if a for-profit business is a fundamentally amoral or even reprehensible activity that we just hope to dress up to look better at parties, rather than an activity that can have intrinsic benefit. There is, of course, nothing wrong with all the many avenues through which business uses its largesse to do good in the world—charitable works, community service, environmental activism, local investment, or other forms of societal good that it may adopt on top of its profit-making activity. These activities are fundamentally positive and deserve our appreciation and applause. But it's unfortunate if our efforts at reform end up being an apology for business rather than an affirmation and an elevation of its inherent potential.

Nothing motivates people or transforms organizations like the possibility of discovering a higher purpose embedded in the essential work of the enterprise itself. For a conscious leader, this motivation is foundational. There are many pathways to leadership in Conscious Capitalism, but all of them involve pursuing, recognizing, affirming, and elevating the intrinsic higher purpose of the organization so that it can reach its full potential—both in impact *and* in profit.

So how does one discover or uncover the higher purpose of a business? For many organizations, it is clearly envisioned by the founders at the outset. Whole Foods Market, for example, was born from a passion to make natural and healthy food widely available to people, and this North Star has continued to guide the company for more than forty years. There are plenty of other successful companies, however, that discerned their higher purpose only once they became established. And even companies that start out with a clear higher purpose often end up evolving it as they grow. A higher purpose is like a living thing: it must be nurtured and frequently reaffirmed in the context of new challenges and opportunities. At every step of the journey, it is the leader's role to seek, refine, and champion that purpose. And for many conscious leaders, the organization's purpose is inseparable from their own raison d'être.

The key to discovering an organization's higher purpose, if it isn't already clear, entails discerning the intrinsic good that is at the heart of its value proposition. All viable organizations, and especially for-profit businesses, must continuously create value in order to survive. And it's in this activity of value creation that the essence of an organization's purpose can usually be found. At one level, the value creation can be defined straightforwardly as the immediate benefits of the product or service being sold. But the deeper meaning of that value creation—the "higher" part of the purpose—is found in the general inherent improvement or betterment that the value creation helps bring about. There may be some cases where this betterment is obscure or barely exists, or is swamped by other problems. But all authentic forms of value make the world incrementally more beautiful, true, or good to some extent. It is in that discernible arc of positivity that the deeper meaning and purpose of an organization can be seen.

For Whole Foods, the intrinsic good behind our value proposition is health and vitality—both for people and for the planet. For an information company like Google, their essential value is found in the growth of knowledge, in helping humans skillfully negotiate the burgeoning world of data in the information age. For an outdoor retailer like REI, connecting people with the beauty of nature is the intrinsic value behind their work. One way that REI powerfully expresses this commitment is by closing all its stores on what for many U.S. retailers is the most profitable day of the year—Black Friday. Instead, the company gives all its team members a paid holiday and encourages them and their customers to "opt outside" and spend the time in nature. In 2019, it took this tradition a step further, in recognition of the seriousness of the climate crisis, and used the day to encourage its community to take action to protect the environment.

In claiming that purpose runs deeper than profit for many organizations, we don't mean that every single activity is perfectly oriented toward that end, or that there aren't competing goals and other motivations. It doesn't deny that the day-to-day realities of business are full of all the grit and grind of competing in a challenging marketplace. But, nevertheless, there is a real, beneficial impact that the company is leaving in its wake as it grows and develops. Even if the intrinsic good the customer receives seems small or mundane, when this good is magnified by the scale of a large market, the value creation becomes socially significant. Conscious leaders therefore "live out" their higher purposes by helping all their stakeholders feel the self-actualizing satisfaction that results when their organization delivers on the promise of that intrinsic good.

We understand that talk of "intrinsic good" will raise hackles in today's anti-business social climate. So many today seem to think that the purpose of business is simply to squeeze out maximum reward, fleece customers, and enrich shareholders at the expense of all other stakeholders. This is an unfortunate, though persistent, misunderstanding. Doctors make a lot of money, but their real purpose is to heal people. All professionals are paid for their efforts—from professors to architects to engineers—but this is not the higher purpose that gives meaning to their work. The value creation that makes these activities noble always relates to the benefits they bring to people. Likewise, the central goal of most businesses is to bring benefits to other people, not simply to make money.

Business professor Ed Freeman illustrates this point through a physical analogy: Our bodies produce red blood cells. It's absolutely essential, and if they were to stop producing red blood cells, we would die fairly quickly. But it doesn't necessarily follow that just because we need red blood cells to live, the purpose of our lives is to grow red blood cells.[5] Similarly, businesses need to make money—as *Conscious Capitalism* argues, it is socially irresponsible of them not to[6]—but for most companies, and especially those with conscious leaders, making money is not the primary reason they do what they do. They may be trying to solve problems, change behavior, upgrade our lives, invent new technologies, or provide new and better services. But they are rarely just "in it for the money."

Of course, there are exceptions. Some companies do behave with little more than profit in mind. But when we talk to entrepreneurs and business leaders, what we find, almost always, is that they are in it for the purpose, the meaning it brings to their lives, and the value it brings to others. Purpose is central to their motivation. Money is part of the equation, and there is nothing wrong with that. It's one marker of success, of the organization's ability to actually deliver on its value proposition in the marketplace. In fact, they should feel satisfaction when customers pay well for their products or services, because it affirms and ratifies their purpose. Profit is an important thing; but it's not the most important thing. Organizations work every day to make money, but they exist to deliver on their purpose.

PURPOSE, PRAGMATISM, AND PROFIT

The great challenge—and also the great opportunity—facing leaders of purpose-driven for-profit enterprises is that they also have to be pragmatic and market-oriented. Any business must follow the customer's needs—at least to some extent. It doesn't have to be a slave to the market, but it needs to be connected to the reality of what people are willing to exchange value for. If you don't stay in touch with existing tastes and desires, you won't last very long in business, as I learned the hard way.

Before we became Whole Foods Market, we opened a store named

Safer Way that sold natural food, with absolutely no meat, poultry, seafood, highly refined sugars, or coffee. It was driven by a higher purpose, but disconnected from the market. As you might imagine, we were not very successful initially, because we weren't running a business that was adequately engaging a large enough customer base. We were young idealists, full of the joy of elevated thoughts, and we let our sense of purity overshadow other important concerns. After all, what use was a grocery store with a higher purpose if we couldn't sell enough groceries to be a viable business?

After two years as Safer Way, we moved to a larger location, merged with a very similar store, changed the name to Whole Foods Market, and added back some of those forbidden items—meat, poultry, seafood, coffee, sugar, beer, wine, and some refined grains. Within just six months of opening, we had the highest total weekly sales of any natural foods store in the country. We still sold natural and organically grown products, without artificial colorings, flavorings, or preservatives. We still offered great options for those looking to eat healthier. We still provided a retail outlet for all kinds of fledgling natural foods businesses. We still helped drive forward the healthy eating trend. But now we had something else: impact and influence. We stopped trying to remake the market and started trying to engage the market. We began having an actual conversation with our customers. With the advent of Whole Foods, that dialogue, like any good conversation, became two-sided. Yes, we had things we wanted to say in that conversation, messages to deliver about healthier food and lifestyles—but now we were listening as well.

The inherently two-way, transactional nature of commerce necessarily constrains a for-profit business, but it also empowers it. It provides a pathway for a purpose-driven business to have a demonstrable impact. A business derives much of its value from having to engage market forces on their own terms. In doing so, it has two great advantages. First, it has real potential to lead, because, like a pace car, it needs to stay connected to the market forces that trail it. Second, it has the potential to be self-funding. So what it lacks in exclusive pursuit of high-minded ideals, it can make up for in sustainable and measurable impact. It may not be able to uncompromisingly adhere to a principled purpose no matter the cost, but, in its own way, a business can be a powerful change agent.

Society needs both for-profit and nonprofit organizations, as well as purpose-driven leaders who are engaged in both. For example, consider an issue close to our hearts: animal welfare. There are many well-funded and important nonprofits pushing this worthy cause, doing critical work, and making an enormous difference in the lives of our fellow creatures. They should be celebrated for it. At the same time, innovative businesses such as Beyond Meat and Impossible Foods are seizing the opportunity to move consumer habits by meeting the market on its own terms, with new products that appeal to the mainstream, generating significant resources rarely available outside of a for-profit context. They also pursue a higher purpose, but it's the promise of market impact that has allowed them to grow and flourish.

PRACTICING PURPOSE: Develop Purpose Champions

Every company needs individuals who keep alive the higher purpose of the company. There will inevitably be moments when you need influential people who are so aligned with the organization's purpose that they can represent its significance in any important situation. Maybe it's the chairman of the board, who is above the day-to-day fray. Maybe it's the original founder, who preserves a deep connection to the higher purpose of the company. Perhaps it's some other person or group. Whatever the case, every company needs "purpose champions" who can stand for the purpose when big decisions are being made, and continue to skillfully infuse the significance of that purpose into the stakeholder community, and ultimately into the culture.

THE IDEAL AND THE REAL

Consider some of these purpose statements from today's most successful organizations, both for- and nonprofit:

- **Nike:** "To bring inspiration and innovation to every athlete* in the world." *If you have a body, you are an athlete.
- **Unilever:** "Make sustainable living commonplace."
- **Tesla:** "To accelerate the world's transition to sustainable transport."
- **Whole Foods:** "To nourish people and the planet."
- **Zappos:** "Delivering Happiness."
- **ING Financial Group:** "Empowering people to stay a step ahead in life and in business."
- **U.S. Humane Society:** "Celebrating animals, confronting cruelty."
- **NPR:** "To create a more informed public—one challenged and invigorated by a deeper understanding and appreciation of events, ideas and cultures."
- **TED:** "Spread Ideas."

Most of those statements accurately capture the high-level value-creating activity of the company or organization. We can see here that, in terms of purpose, nonprofits and for-profits are more alike than different. These are both idealistic and pragmatic. They point to lofty goals, and they also represent a benchmark against which to evaluate the relevance and importance of strategic activities. But, inevitably, leaders need to translate that lofty ideal into practical outcomes. Pursuing a higher purpose in a business context is always about serving twin gods, both of whom require our attention: the ideal and the real.

We love an idealistic, inspiring purpose. We also love pragmatic, successful businesses focused on results. Either one pursued independent of the other can be problematic. A conscious leader's daily practice is to make sure neither of those twin gods—purpose and pragmatism—ever fully dominates the other. The ideal and the real each point to an indispensable element of success in Conscious Capitalism. Like two legs, both sides of this polarity are important to walking forward (for more on managing polarities, see The Conscious Leader's Tool Kit: The Art and Science of Polarities, p. 22). If an idealistic purpose ever takes complete power over the everyday work of the organization—serving customers, being efficient in allocating resources, innovating new products and services, and making money—it may quickly quell many of the healthy "animal spirits" that empower the capitalist endeavor. Zappos may aspire to "deliver happiness," but it had better deliver lots of shoes at the same time! If not, the company may begin to falter in its essential value-creating activity and lose its edge, even if it temporarily seems to gain an extra halo.

Likewise, if the everyday concerns of sales, finance, resource allocation, customers, competition, and growth take over completely and the business becomes disconnected from its core purpose, the organization may eventually find itself rudderless. Higher purpose provides clarity of direction in decision-making and creates a positive pressure for forward-looking growth and innovation. Losing that is always dangerous for the long-term viability of any business. If Zappos loses its signature customer service mojo—if it forgets that "delivering happiness" is core to its brand—it's well on its way to losing exactly what gives it a unique position in the marketplace. That will impact morale, motivation, and ultimately its essential value creation, even if it temporarily seems to boost the bottom line. Conscious leaders understand that purpose and pragmatism must thrive under the same roof.

At the beginning of this chapter, we highlighted Lincoln's remarkable ability to connect people to a higher purpose. Negotiating the relationship between the ideal and the real was another thing he did with unmatched skill—a quality that made him uniquely suited to shepherd the country through the immense challenges of the Civil War. Even as he articulated a renewed higher purpose for the nation, he understood that embodying that higher purpose is a continuing journey for all of us, not a final destination to be reached once and for all. And while that purpose may shine bright and clear, and provide a "true north" that points the way, the pragmatic road toward it is not always straight and narrow. An idealistic commitment may provide a general clarity of direction, but the steps taken inevitably require unexpected turns and necessary deviations. In a more contemporary context, the same is true for a business delivering on its mission. The necessity to follow the market creates strategic and tactical flexibility, even as the responsibility to deliver on purpose creates direction and discipline. Both are indispensable. Purpose without pragmatism is impotent; pragmatism without purpose is aimless. Market realism, in the hands of a conscious leader, is a powerful ally to an idealistic purpose.

PRACTICING PURPOSE: Create Conscious Reminders

In order to successfully use a higher purpose to guide and motivate an organization, the purpose must be kept at the forefront of people's awareness. Maintaining mindfulness of the purpose involves continually communicating and demonstrating it in fresh and creative ways. A great example of this comes from Jeff Bezos, who, in the early days of Amazon's growth, famously communicated the company's stated purpose of being "Earth's most customer-centric company" by leaving an empty chair open in his meetings to represent the customer. Physical symbols such as this create a powerful reminder that infuses the mission of the company into everyone's decision-making.

PURPOSE CREATES ALIGNMENT

Believing that business can and should pursue a higher purpose doesn't mean we should take at face value every marketing slogan. In a society awash in high-minded platitudes, it's easy to grow a bit weary or even cynical about one more claim that this or that product or technology is going to "change the world." Real purpose can exist in packages of all shapes and sizes; it need not always take on universe-altering proportions. The question that matters is this: Is it the right purpose at the right moment for the right organization?

An organization's true purpose is something that all its stakeholders can participate in discovering and realizing. Stakeholder participation is crucial if the higher purpose is to be effective in energizing the organization and fostering emotional engagement. It won't impact every decision, but it had better impact the important ones. Conscious leadership involves recognizing and affirming that higher calling, so that it doesn't get left aside amid the day-to-day demands of organizational life. It helps everyone feel connected to the organizational purpose and provides a context in which leaders throughout the organization can make decisions.

The art of generating higher purpose out of ordinary work was poetically expressed in a quote often attributed to Antoine de Saint Exupéry: "If you want to build a ship, don't drum up the men and women to gather wood, divide the work, and give orders. Instead, teach them to yearn for the vast and endless sea." It's been a couple of centuries since the "vast and endless sea" has captured the human imagination as it once did. Today, the explorers among us direct their yearning not across the oceans but into space. But the same principle applies. Many are familiar with the famous story of John F. Kennedy's visit to the headquarters of NASA in 1962. As Kennedy toured the building, he came across a janitor carrying a broom and asked the man what he was doing. The janitor replied, "I'm helping put a man on the moon."[7] One of the secrets of business and life is that most people are more motivated by meaning than by money. If we can provide that meaning, there is very little we can't achieve, and people will line up to help us accomplish it.

When stakeholders participate in and help evolve an organization's higher purpose, it can be infectious. The whole company receives an extra boost of alignment. There are few things more powerful than a shared commitment to a higher purpose among all relevant stakeholders. It allows everyone to feel connected to the beating heart of the organization, at least to some degree.

Still, the assumption that all businesspeople are just "greedy bastards" is widespread in our society, and this jaded view can undermine the sincerity and commitment necessary to keep an organization's stakeholders engaged with its higher purpose. Conscious leaders work to overcome this resistance by demonstrating the preeminence of the higher purpose through their actions, affirming that it means something much more than words on paper. In fact, it is by consistently prioritizing the purpose when faced with hard choices that the deeper dimensions of that very purpose are continually discovered and renewed.

When stakeholders see important decisions being made in ways that are aligned with the company's core values, and when they see leaders actually engaged with that higher purpose, it has an enormous impact. For lack of a better word, it gives people faith.

THE CONSCIOUS LEADER'S TOOL KIT

The Art and Science of Polarities

What made the Beatles one of the greatest rock bands in history? Talent? Good timing? Years of practice? All of those played a role. But at least one of the secrets to their success was a powerful combination of two seemingly opposed attributes: *competition and cooperation*. The Beatles had a highly developed cooperative relationship, and their musical synergy was extraordinary. Yet they also had a powerful competitive dynamic, especially between Lennon and

McCartney. That competition spurred the band to greater creative heights. Cooperation and competition—both were essential. It was a polarity that helped define their success.

Without knowing it, the Beatles were demonstrating an important concept that every conscious leader should be aware of: *polarity theory*. It suggests that, while some polarities are *positive/negative* (war and peace, profit and loss, wealth and poverty), others are actually *positive/positive*. Which means both sides are actually desirable. As clinical psychologist and leadership coach Bert Parlee suggests, "A fundamental question to ask when encountering a difficulty is: Is this a problem we can 'solve,' or is it an ongoing polarity we must manage well?"[8] Indeed, positive/positive polarities are better viewed as *systems to be managed* than problems to be solved. Polarity Management consultant Barry Johnson explains that in this type of polarity, "because the two sides . . . are interdependent, you cannot choose one as a 'solution' and neglect the other. The objective . . . is to get the best of both opposites while avoiding the limits of each."[9]

As described above, one positive/positive polarity is *competition and cooperation*. Competition is healthy when it sharpens performance, encourages creativity, and drives people to do their best. But within an organization, unrestrained competition, in the absence of a larger agreement to cooperate, can quickly devolve into a toxic environment that interferes with essential trust and mutual support. Likewise, cooperation is a great quality in any organization, but by itself, without the incentive or opportunity for individual excellence or creativity, it can similarly devolve into groupthink or stifling bureaucratic mediocrity. However, when competition and cooperation are brought together in a mutually correcting relationship that encourages the best aspects of both, beautiful things can occur. Instead of mistrust and one-upmanship, you get synergy and creativity. Instead of groupthink and stagnation, you get productive autonomy and creative collaboration.

The great physicist Niels Bohr once stated, "It is the hallmark of any deep truth that its negation is also a deep truth."[10] This is polarity theory in a nutshell. Similar interdependent polarities that leaders are likely to encounter include: challenge and support, structure and flexibility, defense and offense, simplicity and complexity, liberty and equality, and even individual and group. As discussed in this chapter, a critical positive-positive polarity that relates to purpose is *real and ideal*. In these examples, each set of values exhibits an opposing yet mutually correcting relationship, and a healthy, creative tension is produced by the ongoing relationship between them. The strengths of each pole serve to mitigate and moderate the downsides of its opposing pole in a recurring stepwise process that results in "both-and" progress instead of "either-or" choices.

Living and working with polarities challenges us to embrace more complexity in our leadership style. It helps push us beyond black-and-white, binary thinking. It engages our ability to understand nuance and can address the inevitable shades of gray that we face every day as leaders. It gives us a powerful tool through which to examine the overall health and vitality of our organizational culture. Polarities are real; you'll face them every day of your leadership career. Conscious leaders learn how to skillfully manage them.

LEAD WITH LOVE

> Love alone is capable of uniting living beings in such a way as to complete and fulfill them, for it alone takes them and joins them by what is deepest in themselves.
>
> —PIERRE TEILHARD DE CHARDIN

AT WHOLE FOODS MARKET, before we end any meeting, we ask a question: *Would anyone like to appreciate a fellow team member?* Whether it's a store team meeting or a strategy session with the executive leadership team, we never leave without opening the floor for people to honor one another's positive contributions. These appreciations are voluntary, and they happen at every level of the company. They might highlight simple acts of kindness or significant business achievements. It's one of the more unconventional elements of our culture, yet over time it's become one of the most popular. And it's one of the many ways that we strive as a company to operationalize a virtue that's too often overlooked in business: *love.*

In principle, few would argue with the statement that love is extremely important in every domain of human life. And yet, when it comes to business, this core human virtue is striking in its absence. Love rarely makes the list alongside traditional leadership virtues like integrity, hard work, and courage. Of course, we're not talking about romantic or sexual love here—there are good arguments for leaving that outside the workplace. But it is unfortunate that love in a broader sense is so often missing from our professional lives. As a consequence of this omission, corporations are far less satisfying places to work than they should be, organization cultures are suboptimal, and their highest potentials are stunted. Love is very much in the corporate closet. But it doesn't have to be that way. We need to practice the virtue of love in all domains of our lives—including when we show up at work. And leaders who do so will discover that in fact, as consultant and author Steve Farber likes to say, "Love is just damn good business."[1]

While the emotion of love is intrinsic to human nature, and its expression may be instinctive when it comes to activities like raising a family, leading with love in business is a skill that must be learned, practiced, and developed. For conscious leaders, that challenge is complicated by a number of common metaphors that define how we think about this area of our lives. After all, humans are storytelling creatures, and the language and imagery we use tend to shape our ways of thinking. Some of the stories we tell about business are almost antithetical to the virtue of love. Let's examine a few.

BATTLEFIELDS, JUNGLES, SHARKS, AND SPORTS

Judging by how we tend to speak about it, you might think business was an all-out bloody battle every day of the week. One of the most common metaphors used to describe business is that of a war. We see our competitors as "the enemy" that must be "killed," "destroyed," or "crushed" before they do the same to us. The hierarchical structure of the business organization often takes on a quasi-military "chain of command," and team members are frequently called "the troops." We create competitive "battle strategies" and "campaigns" to win market share and defeat our business rivals. Cash reserves for future needs are sometimes referred to as "war chests" that can potentially be used for "hostile takeovers." We have meetings in the "war room" to plan competitive strategies. If the battle with our competitors is lost, the executives responsible for the defeat might negotiate "golden parachutes" that allow them to escape the consequences.

If a company is at war, how can there be space for leading with love? There is a classic scene in the 1970 World War II movie *Patton* where General Patton (played by George C. Scott) is visiting wounded and dying American soldiers in a hospital. He encounters one soldier who is crying and undoubtedly suffering from post-traumatic stress syndrome. Rather than showing any empathy or care for the man, Patton is outraged and begins verbally and physically abusing him for crying, repeatedly calling him a coward who is dishonoring America. He promises to send him back to the front immediately or have him shot for cowardice and goes so far as to start reaching for his gun. Finally, he is physically constrained by the doctors and his staff before he is able to carry out this rough justice.

This scene was based partially on several real incidents; Patton was truly old school. Of course, our standards and perspectives have evolved over the intervening decades, and so have our understanding and appreciation for the reality of conditions like PTSD. Nevertheless, *Patton* portrays a type of alpha-masculine leadership that is common in war and still celebrated in many circles, including in the business world. We have historically admired "strong leaders" such as General Patton because they have done whatever was necessary to defeat dangerous enemies and win wars. That may, to some extent, be a necessary quality in true conflict, but why are we thinking in such terms for business? When thinking about leadership from the perspective of war, love and care are not necessarily virtues, but potential weaknesses! Such life conditions demand very particular styles of leadership. Of course, love will take a back seat in such urgent, life-or-death circumstances. But maybe it's time to reconsider whether business is actually a battlefield?

Another popular lexicon we draw on when describing business is that of Darwinian evolution. Without question, evolutionary language and imagery such as ecosystems, niches, novelty, adaptation, and so on can be quite useful in describing business activities. But too often we use Darwinian terms that invoke an unrelenting competition for survival. We regularly hear phrases such as "survival of the fittest," "natural selection," "it's a jungle out there," and "it's a dog-eat-dog world."

Andrew Grove, former CEO of Intel, often said that "only the paranoid survive."[2] The popular television show *Shark Tank* has done much to positively encourage entrepreneurship in our country, but the entire framing of the show is regrettably Darwinian. Various entrepreneurs pitch their business ideas to hard-nosed venture capitalists, or "sharks," and only the very best ideas survive the "ruthless competition" to receive funding. The term "shark tank" has itself become a common business metaphor, reinforcing the idea (or myth) that bloodthirsty conflict is the fundamental reality of business.

Who but a very brave or foolish person would climb into a tank full of hungry sharks? If business is truly a "survival of the fittest" world, what place does love have in it? If we are fighting for our very existence, surely love will need to wait until after we've vanquished the competition. Will that day ever actually come? Not if we are stuck in that metaphor!

While both war and natural selection are quite commonly evoked in descriptions of business, probably the most popular metaphors today are borrowed from the world of sports and games. We talk about "hitting a home run," "throwing a touchdown," "making a slam dunk," "getting together for a huddle," "executing the game plan," "organizing into teams," and so on. An excellent book that shows how sports have pervaded the way we think about business is Robert Keidel's *Game Plans: Sports Strategies for Business.*

In many ways, the language and imagery of games and sports is a great improvement over wars and jungles. They necessarily imply important constraints such as rules, sportsmanship, and fair play, as well as positive virtues such as challenge, fun, creativity, teamwork, and excellence. The game metaphor translates well to the competitive matchups between businesses striving to win market share through higher quality, lower prices, and better service. This kind of competition is critical to success, no doubt, but there are still several flaws in this conception of business that should be addressed.

For one thing, it can give rise to an obsession with winning above all else, which can be harmful to the overall well-being and morale of the organization. UCLA Bruins football coach Henry Russell Sanders famously said, "Winning isn't everything . . . It's the only thing."[3] Furthermore, traditional games and sports usually result in only one winner, leaving every other competitor or team in the category labeled "losers." "No one remembers second place" is another pithy statement that captures the preeminence of standing atop the podium. Notably, this is *not* the case with business, which always has multiple winners. Indeed, when game metaphors are applied to business strategy, it is better to consider them in the context of win-win-win strategies whereby all the major stakeholders are "winning" in their voluntary exchanges with the business—otherwise they wouldn't be making the exchange in the first place. (See chapter 4 for more on win-win-win solutions.) Ironically, the *business* of sports follows this win-win-win ethos, with communities, teams, owners, team members, advertisers, sponsors, and media companies all participating in a growing, mutually beneficial ecosystem. But if so many of the metaphors we use are based on a win-lose idea, we easily forget that.

The idea of business as a game completely fails to take into account that very few of the stakeholders trading with a business are actually playing a game at all. Customers, team members, suppliers, investors, and communities are voluntarily trading with the business in a variety of ways for mutual gains—they are not seeking exclusive victory in some high-stakes competition. For that reason, even if the competitive game metaphor animates the senior leadership of a company when they are thinking about how to get ahead of their rivals, it seldom energizes the larger stakeholder community that the business exists to serve.

Nevertheless, game and sports metaphors allow for the possibility of the existence of love in the organization. After all, in the spirit of healthy competition, we often love our own team, have deep connections with our teammates, appreciate the joy of camaraderie, and care about people who are helping us, such as our customers. However, when the winner-takes-all mindset becomes dominant, love is quickly relegated to the sidelines.

There's another metaphor we've begun to hear recently that combines many of the elements described above, including war, Darwinian competition, and games. It's a reference to HBO's hit show *Game of Thrones*, which aired in more than 170 countries around the world. Many people, it seems, have latched onto the series as an apt parallel to the world of business. We beg to differ. For those readers who might not count themselves among the show's tens of millions of fans, all you need to know is that the various characters in the fantasy world created by author George R. R. Martin are striving to be crowned king or queen of the Seven Kingdoms and to sit on the Iron Throne of Westeros. Most prove to be utterly ruthless in this quest, and only the strongest, smartest, and fittest survive. War is a constant strategic tool in this deadly game. As one of the would-be monarchs, Cersei Lannister, says: "When you play the game of thrones, you win or you die. There is no middle ground."[4]

Needless to say, there is very little real love in this series—almost none that isn't fueled by familial bonds. Even then, love is frequently trampled upon in the quest for power. "The more people you love, the weaker you are"[5] is another pithy leadership lesson from Cersei, who is unlikely to be invited to any future Conscious Capitalism leadership conferences (although—spoiler alert—she does temporarily become queen of Westeros before meeting a fiery end).

We have enjoyed the many enthralling seasons of *Game of Thrones*, but that doesn't mean we want the ethos of Westeros to define the ethics of business! In this hostile world of alpha males and females jockeying for power, authority, and status, love can hardly be anything but a chink in one's armor. Surely, we can do better than to interpret our business activities through this lens. Nevertheless, too many people do, even without realizing the consequences, and that in a nutshell explains why love is kept hidden away in our corporate closets. It is inconsistent with the mental models that so many of us see as the fundamental necessity for doing business. It has no place in a world where we are at war with our competitors, where only the strongest and fittest survive, and where there can be only one winner.

IN SEARCH OF NEW MAPS AND METAPHORS

If we want to bring love out of the corporate closet, if we want to be conscious leaders who skillfully practice this powerful human virtue not just at home but at work, then we are going to need to think about business in entirely new ways. We need to seek new mental models and metaphors that are truer to the essence of what business is and highlight the best it can be.

That's not to say the old metaphors are entirely useless—they each represent partial truths about business. Competition, for example: striving for excellence above and beyond competitors is an important driver of business development. It can and should inspire virtues and strengths that we discuss in detail in this book, such as innovation and continuous improvement of the leader and the team. But as we've pointed out, competition without a balance of other attributes, like cooperation and service, can quickly become counterproductive and toxic. Competition won't disappear from leadership when love comes in, nor should it. But it will take its rightful place as one among many ways we think about our enterprises, rather than being seen as the sine qua non of business reality.

We encourage you to come up with your own metaphors for a purpose-driven, love-powered business. Here's one that we like. Instead of thinking of business as a battlefield or a jungle, what if we think of it as a community? The recognition that every enterprise is composed of a variety of stakeholders who are all voluntarily exchanging with the business for mutual gain and benefit is one of the foundational tenets of Conscious Capitalism (see "The Conscious Leader's Tool Kit: Stakeholder Integration," page 51). It follows that one of the higher purposes of a business is to create value for all of its primary stakeholders. When we do that, every stakeholder flourishes, the business flourishes, and our larger society flourishes.

If we think of business as a community of stakeholders that are connected through mutual interests and benefits, then we can appreciate that leadership's job is to create value for every member of that community in a continuous series of win-win-win decisions. Because we are so used to thinking in terms of win-lose, it can be difficult for many leaders to make the shift to this new way of thinking. The community metaphor helps with this reframing, giving our minds permission to create new, innovative solutions that benefit all key parties. It also helps us to appreciate how important liberating love is to the entire organization. Love helps us to do a better job of creating value for all those different stakeholders, because it enables us to better understand their needs and desires and care more about fulfilling them. Love is the glue that holds it all together.

When stakeholders feel loved by a business, they will tend to love the business back and appreciate the value it is creating for them. That means more than a transaction—it builds the experience of a community. And authentic community is practically the holy grail of business brands in today's world. How many marketing dollars are thrown away trying to manufacture a community around a brand, when a little bit of authentic love would go so much further? The conscious leader strives always for the flourishing of the whole community, and unleashing love is essential to accomplishing that. If customers feel like members of a community, they will become the biggest advocates and the best marketers of the business. Likewise, team members will stick around and work for the business for decades. Suppliers will give preferential treatment to the company and will work closely with the business to innovate new products and services.

What other metaphors can we use to capture the spirit of the human entrepreneurial journey from nascent startup to small business to large corporation? In some ways, the answer to this question has to do with how we interpret the human experience itself. Human beings are unique animals in the evolutionary journey. The higher mammals have some extraordinary characteristics and have demonstrated remarkable intelligence and forms of consciousness worth honoring and protecting, but they have not developed the remarkable cognitive capacities that distinguish *Homo sapiens.* We need new myths, new stories, and new ways of conceiving the arena of business and leadership that encompass the many dimensions of what makes us human. War is one unfortunate part of the human condition, but it is not all of what defines us. The Darwinian struggle for survival is very real, but there is more to life than such primal instincts. Our tribalism is certainly part of our social organization, but we are not purely creatures of status. At times, we manage to transcend all of this. Shouldn't our metaphors transcend it as well?

Humans are also creatures of elevated emotion, artistic imagination, joy, laughter, and leaps of faith. We imagine new realities, invent amazing things, embrace larger perspectives, create extraordinary beauty, discover new realities, build communities, and carefully reflect on all of it. We love. Our species contains all of those capacities and more—and so should business! It's too easy to default to modes of thinking that may accurately represent our biological drives or a few of our evolutionary instincts but that fail to truly capture what it means to be fully alive.

SERVANT LEADERSHIP: LOVE IN ACTION

Another recent model that encourages the virtue of love in business is the practice of "servant leadership." In a business landscape still rife with conflict-based metaphors, this trend that's emerged in the past few decades stands out in stark contrast. It's a business philosophy that, like the Trojan Horse, has smuggled love into the upper echelons of corporate America, openly practiced by companies like Starbucks, Southwest Airlines, the Container Store, and Marriott hotels and espoused by influential business thinkers like Stephen Covey,

Peter Drucker, Ken Blanchard, Warren Bennis, and Peter Senge. In essence, servant leadership reenvisions the role of the leader as one who serves the organization, rather than wielding power over it.

The idea originates from the 1970 essay "The Servant as Leader," by former AT&T executive Robert Greenleaf. In the midst of the countercultural revolutions of the era, as traditional sources of authority were being questioned and overturned on all sides, Greenleaf was conducting his own soul-searching. His guiding question: "Where can we find the natural sources of rightful authority that are necessary for effective leadership?" He found the seeds of an answer in Hermann Hesse's novel *Journey to the East*, which tells the story of an unassuming servant named Leo, who guides a group of pilgrims through the desert in search of ultimate truth. It is only after Leo disappears and the group falls apart that they eventually realize that the man who has been carrying their luggage and taking care of their needs is in fact the great and noble leader of their religious order. Inspired by this story, Greenleaf penned his now legendary essay, and sparked one of the most influential leadership movements to arise over the past fifty years. In the decades since its inception, it has only become more relevant as traditional corporate power hierarchies have come under criticism from all sides and a new wave of leaders have begun to experiment with more democratic, egalitarian systems.

A servant leader is defined as a person who prioritizes the needs of others, deriving his or her authority from the heartfelt impulse to help. Leaders are traditionally thought of as those who "go out in front," directing affairs from above. The philosophy of servant leadership, however, turns this idea around. Rather than viewing themselves as being at the top of the hierarchy, where they need to use their power to control things, servant leaders place themselves at the bottom of the hierarchy, adopting the role of servant for all the organization's stakeholders. Some advocates of this approach focus their service on the needs of customers, on providing them with an exceptional product or experience. Think of companies like Trader Joe's, Amazon, Zappos, The Home Depot, and Ritz-Carlton. Others make it a priority to support and empower their people, serving their development and growth and earning loyalty and high performance in the process. Companies like Nordstrom and Southwest Airlines have employed this strategy with great success. Whatever the particular emphasis, servant leadership is an expression of love in action, and a much-needed antidote to the battlefields-and-shark-tanks approach.

Indeed, the reason the idea of service is so radical is that it upends the traditional conceptions of power and dominance and the drive to win that so many see as inextricable from success in business. Just ask Jonathan Keyser, a commercial real estate broker from Phoenix whose journey in business has moved from one extreme to the other. Reflecting on the early years of his career, he's blunt: "I was a ruthless prick." And it's hardly surprising—he was working in an industry that could rightly be called a poster child for those metaphors with which we began this chapter. As a colleague warned him, "This industry is full of sharks, and every man is out for himself. Nice guys get trampled in this industry. You need to look out for number one."[6]

Keyser soon experienced this ruthless, competitive culture firsthand. It seemed to be routine for brokers to manipulate and undercut one another, to lie to their clients, and to steal each other's leads. "The stuff that goes on—you wouldn't even believe it's legal!" he says. He learned to take important calls in his car—you never knew who was listening. He adopted the behaviors he saw around him, convinced that that was what it took to succeed. And succeed he did. He won "rookie of the year" during his first year in business and went on to reap the financial rewards. He liked the industry, but he was stressed out, constantly looking over his shoulder, and increasingly aware of the gap between his behavior and the values upon which his missionary parents had raised him. After ten years in business, as he describes it, he had lost himself in "the backstabbing drudge of it all."[7]

Everything changed for Keyser when he found himself at an industry conference in a breakout session on networking. The speaker was sharing an approach that involved planting seeds by developing relationships through service and trusting that it would result in future rewards. Keyser was captivated. *Is that even possible?* he wondered. *Does it work? How? Why?* Above all, he wanted to know, if this strategy of helping others led to such success, why weren't more people doing it?

The speaker had a ready answer: *Because it takes too long.* This business model requires a long-term vision, he explained, and few people have the patience to follow through. Keyser recalls his message as follows: "What you're doing now is like hunting. You go out, you shoot a deer, you get to eat it right away. But then you have to get up tomorrow and do it all over again. This is more like farming. If you plant citrus trees and nurture them, they take years to grow, but once they do, you have more fruit than you could ever eat. You have to nurture those relationships, but over time, you'll build this network of people who want to help you—so much so that you're not going to need a sales force."

On the plane home, Keyser's mind was racing. Could he make a service-first model work in the cutthroat, short-term-driven world of commercial real estate? Was it crazy, or inspired? He was determined to try, and he knew that the transformation would begin with him. "I went to work reinventing myself," he says, unlearning the bad habits of a decade of relentless self-interest.

His new approach was to take the spirit of service literally: he connected with people and helped them to get whatever they needed. Rather than pursue leads and promote his services, he got involved in the community and helped local nonprofits. He began actively seeking out ways that he could help everyone he came into contact with—not just potential clients but also his team members, suppliers, and even his competitors. "I booked thousands of coffees, lunches, drinks, and dinners. I sat down with people and listened to their stories," he recalls. At every meeting, he resolved to find at least three concrete, meaningful actions he could take to help. Learning that one potential client had just gone through a divorce, he sent her a book on getting a fresh start. He helped another client find an internship for her daughter. He even helped other brokers get business. His team became, he says with only a hint of laughter, "a concierge service that sells real estate." Even when there was no prospective business to be had, he encouraged his team to tirelessly look for opportunities to help people. When they learned that one prospective client's wife was dying of a rare blood disease, his team spent several days tracking down the leading doctor in the state who specialized in her condition.

As the months and eventually years passed without much financial reward to show for his dedication, Keyser's colleagues, his friends, and his wife at the time questioned the wisdom of his choices. Competitors mocked him as naive and irresponsible. Yet even when doubts assailed him, he remembered the words of the man who'd set him on this path, and he kept planting seeds for the long term. Slowly but surely, those seeds began to sprout, and referrals began to flow his way. People he'd helped out a couple of years before would think of him when they needed a broker. Or they'd tell their friends about him.

Through the committed practice of servant leadership, Keyser's firm has now become the largest commercial real estate brokerage of its kind in the highly competitive Arizona real estate market, and one of the fastest-growing firms in the country. And it all comes from the spirit of service. "I don't have to sell. I don't have to persuade. I don't have to convince. I just serve, and more business comes my way than I can handle," he says. "When I used to be ruthless, I thought I was taking care of number one. What I was really doing was burning every bridge. Now, today, as we love and serve, we're creating greatness for ourselves wherever we go. Everyone is trying to out-help each other!"

THE MANY FACES OF LOVE

Love isn't really one thing—it's a many-splendored virtue. Just like the Eskimos, who famously have many words for snow, we need many words to capture the nuances of love. The ancient Greeks identified several types of love, including *philia* (friendship), *eros* (romantic or sexual love), and *agape* (selfless love). In romance or in family life, love has one set of meanings, but in the realm of conscious leadership it has another. These include qualities such as generosity, gratitude, appreciation, care, compassion, and forgiveness. Love is a type of "master virtue" with many related virtues that, when combined, represent a more complete meaning of the term. We don't fully understand love unless we also understand and practice its many manifestations. Let's take a closer look at a few of these faces of love, and how they might be practiced.

Generosity is an expression of abundance—that's the best way to understand this virtue. It's not an expression of self-sacrifice, which is a common point of confusion. So often, people think that if we give something to someone else, we must also be giving something up—that gain on one side means loss on the other. But true generosity is an overflowing, a movement of the heart that wants to share what we have and help others. It arises not from a feeling of guilt or duty, but from our own awareness of abundance in both ourselves and in the larger universe we are part of. That spirit of abundance naturally wants to give and to share, and to help others. Of course, that can be expressed in many ways. We can be generous with our time, attention, money, knowledge, and even our spirit.

That which we give to others, we give first to ourselves. This is an important spiritual truth that leaders should spend some time reflecting on. The spirit of generosity must first awaken in our own hearts and minds before it can flow outward. Once we consciously recognize that generosity is beneficial not only to the person who is receiving it but also to the one giving, the desire to give will only grow and deepen within us. We will create a virtuous circle of love that nourishes us even as it nourishes others. Imagine an organization in which the spirit of generosity was a defining attribute of the culture!

Conscious leaders can make a habit of this beautiful virtue in many ways. We can mentor and coach younger leaders to help them to learn and grow. If we have reached a place of financial security in our lives, we may even decide to donate most or all of our compensation, and some of our time, to nonprofit organizations we are passionate about—the needs of our world are virtually infinite, and our services are badly needed—while continuing our work with an attitude of generosity.

PRACTICING GENEROSITY:
Keep Company with Generous People

A good way to begin the practice of generosity is by surrounding ourselves with generous people. Their generosity and service will help awaken and inspire our own. Pay attention to those people and the actions they take. Generosity doesn't have to mean grand gestures—it might just mean helping a friend meet a deadline or staying late to mentor a younger colleague. Inspired by such examples, you can stoke the fires of your own capacity to give with small gifts and acts of service. Over time, you will gradually develop an inner "spiritual muscle" of generosity that will grow stronger as you practice it.

Gratitude is one of the single most important keys to happiness in life. Gratitude doesn't always need an object—we can feel gratitude for virtually anything, even for simply being alive. Just to be able to move in this world, to meet other people, to love, to experience the abundance of life—it's amazing! The great writer D. H. Lawrence perhaps said it best when he wrote, "Whatever the unborn and the dead may know, they cannot know the beauty, the marvel of being alive . . . The magnificent here and now of life in the flesh is ours, and ours alone, and ours only for a time. We ought to dance with rapture that we should be alive and in the flesh, and part of the living, incarnate cosmos."[8]

If we can recognize and reflect on this truth daily, we will expand our hearts and minds, and joy and happiness will be a more constant companion on our life journey. More important, this type of gratitude gives a leader perspective. Amid the inevitable challenges and difficulties of leadership, there is a strong tendency to contract inward. It's so easy to end up myopically focused on our own personal problems or grievances. We end up focused on things that we're dissatisfied about, on ways we've been wronged by others—and there are always plenty of those!

You've heard of the power of intention? Well, don't underestimate the power of *attention*. One of the secrets of life is that our own experience is highly influenced by what we focus on, by where we place our precious attention. If we focus on grievance and pain, it inevitably leads to unhappiness. We collapse in on ourselves. Whereas if we focus on gratitude, we naturally expand our consciousness outward and we make room for a deeper perspective. This shift of attention, this practice of gratitude, allows us to put real problems and grievances in their proper context and perspective. Gratitude is a key that unlocks the heart. If we find ways to express gratitude every single day, we will be more successful leaders *and* experience more joy and happiness than we ever thought possible.

PRACTICING GRATITUDE: Morning, Noon, and Night

Consider beginning each day with just one minute of gratitude—reflecting upon how amazing the universe is and how incredible it is to be alive! If you have a morning meditation or spiritual practice, then beginning that practice with gratitude will help deepen the practice and enrich your entire day. You can try the same before your morning exercise routine.

Mealtimes are a wonderful time to express gratitude—as many of our cultural traditions tell us. Beginning our meals with a few seconds of thankfulness for what we are about to eat can be a bonding experience and help us more deeply appreciate the experience of sustenance and life. (It also has practical benefits: we'll tend to eat our meals more slowly and conscientiously, which helps digestion and discourages overeating.)

Many people keep a "gratitude journal." At the end of each day, before retiring for the night, they will jot down a few thoughts on how their day went, focusing especially on whatever they are grateful for. It is a perfect way to calm our minds and open our hearts before sleeping. This often results in deeper and more peaceful repose.

Appreciation. In his 2019 commencement address at Princeton, the columnist George Will had a message for the future leaders at the prestigious Ivy League institution. He warned them to beware of the tendency in contemporary culture to lean on rage and outrage as normal in public expression. "In this age of rage, disparagement is the default setting for many Americans," he lamented. And then he implored his young audience to embrace the virtue of appreciation and praise. "Intelligent praising is a talent. It is learned. Like all virtues, it is habitual. It is a habit. And it is a virtue we need more of, right now. It is the virtue of recognizing virtue, and saluting it."[9]

One of a leader's most important jobs is to salute excellence—to see it, recognize it, and appreciate it, as we do in our meetings at Whole Foods. But remember, appreciation needs to be authentic. People have highly tuned antennas for misleading or disingenuous compliments. What we've found is that when we authentically appreciate somebody, it not only makes the person receiving the appreciation feel good; it also helps build trust and break down barriers between people. After all, it's hard to maintain judgments about another person if they are authentically appreciating us! And this works both ways. It's almost impossible to authentically appreciate someone without opening our hearts to some degree. We so often spend so much time judging what others are doing and saying. Most of us have an internal critic that constantly measures both ourselves and other people. Real appreciation temporarily breaks the power of that critic. When we truly appreciate others, we silence that part of ourselves and it allows us to open our hearts. Suddenly love is released. This practice has been enormously beneficial for our work culture, and yet it's so simple.

A conscious leader needs to be actively appreciative. We can be tough leaders at times, we can and should be strong, but at the end of the day, human beings respond best to care and appreciation. It's important to remember that in business, everything we accomplish is ultimately done with and through other people. That is what conscious leaders do—we inspire, motivate, develop, and lead others. To be appreciative of the gifts that other people share with us and with our teams is uplifting and creates a rewarding feeling of fulfillment.

Appreciations are easy for leaders and organizations to implement, as we have done at Whole Foods, and they have very powerful reverberations. They unite people, create camaraderie, and help build trust. Conscious leaders should consider ways to institutionalize a culture of appreciation—their teams will thank them for it.

Let me end this section on appreciation with a personal note. I have always felt so grateful for the truly amazing people I have worked with over the past forty-plus years at Whole Foods. Without them, the company never would have amounted to much of anything, and neither would I. Every day I work with people who I know are incredibly smart, talented, caring, and passionate. I try to go out of my way to appreciate and thank people every day. I am deeply grateful for all the things that people do to make Whole Foods better. I am grateful to all of our stakeholders—to our team members, customers, suppliers, and communities and to our parent company, Amazon.

PRACTICING APPRECIATION:
Catch People Doing Something Right

In his bestselling book *The One Minute Manager*, Ken Blanchard popularized a practice that he called "catching people doing something right." In our normal lives, most of us tend to do the opposite—we are fault-finders ready to catch people doing something wrong. Turning our attention to the good work people are doing helps shift our consciousness to a quality of deep appreciation. You can do this every day in your normal work life. But don't restrict it to work. Practicing authentic appreciation with the people you love most will help elevate those relationships to new levels of mutual happiness.

Care. People always know if the leader truly cares about them or not. When we as leaders express indifference or apathy at work, we are communicating that we don't really care about others as individuals. When we treat others as objects—"human resources" to be used purely for their utilitarian value—and not as individual subjects we appreciate and value on their own terms, it doesn't go unnoticed. Social capital is significant in any work environment, and every time a leader falls below a certain threshold of care, they lose the respect of those around them. "People will try to convince you that you should keep empathy out of your career," says Apple CEO Tim Cook. "Don't accept this false premise."[10]

It's worth remembering that everything a leader does is amplified, whether positive or negative. A leader's whispers are heard as shouts, as the saying goes. So when we go out of our way to extend ourselves and care for a team member, customer, or other stakeholder, the ripple effect is enormous. We will start to accumulate goodwill, and that can have a hugely positive impact over time. It's also so important to be very aware of what behavior we are modeling to our team. If we as leaders don't care, then why should our people care?

Authentic care is an act of moral imagination. Why? Because it requires us to take a cognitive leap of perspective, to actually put ourselves into another's shoes. Of course, we talk about such things frequently, but it's very hard to deeply care for another if we can't see life from their perspective. And that involves an ability to transcend our own myopic worldview, at least to some degree. This is much easier with family—people we are genetically related to. In that respect, evolution helps us out a bit! It's also easier if people are in our close-knit social group, or are members of our "tribe." But to do it for less familiar colleagues, collaborators, customers, team members, and others in our organizational circles—that requires a much more developed capacity for empathy. Many can't do it; it's just too big a psychological leap. But if we can learn to take that step, we'll find it so much easier to naturally express an authentic sense of care and concern toward our customers, our suppliers, and other stakeholders in the organization. We'll be able to understand their needs more deeply, and that is always a boon for our capacity to lead.

PRACTICING CARE: How Can I Help?

Practicing care means constantly asking ourselves, "How can I be most helpful in this situation?" Most of the time there is something we can do, but if we don't keep that question alive, we may let the moment or the opportunity pass. Sometimes care is simple, and the little expressions of it can make a huge difference.

Compassion is a powerful virtue that is often used as a veritable synonym for love itself. "In that fullness of Divine Love blossoms the beautiful, fragrant flower of compassion," claims the Indian spiritual teacher Amma.[11] This ideal is not reserved for the saints and sages; it can also inspire important leadership qualities in the more secular world of business. Traditionally, compassion is seen as arising from a profound confrontation with our impermanence and mortality. When one confronts the suffering that exists in this world, and the truth that we all must die, the natural feeling one will experience is compassion. While we certainly don't believe that somewhat bleak outlook is the final statement on existence, there is deep truth in it nonetheless. We celebrate our existence with gratitude and wonder, but we also accept that we are all mortal beings, and we all experience the reality of pain, loss, death, and grief.

Just as gratitude and appreciation arise naturally out of a recognition of the profound miracle and abundance of life, so does compassion arise out of a recognition of our shared suffering and pain. In light of the reality of suffering, isn't the single best response we can have toward every living being compassion? Leaders who feel and express authentic compassion awaken a deep spiritual quality within their inner selves that will inspire other people. True compassion creates trust, commitment, and loyalty in others. Compassion brings us together and reminds us what is most important in life.

PRACTICING COMPASSION: Be Fully Present

The virtue of compassion may seem like a high ideal, but the first step to practicing it is in fact quite simple. Just pay attention to what is going on around you. Instead of sleepwalking through your life, lost in your own thought stream, wake up and be present to the flow of life around you. When we are fully present in each moment, we begin to notice the fear, sadness, anger, illness, low self-esteem, and depression in other people. Compassion is the normal human response to pain and suffering, but we must be present in the moment to notice it. It isn't easy to be present. As a general rule, we prefer to anesthetize our consciousness to avoid noticing the suffering in both ourselves and other people. As with any skill, the more we practice being present (or "mindful," in the Buddhist tradition), the more we will see the suffering and the more compassion will arise in our hearts.

Forgiveness is an important face of love, and it is also an underappreciated leadership skill. Perhaps this is because it is a virtue that does not come easy to most of us. Too many people hold on fiercely to their grievances and resist letting them go. But, like a hot iron, they will burn us if we hold on to them too long. When we refuse to forgive, it allows us to blame others, and successful leaders don't want to indulge in such energy-sapping distractions. They don't have time to waste feeling sorry for themselves. And it's amazing how much energy is released through the simple act of forgiveness.

Does forgiveness mean condoning the actions of people who hurt us? No. Nor does it mean forgetting or denying the pain they might have caused. But we don't have to compound that pain by hamstringing ourselves with judgment, blame, and victimization. Conscious leaders can model a high level of responsibility by practicing forgiveness.

Whatever our intentions, we are the ones who suffer when we harbor negativity. We become trapped in our own small prison of victimhood. Forgiveness, authentically practiced, allows us to escape. As the psychologist Lewis B. Smedes insightfully writes, "When we forgive, we set a prisoner free and then discover that the prisoner we set free was us."[12] Practicing forgiveness will expand our inner universe into a space of loving-kindness, where we can flourish and be truly happy. In fact, in a world where there are endless opportunities to take offense, and outrage culture dominates social media, forgiveness is even more relevant and powerful. It's essential to living an authentic and loving life. When we practice forgiveness, all the guilt, self-judgment, and suffering we have endured from our own past mistakes can finally be let go. As we forgive others, we will come to discover something quite wonderful: we, too, are forgiven.

PRACTICING FORGIVENESS: Water Wears Away the Mountain

Forgiveness isn't always easy. Choose a person you find it hard to even imagine forgiving. Perhaps the notion of walking up to that person and saying "I forgive you" is unthinkable. That's okay. Remember, forgiveness doesn't mean condoning or forgetting. It doesn't even have to mean telling the person directly. But it does mean that, inwardly, you let the grievance go. To start, you can simply focus on having the clear intention to forgive. Initially, there's likely to be resistance, especially if the grievance is deep. But if you continue to practice sincerely, like water wearing away a mountain, the resistance will slowly but surely erode. Persistence is the key to forgiveness. Eventually, you may feel so free of the emotional baggage that you are able to reconnect in person with the one who hurt you.

LOVE AS A SOURCE OF STRENGTH

When we consider the virtue of love, we primarily think of its supportive, nurturing, and gentle faces, many of which we have highlighted in this chapter. Too many leaders are, frankly, deficient in these qualities, which is why we're arguing that they need to be brought to the forefront in business. But we should not forget that there is also another face of love, one that wears a more resolute expression. Just as compassion and devotion are exemplified by the saints and deities of the world's wisdom traditions, so, too, do we find representations of righteous and demanding passion. This strong side of love cares deeply about each of us rising up and reaching our potential. Like the intense concern that parents have for their children's success, this expression of love can be tough, challenging, and even uncompromising at times. It is not a love that accepts and reassures; it is a love that demands and inspires. For conscious leaders, this kind of love takes the form of a deep desire for individuals and organizations to reach further, achieve more, and live up to their higher purpose.

Leading with love does not always mean an appreciative gesture, a selfless act of service, or a sensitive, supportive culture. There are situations in which conscious leaders need to go beyond nurturing their people and stakeholders—they also need to embody the strong side of love and *challenge* them. This is not a license to be high-handed, but merely a recognition that there is a time and a place for calling people to higher levels of performance, achievement, and excellence. Such actions need not be antithetical to leading with love; they can be an important expression of it.

THE HEART OF A CAREGIVER

Andy Eby grew up with a dream, and it wasn't to love people—it was to hit, block, and tackle them. From an early age, he wanted to play in the NFL. There was just one minor problem: he wasn't a natural athlete. Luckily, he had something even more powerful. He was fully committed. And he trained himself to get the most out of what talent he had. Step by step, he made his way, eventually playing for the Green Bay Packers and the St. Louis Rams, snapping the ball for some of the great quarterbacks of that era. But while his dream was fulfilled, his life was far from it. Sometimes when you get what you want, you come to realize that you didn't really want it after all. For Andy, the NFL lifestyle and its focus on individual achievement and chasing the next contract lacked something and he felt adrift, longing for purpose and a more meaningful life. It would come in the form of love—because love was the family business, literally.

Andy's grandmother had suffered from Alzheimer's, and his family had struggled to find good care for her toward the end of her life. The cold, institutional nature of many of the nursing homes of the time left much to be desired—so much so that Andy's entrepreneurial father decided to start his own assisted living business, Bickford Senior Living. Andy's grandmother was the first customer. The business was purpose-driven and successful, and it grew over the many years that Andy was off playing football. However, by the early 2000s his father was sick and the business had fallen on hard times and was losing money. Around this time, Andy's brothers invited him to lunch. Would he be interested in leaving the bright lights of the NFL to come work for the family business? Andy surprised everyone, including himself, by how quickly he said yes.

After joining the business. Andy began to understand that changing the trajectory of the company meant more than simply fixing what was wrong with the income statement and the balance sheet. Turning around Bickford Senior Living had to start with the company's original purpose. It would mean revitalizing the ethos of care that had been at the heart of his family's vision. Andy and his brothers realized that they needed to deepen their capacity—and, by extension, the whole company's capacity—to lead with love. After all, that's the business they're in.

As the debt-ridden business went through a series of near-death experiences, Andy encountered an inescapable truth about organizational change: *Leadership matters.* He recognized, "If you want to grow the business, you have to grow the leader." After some deep soul-searching, he started on a path to become a more conscious leader. As part of that effort, he decided to write a manifesto for the company. And he didn't just farm it out to a marketing agency. He worked on it himself, mulling over every word, slowly developing the language and ideas. At every visit to one of their facilities, he would discuss it with the local caregivers. *Are these words authentic? Do they resonate? What needs to be added? What themes are important?*

Were the words he'd chosen truly capturing the heart of a caregiver? He worked on it for a year, getting feedback from caregivers all over the country, and by the time he got done, the very process of creating it had changed him. Thinking he had written it for others, he realized that the process had awakened the caregiver inside of him. "I realized that I needed to infuse a caregiver's love into all aspects of what I do. I needed to learn how to lead with that kind of love."

Andy attended the opening of the next Bickford assisted living center, in Virginia Beach, Virginia, as he does every new opening. But this time, it was different. He was armed not just with the new manifesto, but with his own transformed understanding of what Bickford's work was truly about. While leading the new team through a training process for their roles as caregivers, something came alive in the group that he'd never seen before. People started standing up and sharing their own feelings of responsibility to love, care, and create a beautiful atmosphere in the new center.

"I couldn't believe it," Andy recalls. "I hardly had to say anything. They were all sharing and teaching our values—one after the next. I know this is ridiculous to say, but I don't think there has been a better training day in the history of corporate America." By learning to lead with love, Andy was able to create a space in which others could do the same. His journey from toughened NFL lineman to champion of the most tender and delicate act of caregiving had changed him. But, more important, it was changing the entire organization and allowing it to truly fulfill the spirit of its original mission.

When it comes to leadership, love is the most underutilized virtue, and it's also potentially the most powerful. Once we reenvision business as being fundamentally about fulfilling a higher purpose, and create new metaphors that align with that, we will be able to liberate love in our organizations. In this new conception, maximizing profits is no longer the raison d'être of the business, although profit is still recognized as necessary for fueling the pursuit of purpose. As the context shifts in this way, the virtue of love, which takes the form of service, generosity, gratitude, care, compassion, appreciation, and forgiveness, begins to come alive. This courageous step of letting love out of the corporate closet is perhaps the single most important task for leaders who feel inspired to contribute to a more conscious capitalism.

THE CONSCIOUS LEADER'S TOOL KIT

Stakeholder Integration

One of the foundational tenets of Conscious Capitalism is *stakeholder integration.* As discussed earlier, this is a shift away from the traditional conception of a corporation, in which increasing profits for shareholders is seen as the primary responsibility of the business. Instead we think of businesses as serving a wider community of stakeholders, all of whom are connected through mutual interests and benefits.

Ed Freeman, the father of stakeholder theory, described the idea as follows: "Every business creates, and sometimes destroys, value for customers, suppliers, employees, communities and financiers. The idea that business is about maximizing profits for shareholders is outdated and doesn't work very well, as the recent global financial crisis has taught us . . . The task of executives is to create as much value as possible for stakeholders without resorting to trade-offs. Great companies endure because they manage to get stakeholder interests aligned in the same direction."[13]

A stakeholder, in the broadest sense, could be any person, company, or other entity that interacts with the business. In Conscious Capitalism, we divide stakeholders into two groupings: an *inner circle* of primary stakeholders and an *outer circle* of secondary stakeholders. Primary stakeholder relationships are two-way relationships that create mutual value and are usually ongoing and voluntary. For most businesses, this inner circle might consist of customers, team members, suppliers, investors, communities, society, and the environment. Secondary stakeholder relationships are more episodic and sometimes involuntary. This outer circle might include the media, activists, critics, governments, unions, and competitors. These stakeholders are connected to the business but may not be voluntarily exchanging with it for mutual benefit in the same way that primary stakeholders are.

It's critical that conscious leaders understand the web of stakeholder relationships within which their businesses operate. We encourage you to spend time mapping out your own inner and outer circles and actively considering each stakeholder group in your decision-making. All stakeholders, both primary and secondary, require leaders to take their interests and perspectives into account, because all of them have a "stake" in the business and can impact it in both positive and negative ways.

3

ALWAYS ACT WITH INTEGRITY

> The supreme quality for leadership is unquestionably integrity. Without it, no real success is possible, no matter whether it is on a section gang, a football field, in an army, or in an office.
>
> —DWIGHT D. EISENHOWER

WHAT WOULD YOU DO IF your company had doubled in size, your shareholders were happy, profits were up, and everyone thought you were doing a fantastic job as CEO?

If you're Ramón Mendiola, back in 2008, the answer is not "Double down on what you're doing." Despite the looming financial crisis and a board that saw no reason to mess with a good thing, Ramón was listening to an inner voice that told him he could do better. He could create a company that not only was profitable but had integrity—a company that not only enriched its shareholders but also did the right thing by all of its stakeholders, including the larger society and the environment.

Five years earlier, Ramón had taken over as CEO of Florida Ice & Farm Company (known as FIFCO), a Costa Rican beverage company whose main business was brewing beer. Under his leadership, the company improved its efficiency and expanded into new markets, adding non-alcoholic drinks, wine, and spirits to its portfolio and growing through acquisitions in other Central American countries.

The seed of Ramón's discontent was sown by one of his executives, Gisela Sanchez. She told him about the concept of the "triple bottom line," which elevates environmental and social impact metrics to the same status as financial results in the accounting of a company's success. She also pointed out that the company's philanthropic giving amounted to only about 1 percent of profits, a far cry from companies like Microsoft, which gives 8 percent. "I realized that we needed to evolve in the way we were doing business," Ramón reflects. "We needed to embrace a more conscious, inclusive, holistic view in which we are sharing the wealth that we create among all our stakeholders."

Once he'd been exposed to this way of thinking, Ramón couldn't ignore the ramifications or go back to business as usual. Like any conscious leader with a strong sense of integrity, he felt compelled to bring his company into alignment with his newly awakened sense of purpose. He set out to bring to the company's environmental and social impact the same rigor that they brought to financial performance.

"You can have the consciousness that you want to be more responsible, serve more stakeholders, and so on. But how do you really go about it? That's the question that matters." Luckily, Ramón is a master of implementation. He created a process that began with hiring a third party to gather feedback, both quantitative and qualitative, from a wide circle of stakeholders, including team members, partners, shareholders, financial institutions, retail partners and suppliers, NGOs, government regulators, media, and more. They asked each of these stakeholders, "What can we do to be a more responsible company? How can we improve our social or environmental footprint?"

In 2008, the feedback they received fell into four clear categories. First was the misuse of alcohol: NGOs like Mothers Against Drunk Driving accused companies like FIFCO of marketing to kids and promoting irresponsible consumption. Second was waste: people saw their bottles littering the beaches and floating in the rivers. Third was water: access to water is always a big issue in Costa Rica, and there were fears that companies like FIFCO were diverting water away from the communities. Fourth was carbon: FIFCO's five hundred trucks were a common sight on Costa Rica's roads, and people were concerned about emissions as well as contamination from their manufacturing and bottling facilities.

The next step was to get buy-in from his senior leaders. "They all needed to agree that we should do something to try to mitigate or minimize these footprints," he said. "If I just come in and tell them this is what we're doing, but they don't understand why it's important, things will get complicated." Once he had his leadership team on board, it was time to set specific targets. "If you can't measure it, you can't manage it," the old business adage says, and Ramón knew that to be able to measure, you need a specific objective to measure against. The company was accustomed to setting ambitious key performance indicators (KPIs) related to profit, customer satisfaction, and market share. Now they set equally ambitious objectives related to their environmental impacts. In 2008, he declared that FIFCO would generate zero solid waste by 2011, be water neutral by 2012, and be carbon neutral by the end of 2017. "I didn't know how we were going to get there," he says, "but I believed we could do it."

He set targets on the social side as well, aiming to reduce the downsides of his products: alcohol and sugar. This was not driven only by altruistic motives; it made solid business sense, too. He was well aware of how regulators had clamped down on the tobacco industry, and he wanted to avoid a similar fate. So he worked with regulators and other government officials, taking the initiative to reduce sugar content in his sodas and promote safer and healthier drinking habits.

Measurable objectives were all well and good, but Ramón knew that there was a further step he needed to take. He had to put his money where his conscience was. And not just his money, but his executives' as well. FIFCO's compensation model for the top executives was 50 percent variable, meaning that half of each of their paychecks was dependent on traditional measures of the company's financial performance. Ramón's own compensation was 60 percent variable. He now proposed that the social and environmental metrics be included in that calculation. In other words, if the company didn't meet its new targets, the executives would be paid less. This was no longer a side project; it was a fundamental restructuring of the incentives of the organization.

The board balked. This was a step too far. What kind of fool decides to change the company's compensation model in the middle of a financial crisis? One board member, a New York banker, told him point-blank, "This is the most crazy thing I have ever seen and heard in my entire career." Ramón's whole initiative could have been killed, or significantly watered down, right there. But he was not to be dissuaded, and at the end of the heated discussion, he got the board to narrowly pass the initiative, on a 4–3 vote. Economic KPIs now accounted for only 60 percent of their "scorecard," with the remaining 40 percent being social and environmental.

"You need to touch the hearts of your executives, your leaders," Ramón says, "but when you change the compensation, that's what leads to behavioral change, because they are actually on the hook for it." Some left, including his CFO. But the remaining executives rose to the challenge.

With these key changes in place, Ramón and his team got down to work—measuring, reducing, adjusting, offsetting. FIFCO met each of the environmental goals Ramón had set and has now exceeded them. For example, the company became water neutral by 2012, as he had said it would, and then went on to become water positive, putting more water back into the community than it takes out. They made measurable progress on their social priorities too, changing patterns of alcohol consumption. And the company steadily increased its philanthropic commitment, now dedicating 8 percent of its net profits to strategic social investments. None of these changes damaged the company financially. In fact, it has continued to profit and grow. Over time, the once reluctant board came to take great pride in its social and environmental accomplishments.

Today, FIFCO is thriving and attracting young, talented people who are excited by the company's holistic approach to serving all its stakeholders. It has become a kind of flagship corporation for Costa Rica, something that government officials and local leaders can point to as a source of national pride. Since Ramón came aboard, it's grown from around 1,800 team members to 6,500, and its revenues have grown from $150 million to $1.2 billion. Another of the rewards, he believes, has been a more stable legislative environment in which the regulators truly see him as a partner. But by far the greatest reward, from his perspective, is the loyalty and enthusiasm of his team members and customers. "We're not perfect," he says, "but we have a conscience, and they can see it. We are doing everything we can to have integrity as a company, and when we see an area in which we fall short, we take concrete steps to address it."

THE MEANING OF INTEGRITY

Integrity is a virtue that every leader should aspire to, but we won't pretend that it is easy or common. In some sense, we can more easily define integrity by what it's obviously not. It's not lying. It's not stealing. It's not fudging your accounting, or mistreating your team members, or greenwashing your marketing. It's not making unsubstantiated claims and false comparisons. It's not misleading your customers or hiding facts from the public. All of those are easily grouped into the "lacks integrity" bin of failed leadership. But what goes in the "act with integrity" pile? How do we capture the qualities of character that make someone like Ramón Mendiola feel an inner compulsion to upgrade his company's behavior and impact, despite the uncertain payoff and personal risk? How can we cultivate these same character traits in our own approach to leadership? Is a virtue like integrity simply innate? Or can it be developed?

Perhaps the best way to understand and ultimately embody this critical virtue is to separate the white light of integrity into its many-colored components. We have chosen to focus on five qualities that we believe are core to understanding and practicing the virtue of integrity when it comes to leadership: truth-telling, honor, authenticity, trustworthiness, and courage. None of these by themselves can adequately capture the meaning of integrity. But an exploration of each in turn helps us identify the many qualities of character that together constitute this elusive but essential virtue.

TRUTH-TELLING: THE FOUNDATION OF INTEGRITY

Tell the truth. There are few more basic moral injunctions. As Thomas Jefferson wrote, "Honesty is the first chapter in the book of wisdom."[1] Indeed, honesty and truth-telling are essential elements of integrity, along with adjacent values like sincerity, fair-mindedness, and promise-keeping. And while these are commonly referenced in our cultural value system, they are hardly common in practice. In fact, many people lie all too readily. Perhaps not in egregious or noticeable ways, but in ways that still betray an insufficient fidelity to the truth.

Many of us tell small lies every day, almost without noticing. In the scheme of our daily lives, they may not make much difference at all. Nevertheless, the lines between seemingly small lies and significant ethical breaches are not always crystal clear, and those lines can blur even more when we become habituated to traversing the territory. How many ethical, even criminal, lapses in the business world have started with small, seemingly innocuous forays away from truthfulness? There are sometimes areas of genuine ambiguity, but that should never be an excuse to conceal mistakes or bend rules.

Truth is powerful, but it's not always popular, which means truth-telling can be an uncomfortable endeavor. Sometimes transformative truths must be spoken. We never know exactly when the circumstances of life will demand that we give voice to a larger truth, one that may be subtle, difficult, or even dangerous. Occasionally, it may involve upsetting colleagues or challenging convention. Do we have the commitment to follow through, to risk rocking the boat in the name of honesty and truthfulness? Few have that kind of integrity. But real leadership occasionally demands it.

Our culture has a love-hate relationship with truth-tellers. We respect them. At times we revere them. History may even celebrate them. But they also make us uncomfortable. They don't simply "get along and go along." They confront us and challenge our assumptions. They bring to light cultural shadows. They ask us to look more closely at areas of our collective lives we don't always want to examine.

Leaders who understand the importance of honesty strive to create an environment wherein the truth can readily be told—whether it's good news or bad. Former Medtronic CEO Bill George once told a colleague who was selective about giving his boss negative information, "Integrity is not the absence of lying."[2] We wholeheartedly agree, but for that standard of transparency to become embedded in any corporate culture, it needs to start at the top.

The leadership virtue of integrity requires honesty not only in what you say but also in what you allow yourself to hear. An anecdote from Ford describes this well. Alan Mulally, who was CEO of the auto maker from 2006 to 2014, described a first meeting with his senior executive team, one that would be critical to changing the culture of the struggling car company. In those days, Ford was actually losing billions of dollars, yet the message the new CEO was receiving about the company was bizarrely positive. After a few minutes, he stopped the meeting. "We're going to lose billions of dollars this year," he remarked incredulously. "Why is every line green? Isn't there anything that's not going well here?"

As it turned out, the tendency of the executive culture at Ford was to put a positive spin on things and try to please the boss, not to tell the honest and sometimes brutal truth. In the next business review meeting, things looked different as the Ford team began to get the message—honest communication was expected, even demanded, by their new leader.[3] It's natural for people to emphasize the good news, but sometimes tamping down the bad is akin to lying. If leaders react poorly and condemn the messenger when receiving bad news, they make it all the more likely that people will hesitate to deliver it. Conscious leaders don't just practice truth-telling in their own lives; they encourage honest feedback from those around them.

HONOR: A CONSCIOUS LEADER'S IDENTITY

Imagine you are playing a card game, and the stakes are high. At a critical point in the game, your opponent is distracted by a visitor, gets up from the table, and, for a moment, accidentally leaves his cards faceup. They can easily be seen with just a glance. There is no way your opponent would know. Do you look? Do you take advantage of a careless moment? If not, then why not? When there is no chance of repercussions, when no one else in the world would ever know, why not give yourself an edge?

If you ask a person of integrity that question, they will say something like "I'm not that kind of person." That's exactly what we mean by honor. It's a deep, inner ethical self-identity that knows when an inappropriate line is being crossed. The honorable person stays well on this side. It has little to do with what others think or see or imagine about you; it's between you and you. When there is no one else to impress, nothing to be personally gained, no external image to be burnished, no social standing to maintain, what guides our actions? Independent of rules, regulations, customs, or laws, what "kind of person" am I?

Honor is one of the highest forms of integrity, and one of the most important in business, because the business community thrives, and society along with it, when the all-important value of fair play is alive and well. It can't truly thrive as long as the participants are endlessly trying to game the system, take advantage of every possible loophole, and violate every unwritten rule whenever an authority turns their head. In the end, the virtuous functioning of our economy and our society doesn't simply depend on the enforcement of rules, regulations, and laws, though they are important. An external authority can never ultimately elevate the standards of a community. Individual leaders must do that—leaders with honor. When those individuals consistently hold themselves to their own ethical standards, the fabric that binds that social system together becomes stronger. No regulatory restriction could ever accomplish what the intrinsic power of leaders with honor and integrity makes possible. The quality of the entire community is elevated.

INTEGRITY AS AUTHENTICITY

An individual who has integrity doesn't live behind a carefully calibrated mask. Everything is not focus-grouped and preapproved for public consumption. They are *authentic*—which means they are not one person when they are presenting to the board and someone else when onboarding new interns. They aren't two-faced or three-faced. Integrity has one authentic face: the undefended countenance of simple consistency. An authentic person doesn't just play to the crowd, afraid of what people think and what they will say. They don't endlessly curate their own image. Free of hidden agendas, they exude a refreshing transparency.

Authenticity means being true to ourselves and straightforward with others, whatever situation we may find ourselves in. Of course, this doesn't mean being blind to circumstance. Obviously it's not appropriate to speak out on every subject whenever someone asks us a question, and that's even more true if we represent a larger institution. Some things are private; some are personal. But conscious leaders aren't obsessed with a need-to-know secrecy, and they don't parse out information at every link on the chain of command as if national security was at stake. Whenever possible, frankness and transparency guide their actions. Authentic leaders don't hide behind titles or positions or status, so they are more free to forge the kinds of relationships that great businesses are built upon.

Authenticity also springs from a self-consistency between inner values and outer behavior. In this sense, the core of our personal integrity is forged in the relationship between our values, aspirations, and convictions and the way we behave in the world. It is for this reason that "being true to oneself" is often cited as a foundational element of integrity. Are we showing up in the world in a manner that is consistent with our own sense of what is real, what is true, what is most important? Is there integration between word and deed, between values and volition? When anyone violates that connection, they lack integrity, almost by definition. On the other hand, if someone has integrity, there is a sense of integration in an individual's character that is powerful, even magnetic. They shine with an extra strength and inner confidence. We are naturally drawn to those in whom we sense a predictable, reliable connection between inner conviction and outer behavior.

All of that being said, we must also acknowledge that human beings are complex creatures, and that our psychology inevitably contains dualities, polarities, and different, sometimes even contradictory, parts of the self. Integrity does not mean ironing out all of the inner creases and wrinkles in the human character. Purity is not the goal. But conscious leaders should strive for a level of self-awareness that prevents them from falling blindly or unconsciously into expressions of self that are inappropriate, destructive, or self-contradictory. We've all heard stories of otherwise impressive leaders who had unintegrated sub-personalities, fatal flaws that undermined their authority and credibility, creating confusion and disillusionment. We get into trouble when one part of our personality exists as a kind of outlier to the self—an unseen "shadow" that we aren't able or willing to integrate into our larger umbrella of identity. (See "The Conscious Leader's Tool Kit: Shadow Work," on page 74, for more on this important idea.) One important element of being "conscious" is acquiring enough self-knowledge to better recognize our strengths and weaknesses and take responsibility for their impact, positive and otherwise, on those around us.

PRACTICING INTEGRITY: Authenticity Doesn't Always Come Naturally

It sounds like a bumper sticker, but it's true: To be oneself, one has to know oneself. The deeper one's self-knowledge, the more profound and authentic is one's self-expression. But that doesn't always come naturally; sometimes it must be earned. We're not suggesting that today's corporate leaders immediately drop everything and take a self-help sabbatical. But a little self-knowledge, however it is gained, translates into a treasure trove of leadership wisdom. It may arise from honest feedback, 360-degree leadership reviews, contemplative insight, or another form of practice or reflection, conventional or unconventional. But your career and your colleagues—and, most important, your own character—will be better off for your efforts.

INTEGRITY AS COURAGE: DO THE RIGHT THING

Don Davis became something of a legend in the twenty-two years he spent at MIT Sloan School of Management. A former CEO of Stanley Works turned business and ethics professor, he enjoyed a kind of popularity among his students that went deeper than merely the charisma of success. He was someone they trusted and felt able to turn to for sound advice on important career decisions. Among his many students in those years was a young man named Jeff Wilke, who came to the school after a stint at Andersen Consulting (now Accenture), and for whom Davis became an important mentor.

After his time at MIT, Wilke was confronted with the dilemma facing all graduating students: *What's next? How do I take the learned skills of the classroom and translate them into lived experience in the business world?* Many of his fellow graduates were accepting prestigious jobs on Wall Street or in other celebrated industries, but as Wilke reflected on his next steps, he remembered something Davis had told him. In one of their many conversations about ethics and integrity, he had encouraged Wilke to "seek out tough situations, because you'll get better as a result, and then develop the courage to do the right thing when faced with tough decisions."

For Wilke, "seeking out tough situations" came to mean something very specific. Instead of taking a more prominent, high-paying job, he decided the right thing for him was to do something unexpected—to start his career on the factory floor. He had many offers for jobs in finance, but he was convinced that he needed to work in a manufacturing plant in order to truly cement the leadership virtues he had been studying at MIT and give him a solid foundation from which to earn the trust and respect of others.

"Maybe it was growing up in Pittsburgh, a blue-collar town," he explained, "but I had this instinct that understanding what the people in the operation who are actually doing the work go through—understanding how they work from the ground up—would be very precious later when I was leading those people." He set his sights on a company called AlliedSignal, led by someone he admired. And so it was that this young graduate with hundreds of offers and options ended up in a nylon plant in Virginia, working as an engineer and plant supervisor on the floor.

It wasn't a job that came with the trappings of success, but for Wilke it was priceless. He relished the experience. He learned the business from the ground up, gaining experience in all of the fine details that add up to operational success: making the machines function perfectly, the factory operate smoothly, and the people work productively. He recalls, "Every day I'd go home and say, 'How am I doing?' And then I would think through the things I had encountered that didn't match my mental model and say, 'How do I correct my mental model and do better the next day?'" Little by little, as his operational competence increased by leaps and bounds, Wilke felt his unconventional choice was paying dividends. But he still had no idea how critical this early experience would prove to be to his future career trajectory.

In 1999, an e-commerce company reached out with an offer. They needed an operations guru for a fast-growing distribution and delivery system. They wanted someone who could bring order to the extremely complex supply chains and distribution networks that were developing on the back of the dot-com boom. For Wilke, it was a perfect fit. The name of the company? Amazon.com. He stepped into the new job at the height of the 1999 Christmas season, when online shopping was exploding and the company was scrambling to respond fast enough to its burgeoning business. By the end of the holiday season, he had found a home.

Today, Wilke is one of Amazon's three CEOs and widely credited with helping build what is perhaps the most operationally sophisticated company in the world. The lessons learned on the floor in the nylon factory paid extraordinary dividends. Even to this day, Wilke still credits Davis's words with helping him see the wisdom of following his own instinct and taking the less-traveled road that matched his own values and convictions. It wasn't easy, it wasn't for everyone, and it wasn't what his classmates were doing. But for Wilke, it was the right thing. And somewhere in the vicinity of that "rightness" lives the virtue of integrity. Being true to oneself—in the best sense of what that means. In fact, we would be hard-pressed to come up with a better all-encompassing definition of *integrity* than "doing the right thing."

INTEGRITY AS TRUSTWORTHINESS

When leaders demonstrate the courage to act with integrity even under challenging circumstances—when they do the right thing in the face of complexity, temptation, or confusion—they earn a kind of natural authority and build trust among those they lead. That kind of authority is powerful. It inspires deep loyalty. It's not easy to counterfeit.

Are you a leader who inspires trust? Trustworthiness is a critical component of integrity. As Professor Don Davis expressed it:

> Trust cannot be commanded—you have to earn it. And you do this by being a leader of unquestioned integrity—an authentic human being who has a highly developed sense of straightness and fairness in all human interactions. As a leader, your ethical standards will have a major impact based on your behavior, not your words. It takes courage and a sense of self-worth, together with a certain amount of wisdom, to stay off that slippery slope of temptation. But, when you do the right thing (and you'll know what it is), you win in every direction—and at every level of the organization.[4]

Being a trustworthy leader and practicing these qualities of character can be infectious. When we're responsible, transparent, honest, and authentic, it can help establish a deeper sense of confidence among those we lead. It cuts through the negative politics and discourages the backbiting and jockeying for power that can be so debilitating to any team's productivity and creativity. When we create an environment of shared confidence, it allows our organizations to "move at the speed of trust," as Stephen M. R. Covey puts it. Trust, he explains, is a "hidden variable that affects everything."[5] In its absence, without even realizing it, organizations fall back on politics and time-consuming bureaucratic processes. When trust is established, these become unnecessary, and everything moves faster.

Conscious leaders also understand the limits of their own expertise, and honestly admit when they're wrong or don't know something. By taking responsibility for our own shortcomings and failures, we make it easier for those we lead to do the same. And by reducing defensiveness in this way, we encourage the risk taking required for innovation. In other words, forgiving reasonable or unavoidable mistakes, both our own and those of others, creates a culture of trust that fosters the autonomy necessary for resourcefulness and managerial creativity.

PRACTICING INTEGRITY: Keep Information Transparent

Trust is a two-way street. If you want people to trust you, then you have to return the favor. As a leader, one of the best ways to demonstrate that trust in people is to share information with them. So, unless there's a very good reason not to disclose information, it should be transparently made available. Better still, leaders can be proactive in delivering information and answering questions, in informal settings like team member lunches or larger forums like "town halls." The worst thing a leader can do is refuse to acknowledge something that everyone already knows, because of an overly restrictive communication policy. Of course, not everything can be shared freely, but whenever possible, transparency should be the default posture for the conscious leader.

INTEGRITY TODAY AND TOMORROW

For a conscious leader, integrity should be something that continues to grow and deepen in accordance with one's life experience. It's not just about high ideals. In the moral flush of young adulthood, it's easy to imagine that integrity is all about being a "good person"—being on the "right" side of important ethical decisions, not being selfish, telling the truth, treating people well, and not doing "bad" things like lying or cheating. By the time we're in our early twenties, we've seen countless movies in which the moral dividing lines are neon bright. In that Hollywood version of morality, doing the right thing requires sacrifice and courage on the part of the hero or heroine, but the virtuous path is rarely muddy or complex. There are few shades of gray or matters of degree. Our mandate, as protagonists in such moral plotlines, is "Don't be evil," to borrow Google's famous mission statement. There is nothing inherently wrong with that conception of integrity. It's obviously positive to aspire to ethical behavior, and to not compromise or sell out our own sense of right and wrong because of greed or weakness. We certainly need fewer Enrons in the world, and more courageous whistleblowers. But as we continue to mature, the realization comes upon us that adult integrity is about much more than not being evil. Difficult ethical issues rarely show up in black-and-white terms. Challenging decisions don't often present themselves in cartoonish moral outlines. Yes, it's good not to cook the books, commit fraud, leak confidential information, or deceive our customers. Every day, people fail to make such choices, and we should appreciate those who continue to listen to the better angels of their nature. But once we get beyond those clear ethical choices, the challenge of integrity increases. For the conscious leader, "Always act with integrity" means aspiring to a much higher level of trustworthiness, an expanded sense of responsibility, a superior standard of truth-telling, and more profound depth of character. Integrity, in this sense, includes but also transcends the standard of being a "good person." It's an aspiration to reach our higher potentials, to develop our ability to more clearly see, more deeply feel, and more wisely respond to the myriad of complex situations that an ambitious leader will inevitably face. "Don't be evil" still applies; it can never be taken for granted. But like Google, which eventually updated its moral mission statement to "Do the right thing," conscious leaders do well to aim for more expansive horizons.

EVER-EVOLVING AGENTS OF CHANGE

As we consider this expanded definition of integrity, it's important to understand that it's not only something we "have" (or not). It's also something that we must continually aspire to develop, to deepen, and to live up to. Leadership is a journey, and so is integrity. For example, we would be hard-pressed to find a company that better demonstrates the virtue of integrity than Mendiola's FIFCO, and yet despite all that the company has done in recent years to bring value to its various stakeholders, it has continued to rise to new challenges. In 2014, Ramón and his team were coming off a hectic period of expansion, including a move into North America. They were feeling the need to connect with and unify their team members. They spent time clarifying the company's core purpose and came up with a simple phrase they loved: "We bring a better way of living to the world." Ramón decided to shut down operations for a full day so he could share this purpose statement with all of the team members in Costa Rica—some 3,500 people. After he'd finished his speech, a man stood up, stepped forward, and grabbed the microphone.

"Ramón," he said, "I'm very proud of what the company is doing for the environment. But what about the people working in this company? People who work here are living in poverty. What do you think about that?"

Ramón was surprised, and even more so when a surge of applause rippled through the auditorium. He took back the microphone and thanked the man for speaking up. "I don't know how many of our team members are living in poverty," he admitted. "But I'm sorry. We're going to do something about it."

Once again, Ramón's sense of integrity was challenged. How could he lead a company that claimed to be doing right by its stakeholders when 3.6 percent of its team members were living in conditions of unacceptable poverty? This was not a result of poor wages; the company paid well. But other issues left workers vulnerable. Now that he knew, Ramón called in experts to help him understand the issue, and within six months he had launched the FIFCO Opportunities program, which addresses issues like housing, health, and financial literacy. Each participant in the program is personally mentored by one of FIFCO's top executives. In three years, the company succeeded in lifting every team member in Costa Rica out of poverty. Now they're turning their attention to their other locations too.

It goes without saying that business can't solve all of the problems of society. FIFCO, likewise, is never going to single-handedly transform the social challenges that face Costa Rica. But within their own limited spheres of influence, businesses can have remarkable impact and deploy highly effective resources at targeted issues. At Whole Foods Market, I've seen this happen again and again. Good companies led by conscious leaders are powerful agents of change.

THE DANCE BETWEEN PERSONAL AND ORGANIZATIONAL INTEGRITY

With any virtue or quality of character, a question often arises: What is the relationship between the personal and the organizational? How does our own individual sense of integrity interface with the values of the organizations that we may be involved with? An organization is its own entity, with its own purpose, but inevitably it does take on some of the attributes of its leader or leaders. How far should that go? Where are the boundaries, if any, between personal and organizational values? Let me explore that question by relating a story about a crisis of integrity that I faced in my own life, one that also implicated Whole Foods Market.

I have always had a personal commitment to act with integrity—to live up to my own values and to be authentic, honorable, honest, and trustworthy in my dealings with everyone in my life, both personally and professionally. While that commitment has remained consistent, what it looks like has evolved substantially over the years as

I've learned from my life experience and engaged in relationships with a wider circle of stakeholders. Integrity, I've come to understand, is not an isolated, unmoving moral stance, but rather an authentic, ongoing commitment to *integrate* my own purpose, my behavior, my values, and what I continue to learn. I've made plenty of mistakes in my life, but these mistakes have helped me to learn and grow into a better version of myself.

One of the guiding values in my life is the welfare of animals. Since 2003, I've been an ethical vegan, which means that I choose not to eat any meat, fish, poultry, eggs, dairy products, or other animal products. A few years ago, I was invited to participate in a public debate on the issue at Stanford University. Together with my debate partner, Bruce Friedrich from the Good Food Institute, I was to make the case against eating animals. It's something I feel passionately about, and I've personally gone to great lengths to live in integrity with my belief that for me, animals should not be a source of food. So you can imagine how I felt when, at the beginning of the debate, a group of animal rights activists in the audience got up and began chanting and marching toward the stage, holding placards with shocking pictures of factory farm animals. The target of their protest was not my meat-eating debate counterparts, who were arguing for an animal-based diet. It was me.

This was not an isolated incident. In fact, I am regularly targeted by animal rights protesters, who perceive me as a traitor to their cause and accuse me of being complicit in many of the practices I deeply abhor. Why? Because the company I lead does not mirror my personal lifestyle. In other words, Whole Foods Market is not a vegan store. Is that a lack of integrity?

By way of an answer, let me go back a few years. My own dietary choices have evolved through a series of awakenings—some informed by health concerns, others by ethical considerations. Each time I've come upon new information that has changed the way I think about the topic, I've changed my personal practices accordingly. When I was a child, my diet was quite unhealthy. I ate the Standard American

Diet of highly processed foods and consumed virtually no fruits and vegetables. While a student at the University of Texas back in 1976, I moved into a vegetarian co-op, and my first dietary awakening took place: a recognition of the abundance of delicious natural foods and a discovery that I felt much better when I ate them. I changed my diet and became a vegetarian, eating mostly natural foods that were minimally processed.

Fast-forward to 2003, when an activist came to a Whole Foods Market shareholders' meeting and gave an impassioned speech about animal welfare, accusing the company of failing to do enough. I was initially irritated, because I thought we were doing more than just about anyone else in the industry. But I engaged with her argument, and over that summer I ended up doing extensive reading and research in the field. Even for a relatively informed insider, what I discovered disturbed me. Integrity, for me, meant updating my choices in light of this expanded perspective. I decided that the right response for me was to become an ethical vegan. My health has been positively impacted by that choice, but that was a secondary benefit. In light of this decision, a new question arose: How does my personal conviction relate to the business I run? Should my new ethical sensibility impact company policy? We're trying to lead the market but we are also trying to serve the market. For example, Whole Foods Market has always been about healthy eating, but, as I've often said, that doesn't mean that everything in the store is perfectly healthy. We're a business, not an activist organization.

While I'm the CEO, the overall leader of the company, I've never been the owner of Whole Foods Market—even at the very beginning of the business. This is a common misperception, but my ownership stake has always been very small. I'm also in service to both the higher purpose of the company and all of the diverse, interdependent stakeholders. For the first thirty-nine years of our existence, I was accountable to a board of directors, and with the acquisition of Whole Foods by Amazon, I'm accountable to a senior executive of the larger company. Obviously I have great influence, but I am a servant leader in the organization. That's how it should be. And, to the disappointment of vegan activists, I could not—and would not—announce one day that Whole Foods would no longer sell animal products. Despite my personal convictions, I didn't feel that move would have been in the best interests of the company or any of its major stakeholders. Only about 5 percent of Americans currently follow a vegetarian diet[6] (and back in 2003 it was much less). Though I'm encouraged by the growing awareness and interest in plant-based eating, the United States as a whole remains very, very far from embracing this dietary approach.

But neither did I sit on my hands. That would have been a violation of my own integrity. Instead, I helped lead an initiative in the company to develop a new set of robust animal welfare standards, working to better inform customers about the food they are eating, and to encourage our partners in the agricultural industry to upgrade their animal welfare practices. I'm proud of those standards and the tremendous good they have done. We have led the industry and influenced it for the better. Integrity, when it comes to marrying personal values and organizational behavior, is not always a simple matter. I changed, and then Whole Foods Market changed, but not in exactly the same way. I had to struggle with the question of how to reconcile the evolution of my values with a public corporation that was well over twenty-five years old at that time. In the creative tension of that struggle, a successful initiative has emerged that I believe has improved the lives of—and brought awareness to the plight of—billions of farm animals and ocean creatures.

Today, activists still protest Whole Foods—drawing from a seemingly bottomless well of righteous passion and indignation. And they heckle me regularly, as they did at Stanford. As I sat on the stage that day, waiting for the room to be cleared so I could stand up and deliver my remarks, it was hard to escape the irony. I share many of the values of those who were chanting their outrage at my "betrayal" and at Whole Foods' perceived imperfections. I still question myself and challenge the company I lead to do better. But I also know that the struggle for integrity is not always a solo journey, and moral courage is not always about holding a sign—and a hard line.

Integrity should never be used as a badge of self-righteousness. We live in an age of outrage, and simply refusing to participate in that takes a certain conviction and willingness to not be pulled by the cultural currents into a state of righteous indignation. Always act with integrity, but do it with a light heart and a humble attitude. As one of our favorite philosophers, Robert Solomon, advises, don't regard yourself as "the moral rock around which the rest of the earth revolves."[7] While having integrity means being true to oneself, it also means being open to the opinions of others and being willing to determine the most ethical course of action through careful and considered deliberation, often in collaboration with colleagues or friends. Moral autonomy must be balanced by respect for agreed-upon values and keeping faith with your organization's true higher purpose. Very often, it's about finding a common way forward—a win-win-win. Integrity, Solomon writes, requires "fidelity to self in the midst of others and together with them."[8] It is in the creative tension between those two poles that we, as conscious leaders, must find the energy and perspective to struggle for our own integrity, and ultimately to do the right thing in the communities and organizations that sustain us.

THE CONSCIOUS LEADER'S TOOL KIT

Shadow Work

For those who aspire to lead with integrity, an important skill entails actively working to integrate their "shadow." What is the shadow? The concept comes mainly from Jungian psychology but has been developed by many in the fields of contemporary psychology and spirituality. A simple way to define it is as those aspects of the self that we don't want to see. They're hidden to us, outside of our conscious experience. Often it includes things we don't like about ourselves, or things that make us uncomfortable. Emotions like fear and anger, childhood traumas, things that give rise to shame and guilt—all of these are commonly part of the shadow. We are scared of admitting their presence to ourselves and even more scared of revealing them to others, so we push them outside of our conscious awareness and go about our business as if they don't exist. While it's sometimes described as the "dark side," it's a mistake to think of the shadow as inherently negative. Sometimes we also find it difficult to acknowledge and take ownership of our positive potentials, our desires, our vulnerabilities, even our strengths.

The problem with the shadow is that, while those uncomfortable parts of ourselves may temporarily seem to disappear from awareness, they don't really go anywhere. And as with anything we repress or avoid, sooner or later the shadow aspects of ourselves will surface, often in ways that undermine our conscious intentions and higher purpose. If the shadow remains unconscious, it can control us in ways we don't even see. It may come out in the form of self-sabotage, or addictive behaviors. There is also a tendency to project those things we fear in ourselves onto others. For example, if you're afraid of your own tendency to avoid commitment and break promises, you might find yourself mistrusting other people and questioning their loyalty. If you're uncomfortable with your own anger, you might overreact to the perceived anger of others.

In fact, things that you overreact to are often clues to your own shadow. Because the very essence of shadow is its invisibility, uncovering it takes some detective work. Pay attention next time you're "triggered" in a way that seems disproportionate to the situation. Does the external source of your discomfort point you to an inner aspect of yourself that you've rejected? Is there a suppressed memory of trauma or an embarrassing personal trait that you've hidden somewhere in your subconscious? Feelings of shame or guilt can also act as clues.

Conscious leaders work to integrate their shadows, which means bringing those disowned feelings, tendencies, and experiences out into the light of consciousness and "owning" them. As the authors of *Integral Life Practice* write, you have a choice to either "*own your shadow* by working to become aware of your repressed unconscious drives, feelings, needs, and potentials . . . or *become owned by it* by letting your disowned drives and feelings shape your life outcomes, entirely apart from your conscious choices."[9]

This might involve deep self-inquiry, therapy, or spiritual practice. Whatever path you choose, it should lead you to a more compassionate embrace of all of who you are. Being in a position of leadership can sometimes exacerbate the desire to avoid our shadows—we feel a heightened pressure to set an example, to not reveal weaknesses or risk making mistakes. But that kind of approach, however well-intentioned, is a recipe for disaster. Sooner or later, leaders who set themselves up as perfect tend to fall from grace, and often the shadow is at play. They also implicitly encourage others to suppress or avoid their areas of weakness or insecurity. We're not saying you shouldn't strive to set the best example you can, but part of that example is having the humility and courage to embrace all of who you are, not just the parts you feel good about. Working to integrate your shadow means you are more able to make conscious choices about how you act and are less likely to be blindsided by your own demons.

PART II

MINDSET & STRATEGY

FIND WIN-WIN-WIN SOLUTIONS

Right action focuses on doing what is beneficial
to everyone, including yourself.

—ROGER WALSH

IT WAS AN UNUSUALLY WARM spring day in 2017 when I arrived in New York City, eager to launch a new book. In the days ahead, I was scheduled to speak on several national TV shows about a topic close to my heart: the amazing health benefits of a whole foods, plant-based diet. I was feeling energized and positive about this new opportunity to pursue my life's purpose—until I turned on my phone and it was as if all the sunlight and bright possibility had been sucked out of my world. The thing I'd been dreading and fighting to prevent for years was happening. Whole Foods Market, the company I'd dedicated my entire adult life to creating, building, and nurturing, was facing an existential crisis unlike anything in our history as a public company.

That history began all the way back in 1992. We had opened our first store in Austin in 1978, but 1992 was the year we first sold stock to the public, and I had to learn to balance my long-term, purpose-driven, multi-stakeholder approach to business with the short-term, investor-focused demands of quarterly earnings reporting. This wasn't always easy, but the company was doing well, which helped. Over our forty-two-year history, Whole Foods has achieved tremendous growth. By 2017 we were nearing five hundred stores. We had gone from $300,000 in annual sales during our first year to over $16 billion in sales by the summer of 2017. We had averaged 8 percent same-store sales growth for more than thirty years, which is one of the best track records in the history of food retailing in America. In addition, we had the highest EBITDA (earnings before interest, tax, depreciation, and amortization) percentage among public food retailers, and sales per square foot in our stores, at $1,000 per square foot, were twice as high as the industry average.

But in 2017, that remarkable track record of growth wasn't enough for Wall Street, in part because our sales growth was slowing. Our success had, naturally, spawned a new generation of competitors anxious to participate in the natural foods boom. Conventional grocers were finally waking up to the tremendous opportunity created in the marketplace by people who wanted to eat healthier. More and more grocers and retailers started to imitate Whole Foods and carry larger assortments of natural and organic products. They copied much of our marketing strategy; they increased the space dedicated to organic produce; they even adopted elements of our in-store design aesthetic. From the perspective of our higher purpose—to nourish people and the planet—I was proud of the influence we'd had on the market and the benefits to people who might never enter one of our stores. But, as the leader of a public company, I was keenly aware that our investors might not feel the same way, especially as that competition began to take a toll on our sales growth and our stock price began to fall. Given that I didn't own a huge percentage of the company or have a special share class that gave me a controlling interest, I worried we were vulnerable to activist investors.

Those fears would be proven all too prescient on that spring day, March 29, 2017, when JANA Partners, a New York hedge fund, announced that it had bought 8.8 percent of our stock. Immediately, JANA proceeded to launch a campaign against Whole Foods. Despite our years of consistent success, they had developed a very negative narrative about the company. They wanted us to replace our board of directors and put the company up for sale to the highest bidder. JANA was motivated by one thing only—maximizing short-term profits—and it was determined to do whatever was required to execute its plans. We quickly realized that Whole Foods Market leadership was facing the most significant, high-stakes challenge in the company's history. For me personally, it was an enormous test—how was I to shepherd the company I had led for so many years into the next phases of its existence without losing those qualities that made it special? My book tour was abandoned, my TV appearances canceled, as I devoted every waking minute to finding a way through this crisis.

What eventually transpired over the following weeks and months surprised everyone, including me. Whole Foods ended up merging with Amazon, forming a relationship that has proven to be very beneficial to both companies. For me, it was a time of difficulty and soul-searching. I had some dark moments when I truly feared that so much of what we had built could be lost. But ultimately, it was a period that deeply affirmed one of the leadership principles I have always depended on—the importance of finding solutions in which everyone wins. Before I share the rest of the remarkable story of the merger, or what I have come to call "the marriage" of Amazon and Whole Foods, I want to say a few things about the critical mindset that is at the core of what it means to be a conscious leader.

AN ALTERNATIVE STRATEGY

We all know the archetype: the dealmaker, the negotiator, the shark, the supposedly savvy businessman or -woman who always seems to get the better end of the stick—fifty-one cents or more on the dollar when the deal is made. Their goal is to always "win" the deal. After all, it's a war out there in the business world—isn't it? Think Michael Douglas as Gordon Gekko in *Wall Street*, quoting Sun Tzu's *The Art of War*. Or Alec Baldwin's character in *Glengarry Glen Ross* exhorting his underlings with f-bombs and insults to do anything possible to get people to "sign on the line which is dotted!"[1] Or Kevin O'Leary, aka Mr. Wonderful, on the popular CNBC show *Shark Tank*, rubbing his hands together and saying, "Here's how I think of my money: as soldiers. I send them off to war every day. I want them to take prisoners and come home so there's more of them."[2] In this approach to the art of the deal, business is at best a game, but more often it's a battle. The overriding goal is to survive and prevail, and crush the other party in the process. There is one winner, and the others are losers. That's just the way it works. *Deal with it, sucker.*

Now imagine there was a different way. If you've read this far in the book, you know that we prefer not to view business as a battlefield. What if there was an alternative ethical strategy that we could use in both leadership and life that would result in positive outcomes for both ourselves and everyone around us? Wouldn't that be a marvelous discovery? After all, trying to act ethically and do the right thing can often seem confusing and difficult. Leadership today—and, to be honest, life in general—involves increasingly complex webs of relationships and responsibilities, and it sometimes seems impossible to sort out the best way forward.

Amid this complexity, we have come to advocate and rely on an ethical strategy that is both simple to understand and highly effective: finding win-win-win solutions. It's an all-encompassing strategic approach to leadership for effective long-term success. Employed carefully and thoughtfully, it will result in positive outcomes for everyone involved, including oneself.

You've probably heard the term "win-win," but you may notice that we're adding a third "win." We begin with the basic idea of win-win—creating positive outcomes for both ourselves and the people on the other side of the table. We would contend that a win-win philosophy is at the ethical core of most business dealings. As Alexander McCobin, CEO of Conscious Capitalism, puts it, "A positive-sum worldview is a foundational premise of capitalism, where we seek out mutually beneficial exchanges so that we create more value for everyone than existed before the exchange."[3] A trade happens, and both people do well. One person receives a needed product or service; the other receives a gain on the exchange—both win! There is a double "thank you" taking place wherein both parties are happy. In fact, probably the greatest misunderstanding of business is the failure to appreciate that the vast majority of exchanges are win-win—otherwise they would not have taken place, since they are voluntary.

Conscious leaders, however, take this mindset one giant step further and simultaneously seek positive outcomes for the larger community—a third win. This community can be defined as widely as we wish to define it. In some contexts, the additional win could be for our families, our religious community, our city, our state, our nation, all humans, all animals, or even the health of the biosphere. The key ethical idea in win-win-win thinking is that we are seeking to find strategies and solutions that benefit us, the parties we are directly interacting with, and the larger communities that we exist within. It's a triple victory—good for me, good for you, good for all of us.

In business, that third win typically represents the larger stakeholder group for which the business is creating value—customers, team members, suppliers, investors, and local and global communities. (See "The Conscious Leader's Tool Kit: Stakeholder Integration," page 51, for more on this topic.) The premise is that all the stakeholders are connected and interdependent. By managing the entire system with win-win-win thinking, we create positive synergies that benefit everyone. This helps the organization to be more successful and flourish at much higher levels over the long term. And that long-term view is critical, because some of those benefits aren't fully seen and appreciated if our time horizon is too limited.

Win-win-win thinking is an ethical strategy that can help guide us, as conscious leaders, every single day as we navigate the many dimensions of exercising influence, wielding power, and negotiating deals. More important, this approach can help in a much larger endeavor—transforming our world for the better. But to truly appreciate this philosophy and its power, we have to evolve past our conditioned win-lose, either-or mindset. That can be quite difficult, given how pervasive it is in our society.

Win-win-win thinking is a deeply satisfying approach to our business relationships in part because it represents the essence of the Golden Rule—"Do unto others as you would have them do unto you." In various forms, this has been taught and practiced as a key ethical principle for thousands of years. In evolutionary psychology, it is closely related to "reciprocal altruism"—both parties voluntarily creating value for the other to achieve mutual gain. And let's be very clear: it does not have to involve long-term self-sacrifice. It doesn't mean we put aside our best interests on behalf of the other person. That's win-lose again, only the roles are reversed. In a win-win-win approach, we are looking to create outcomes where *all* parties feel that the outcome is beneficial.

Unfortunately, too much of our culture believes in the win-lose paradigm. It's hard to convince people of another possibility. In fact, that's how business is too often portrayed in contemporary discourse: as greedy, selfish, and exploitative—a win-lose, winner-take-all process whereby the "rich get richer and the poor get poorer." As a result, there are, regrettably, more than a few Gordon Gekkos in the cinematic and literary imagination.

Of course, there are plenty of real examples of greedy, dishonest behavior in business, just as there are examples of bad behavior in all fields. But the idea that business is all about exploitation, and simply redistributes wealth to the top of the social hierarchy, is an unfortunate and inaccurate myth. The percentage of the world population living in poverty has fallen dramatically in the past two centuries, and business has been the major contributor to that trend. Global incomes have increased at an unprecedented rate over the same period, even as global poverty rates have fallen—a process that has accelerated in recent decades.[4] In the magic of trade and voluntary exchange, the uplifting power of mutually beneficial outcomes has been one of the greatest sources of value for human civilization, improving the human condition and upgrading all of our lives in the process.

PRACTICING WIN-WIN-WIN: Is Anyone Losing?

The habit of a win-lose mentality is strong. It's our default mode, which is why we need to retrain our minds. One of the essential practices for developing win-win-win solutions is to ask, "Is anyone losing in this proposal? Does anyone perceive themselves as getting the short end of the stick? Is there anything we can do to fix that for them?" These questions bring quick clarity to any proposal, identify gaps, and help us create better and better alternatives.

THE DYNAMICS OF TRUST

What happens when a person practicing a win-win-win philosophy encounters someone who is engaged in a win-lose strategy? Not surprisingly, this does occur regularly. If that's the kind of person we're dealing with, we must be that much more awake and aware of what's going on. The other person isn't playing by the same rules that we are! We can't be as trusting; we have to be more on our guard. It's imperative to protect our own interests. But that shouldn't deter us from at least trying to seek a win-win-win deal. If we fail, however, the line is clear. Remember Stephen Covey's words in his masterful book *The 7 Habits of Highly Effective People*. He calls for us to embrace the philosophy of "Win/Win or No Deal."[5] If we can't achieve that win-win, Covey urges us to simply walk away.

Trust is so important. If it's not there, do we really want to make a deal? Warren Buffett likes to say that he always wants his deals to be able to be done with a handshake. That doesn't mean he doesn't have lawyers check the details. It simply means that in some basic sense there is a high level of trust and mutual respect. If we don't feel that, we should question the wisdom of going forward. At the very least, we need to be appropriately cautious. "Trust in Allah, but tether your camel," as the old Sufi saying goes.

Research from game theory has provided another boost to the efficacy of this mindset. It has shown that the strategy proven to be most effective over the long term is "tit for tat." In tit-for-tat strategies, the initial approach is open and cooperative. That means we choose to cooperate with everyone (seek a win-win outcome) until a person proves to be untrustworthy (seeking a losing outcome for us). Then our strategy has to shift—we can no longer cooperate with that player. We risk being taken advantage of. This is a very resilient approach, both in game theory and in life. We develop a reputation for being honest and trustworthy, but we don't tolerate being taken advantage of. We protect ourselves, but our basic posture is one of trust and cooperation. It's a win-win attitude with everyone—if possible. When that doesn't work, we channel our inner Stephen Covey and say "No Deal."

PRACTICING WIN-WIN-WIN: Communication Is the Key

When we're looking for win-win-win solutions, particularly when working with other people, good communication is critical. It's virtually impossible to find a win-win-win without all sides being candid about their needs and interests. What does a win look like for them? Don't assume you already know. Transparency helps empower win-win-win approaches. During negotiations, people often hesitate to voice what they truly want or need, because they believe it makes them vulnerable and weakens their leverage. We encourage the opposite. Ask questions like: What would be an ideal outcome for you? What would make you walk away feeling fully satisfied? What elements of this deal are nonnegotiable for you? Once we understand another party's needs and desires, and that information is on the table, we're in a better position to help satisfy them. The dialogue will be more constructive, and a win-win-win solution will be closer at hand.

CRISIS AND OPPORTUNITY

Sometimes it takes a crisis to help us break through conditioned, win-lose ways of thinking and acting. For Cheryl Rosner, as for many Americans, 9/11 was that kind of moment. The entire country felt the devastating social and economic impact of 9/11, but one industry took it especially hard: the travel industry. And Rosner, an executive with Expedia, was right in the middle of it. In the chaos of that tragic day and the week that followed, her team worked around the clock to make sure that their guests and customers, who in many cases were stuck without travel options, had places to stay. Their hotel partners were wonderfully accommodating, so, after the initial crisis had died down, she went on a little tour to thank them personally. What became clear in those meetings was that economic pain was taking a toll. The travel industry had pretty much shut down. "They were getting killed," she remembers, "especially smaller, independent properties who suddenly had very little cash flow." Layoffs and other business disruptions were imminent.

Back at the office, Rosner sat down with her CFO and explained the situation as she'd seen it. Both of them felt the urgency of trying to help these businesses—their partners—who, through no fault of their own, were facing desperate times. And to raise the stakes for Expedia, this was happening at the same time it was preparing to launch a new website, Hotels.com, and needed all the support it could get from these independent hotel operators. Perhaps there was a win-win solution? That evening, over a glass or two of bourbon, they discussed possibilities. After cycling through a number of what Rosner recalls as bad ideas, they finally hatched a plan. After much deliberation, they decided to extend no-hassle, zero-interest loans to many of these small businesses to help them survive the temporary downturn. These loans had a fluid payback period, and they included a benefit to Rosner and her team: preferable rates and pricing when the Hotels.com brand launched and travel picked back up. Not only would those better rates benefit Hotels.com as it entered the market, but they would also help inspire people to get back to traveling, drive business to these struggling partners, and bring benefits to the whole industry.

In 2002, Hotels.com launched and was a tremendous success, powered in part by the favorable terms and relationships Rosner had cultivated with these partners. The travel industry rebounded, and the no-interest loans were paid back sooner than expected. It was a big win for everyone: for the company, for its partners that were able to keep their businesses afloat, for the people who kept their jobs, for the travel industry, and even for the economy itself. All it took was a willingness to find a solution that could help everyone get through the crisis. It was a simple solution, but it took thinking outside the box to get there, and for Rosner the impact was particularly profound. It changed her sense of business, of how connected and interdependent we all are—economically but also in other ways. And it made her want to find ways to bring that spirit of mutual benefit forward as she moved into future entrepreneurial endeavors. It may have taken the shock of 9/11 to jolt her into a new perspective, but she took the lesson and ran with it. Every conscious leader can learn from such experiences, even without the backdrop of a tragedy.

MASTERING THE MINDSET OF MUTUAL BENEFIT

Are win-win-win solutions really possible? Can we adopt such a bold approach on a consistent basis? Is this ethical strategy too idealistic for the "real world"? We don't think so. Of course, life is complicated, and there are occasions when win-win-win solutions prove elusive. At Whole Foods Market, sometimes we've had to close a poorly performing store because, despite many failed attempts, we just couldn't come up with any solutions to make it successful. However, I don't believe this means that a solution didn't exist; it's just that at some point we ran out of time or imagination to find it!

Conscious leaders should dedicate themselves to becoming experts at navigating complex scenarios and finding win-win-win solutions across stakeholder groups, and to do that we need a sophisticated understanding of how systems work (see "The Conscious Leader's Tool Kit: Systems Thinking," page 99). We need to see the big picture and understand how the different components of the system interconnect and behave over time, balancing immediate and long-term needs to create value for as many stakeholders as possible.

If we can master the skill of finding win-win-win solutions whenever time and circumstance allow, we are going to have far more success, not only in business and leadership but also in life. People usually know who's trustworthy, who has their best interests at heart, and if we earn that reputation, it will mean a great deal. We are likely to be much happier and more fulfilled. We will have fewer conflicts, because our attitude will encourage a higher level of trust and cooperation.

What really makes win-win-win such a powerful ethical strategy is that it encourages us to unleash our creative minds and develop more deeply innovative solutions. The win-lose, either-or way of thinking usually comes to mind first, because it's easy and familiar and it requires far less imagination and creativity. It's the path of least resistance. When we practice win-lose strategies, we are often too quick to accept undesirable trade-offs as both inevitable and necessary. If we look for such trade-offs, we will certainly find them. But the idea that someone must lose so that another will gain just isn't true. In fact, we believe that this *zero-sum* mentality, as they call it in game theory, holds back both our own personal flourishing and the collective good of humanity. Instead, when we look for creative win-win-win (or *non-zero-sum*) solutions, our attention will be on finding these instead, often without any onerous compromises. Never underestimate the power of human ingenuity, once liberated from the default mental straitjacket of win-lose. Once we free our imagination to come up with creative solutions where everyone is benefiting, it is amazing how much positive energy and goodwill is unlocked.

PRACTICING WIN-WIN-WIN: Liberate Your Imagination

Conflicts and disagreements present an opportunity for us to liberate our creative imaginations to discover win-win-win solutions. But remember, that kind of creativity takes time and space, and it needs air to breathe. The enemy of creativity is instant judgment. When brainstorming solutions, avoid short-circuiting the creative process by immediately asking, "What's wrong?" or coming up with reasons why a particular solution won't work. There's a time to criticize and a time to judge, but it's not during a brainstorming session. Ideas need to flow freely. Later on, when we've developed a variety of possible solutions, we can go back and analyze them critically. Critical analysis and creative imagination inhabit different dimensions of our mental space—give them both their due.

A WIN-WIN-WIN TO REMEMBER

Win-win-win thinking is not just applicable to the business arena; it's desperately needed in our society right now. If more leaders in both the private and public sectors would begin to adopt the mindset of mutual benefit, the effects would ripple through our economy and our society, rapidly accelerating cultural evolution and progress.

Today, such a scenario seems far-fetched. As we write this book, the United States is more politically polarized than it has been at any other point in our lifetimes. Our culture is divided into angry and aggrieved political tribes. The various value systems that shape our population (see the appendix, "On Cultivating Cultural Intelligence," page 229) are vying with one another for preeminence and control. Win-lose thinking dominates public discourse. People believe that their own values are on the side of the angels, while those values that express a different perspective are stupid, wrong, and evil and must be defeated. It's a battle that seems to have little hope of resolution, and the spillover effects are polluting many aspects of our cultural landscape.

But there is nothing inevitable about this polarized state. Tribal thinking doesn't have to be the default way that we interact. Changing this state of affairs, however, will take courageous leadership. More of our leaders would need to adopt a win-win-win approach to our national issues, employing all of their intelligence and creativity to find innovative solutions that transcend ideological conflicts and generate real value for the larger society. How do we move the society forward, ameliorate the polarization, and do it all in such a way that all of the major stakeholders—which are the various tribes or worldviews—"win" in some way? As conscious leaders, we need to develop a much higher degree of cultural intelligence and a mindset of mutual benefit to achieve those lofty goals.

Yet we can draw inspiration from the fact that it has been done before. Win-win-win thinking has often defined those moments in American history that changed the country for the better. In fact, one of the common threads among all the major social movements that have been successful and sustainable over the long run is that they had an undergirding of mutual benefit. There are many examples of this, but one that we always find deeply motivating and heartening is the Civil Rights Movement of the 1950s and '60s.

Dr. Martin Luther King Jr. was fighting for the rights of his people—but also for more than that. He clearly saw that the Civil Rights Movement needed to seek not only the empowerment of black Americans and their liberation from Jim Crow, but also the ethical redemption of America as a whole from the shameful blight of racism. King's extraordinary vision was a colorblind society with equal rights and dignity for all races and ethnicities. He presented that vision to the rest of America—appealing to the national conscience and to the collective hope that we could create a solution to our racial problems that would benefit all sectors of society.

King and his fellow activists' passionate stance of nonviolence kept the public perception of the movement situated in a win-win-win framework. Their refusal to retaliate, even in the face of violence, appealed to the conscience and goodwill of citizens throughout the nation and helped prevent the movement from slipping into a win-lose stance that would have complicated that inclusive vision. It remains a beautiful vision, an aspiration not only for the country but for humanity as a whole. And it took the extraordinary leadership of King, together with other courageous leaders who stood beside him, to embed it so deeply into the national consciousness.

King's dream of racial equality, dignity, and harmony challenged the American status quo to its core. But it was also congruent with the promise made in the Declaration of Independence that we are all created equal and with rights to life, liberty, and the pursuit of happiness. In that, the Civil Rights Movement created multiple layers of positive outcomes. It offered some measure of justice and opportunity to citizens who had too long been prevented from participating in the American Dream. And it has been deeply beneficial for our entire society—culturally, economically, morally—as we continue our national journey. That journey, of course, is far from finished, as we continue our work to leave behind the inherent racism that was seeded in our country from the beginning. There have certainly been plenty of bumps and setbacks along that road, but, thanks to King's radical win-win-win vision, we have taken significant steps forward.

A HAPPY MARRIAGE

With such lofty ideals and cultural heroes elevating our hearts and minds, let's return to the world of business—the existential crisis that Whole Foods Market faced in 2017. It might not have been a moment of great historic import or national significance, but the stakes were high for me and the many stakeholders who had built, nurtured, supported, and loved our company and its higher purpose. As I huddled with my executive team in the spring of that year, we asked ourselves two critical questions: What is the win-win-win solution here? And what is the best thing for all of Whole Foods Market's stakeholders?

My own fear was that JANA Partners, being motivated by short-term profit-seeking and a win-lose framework, would be able to take control of the company and sell it off to the highest bidder. That highest bidder might not be a company that would honor our higher purpose—our core values, our mission, our standards, and what we stood for. Our culture almost surely would have been deeply harmed, and our headquarters could have been dismantled, with thousands losing their jobs. If our quality standards were overturned, we'd be forced to sell products that no longer fit our mission. The way I saw it, we were in danger of losing everything we had built.

We considered lots of options and strategies. Should we engage in a media war with JANA? Should we pit our vision of the future against theirs in the public mind? Should we commit to a struggle with JANA to maintain control of the board and prevent a sale of the company against our will? If we were to fight, would we win or were we likely to lose?

Though we knew we might ultimately be able to prevail in this struggle, we also recognized that it would likely be a long and expensive battle and a huge distraction for the company. In other words, we could lose even if we won. But it was an alternative that we took very seriously, and we prepared a complete strategy to follow should we opt to go in that direction.

During our discussions, the option of selling the company came up as well. We asked ourselves, "If we were to be sold, is there a buyer that we'd particularly prefer? Is there any company out there that would be a really good fit?" The name Berkshire Hathaway came up in our deliberations, and we contacted Warren Buffett to see if he had any interest in possibly buying Whole Foods. He responded that it wasn't a good fit for him. We considered other food retailers—again looking for a solution that would create a win-win-win for all our stakeholders. I met with the CEO and chairman of Albertsons on an informal basis and concluded that Albertsons probably wouldn't have been a good partner for us.

We also discussed the possibility of taking the company private. There was a strong concern that this would only be a temporary solution and could cause us to take on billions of dollars of debt to finance a private transaction. We were worried that a heavy debt load might bankrupt the company, and that was too big a risk to take. The more we looked for a win-win-win solution, the more frustrated we became, because no clear direction was emerging. However, that all changed in a single flash of insight one morning soon after I had awakened from another restless night of sleep: *What about Amazon? Is there a chance they might be interested?*

I had met Jeff Bezos the previous year and had really liked him—he struck me as a brilliant and authentic man, and his obvious entrepreneurial spirit strongly resonated with me. Moreover, Amazon had long been one of the companies I most admired. As one of the great technology companies in the world, I also imagined that they could really help upgrade Whole Foods in an area that had never been one of our strengths. As we considered the possibility, I grew very enthusiastic. More than simply seeing a way to escape from a difficult position, I began to see the long-term potential of this merger.

PRACTICING WIN-WIN-WIN: The Power of Intention

When you're stuck in a difficult situation, one of the best things you can do is to repeatedly affirm your desire for a win-win-win solution to the specific challenge. Hold that intention in your heart and mind, with great conviction. This doesn't mean you immediately jump to a solution—that's different. Rather, focus on your desire for a win-win-win solution to emerge.

This practice activates your subconscious creative mind to go on an inner "search process" that can yield powerful, unexpected results. When your focus is this clear, your deeper, subconscious algorithms are tasked to work on the problem, and sooner or later a solution emerges. Often, it will do so in unforeseen ways—a sudden insight, a wisdom-laden dream, a breakthrough in the shower, an early-morning intuition, a creative leap. A win-win-win solution presents itself. It may feel like magic, but it's not—it's the power of your own intention.

I often describe the relationship between Whole Foods' and Amazon's leadership teams as "love at first sight." It's not an exaggeration, but a colorful metaphor to explain what happened. After we contacted Amazon to see if they were interested, I flew to Seattle with three of our top executives for a meeting with Jeff and some of his team. That initial discussion took place at Jeff's boathouse. We talked for three hours about all the amazing things we could do together, and the time just flew by. When the Whole Foods team retreated to a restaurant to process the conversation, we were all smiling and happy. We unanimously agreed that these were some of the smartest people we had ever met, and that we had made a special connection. But while we definitely liked them, we didn't know for sure if the feeling was mutual. Like someone in a new romance, we were a bit nervous about it as we waited by the phone. It turned out that we had nothing to worry about. Just four days later, Amazon sent a team of ten executives to Austin to discuss in more detail what a merger between the companies would look like.

A "whirlwind courtship" ensued. We moved from dating to engagement to marriage in just a few short months. Our first meeting occurred on April 30, 2017, we entered into a formal engagement (merger agreement) on June 15, and the deal closed on August 28, after the tribal elders (the government) made the decision to approve the marriage. Reflecting on the years that have since passed, I still believe that the merger represents a win-win-win solution where each major stakeholder has benefited. Let me go through them one by one.

Our customers were always the most likely winners in the merger, especially given that Amazon's explicit purpose is "to be Earth's most customer-centric company." Whole Foods Market has, of course, always cared deeply about its customers, but I will admit that Amazon's customer-obsessed culture is helping us upgrade in that area, and to improve the ways we serve customers by creating an overall shopping experience that is richer and more seamless. Of all the stakeholders, the customer has benefited most from the merger—primarily through lower prices. Everyone loves savings. But it's more than prices; it's taking a long-term approach, which is intrinsic to Amazon's culture. It's been a welcome relief to be freed from the short-term expectations of Wall Street so that we can once again take a long-term, strategic view toward creating value for all our stakeholders.

The merger has also nudged us further out beyond our brick-and-mortar roots, and we are taking full advantage of Amazon's unparalleled expertise in retailing. With Amazon's help, we're working to get ahead in the technology game. In previous years, we were a follower on the tech front, but now we're becoming leaders. The in-store experience and the personalized, high-touch service provided by our team members is still a huge differentiator for Whole Foods, but we are no longer limited to just visiting our stores in person. Prime Now, with its deliveries directly to customers, is revolutionizing our business! Of course, none of these changes would be worth much if we sacrificed our quality. After all, our higher purpose is "to nourish people and the planet," and we've developed industry-leading quality standards over the years. Our customer loyalty is based on that trust. So it's been heartening to me to see Amazon respect and even champion those standards from day one.

Our team members are often drawn to Whole Foods because they feel a personal connection to our core values and higher purpose. We have a unique culture at Whole Foods, and Amazon has shown great respect for that. Of course, with any marriage there are changes. Over time, they will influence our culture, without question. And vice versa. The merger was a way to protect the enormous value we had created with the company and move us forward into the future—not to stay exactly the same. As in any good marriage, we will continue to consciously integrate and evolve together.

Our team members also benefited from Amazon's decision to raise the minimum wage to $15 per hour for all full-time, part-time, temporary, and seasonal workers throughout the United States. Investments like these may raise our costs in the short term, but over the long term they will increase team member happiness and make it easier to hire and retain talent, thus improving our ability to serve customers.

Our suppliers have benefited in several ways. The introduction of our loyalty program, Amazon Prime, has created growth opportunities and increased sales potential for suppliers, which is a win. We've been able to maintain our commitment to sourcing from small and local suppliers, which likely would have been at risk in a different acquisition. Under Amazon, we've been able to continue to nurture local suppliers and leverage the purchasing systems we've developed to maintain our unique product assortment.

Our investors were also very happy. The day that JANA publicly announced that it had bought our stock, it was trading at about $30 a share. Amazon bought us for $42 a share just a few months later. If we hadn't been sold at a competitive price, Whole Foods' stock price likely would have fallen and investors would have experienced a huge loss. Our investors received a price that was 41 percent higher than our closing stock price on March 31, which was a huge win for them.

The sage of Omaha, Warren Buffett, channeling the wisdom of his longtime partner Charlie Munger, is famous for saying that it's better to buy a wonderful company at a fair price than a fair company at a wonderful price. I believe that Whole Foods is a wonderful company and Amazon paid a fair price for it. Essentially, it resulted in an additional $4 billion in value in the pockets of our shareholders.

Let's not forget ***our communities***. Whole Foods continues to distribute 10 percent of its total profits among thousands of nonprofit organizations every year. We actively support all of our communities with local philanthropy, Community Giving Days (aka 5% Days), food donations, and sponsorships, as we always have. Our three global foundations—Whole Planet, Whole Kids, and Whole Cities—have been able to continue to fulfill their missions, and Amazon has been very supportive, even making additional donations, for example through a partnership with Chase Bank that significantly benefited our Whole Planet Foundation. We believe there will be more joint efforts that support our foundations in the future.

As you can see from this story, I truly believe the Amazon merger was the best alternative for Whole Foods and the ideal win-win-win solution to the problems we faced with shareholder activists and new competitive challenges. No merger (or marriage, for that matter) is without challenges, but I think the past few years have borne out the enormous benefits of the deal. The alternatives certainly kept me up at night. At the time of the acquisition, I was acutely aware of the dangers of being sold off, dismantled, and potentially having the company culture destroyed. Now we've teamed up with one of the most successful, innovative, and dynamic corporations in the entire world.

Most of all, this experience has reaffirmed my conviction that when it comes to business negotiations and dealmaking—and really to life in general—if we work hard, think creatively, and bring our best selves to the table, we can almost always discover ways of doing business that increase value, build goodwill, and benefit multiple stakeholders. Through our own conscious leadership, we can strive to increase the circumference of the proverbial pie rather than merely serving up the spoils to a new victor.

THE CONSCIOUS LEADER'S TOOL KIT

Systems Thinking

Systems thinking, sometimes also called systems intelligence or whole systems awareness, is a mental capacity that any conscious leader would do well to cultivate, especially when it comes to working for the win-win-win. Indeed, the very essence of a win-win-win is that it is a solution that works for a whole system *and* for each of the parts within it.

Systems thinking stems from the recognition that our world is made up of complex systems—ecosystems, social systems, economic systems, political systems, and so on—and that within each system, all of the parts are interrelated. Studying the parts of a system in isolation will not help you understand, influence, or manage the whole, because the whole system is greater than the sum of its parts. Rather, it's necessary to grasp the dynamic relationships between all the parts in order to consciously make decisions about how actions in one part of the system may affect other parts of the system. It's a holistic, rather than reductionist, approach.

While the idea has its roots in fields like ecology, biology, mathematics, game theory, and even cybernetics, systems thinking has made its way into business and management theory over the past few decades, as popularized in Peter Senge's classic book *The Fifth Discipline*. Senge illustrates the concept through the analogy of a rainstorm: "A cloud masses, the sky darkens, leaves twist upward, and we know that it will rain. We also know that after the storm, the runoff will feed into groundwater miles away, and the sky will grow clear by tomorrow. All these events are distant in time and space, and yet they are all connected within the same pattern. Each has an influence on the rest, an influence that is usually hidden from view. You can only understand the system of a rainstorm by contemplating the whole, not any individual part of the pattern."[6]

Any organization, large or small, can be viewed as a system in and of itself, and it, in turn, is embedded in larger systems: stakeholders, industries, economies, and so forth. Systems thinking allows us to understand the many patterns, connections, relationships, and interdependencies that exist inside and outside organizations. When thinking about a challenge you're facing, an opportunity you're reaching for, a deal you're trying to make, or a problem you're trying to solve, stretch your mind to take in the entire system within which you're working. Think about not only the individual parts or stakeholders, but the dynamic relationships between them. What impact will your choices have on the system as a whole, and on each of the constituent parts? Will they upset the system's equilibrium? And if so, can you find a way forward that generates positive evolution for the whole, rather than causing fragmentation? How can you increase the health and productivity of this overall stakeholder system? A true win-win-win moves the whole system forward, as well as offering a positive outcome for each part.

INNOVATE AND CREATE VALUE

> If you look at history, innovation doesn't come just from giving people incentives; it comes from creating environments where their ideas can connect.
>
> —STEVEN JOHNSON

"INNOVATION" IS A TERM ON the lips of many pundits these days. We hear it everywhere—in old and new media; in talk shows, podcasts, and panel discussions; at global summits and academic symposia; on broadcast news and social newsfeeds. Innovation represents the powerful engine of a fast-moving global economy, of people and cultures on the rise, of cutting-edge transformations that will improve lives and change our world for the better. It conveys positivity and optimism, the promise of a world that offers hope and possibility to billions rather than millions. We hear the "innovation" drumbeat in business, in science, in technology, in economics—from Silicon Valley executives, social entrepreneurs, and NGO leaders.

Could such ubiquity really be deserved? Well, consider this. University of Illinois economist Deirdre McCloskey credits this single human virtue as being largely responsible for what she calls "the Great Enrichment"—the exponential increase in societal wealth that has occurred over the past 250 years, in tandem with a dramatic fall in poverty rates.[1] (In 1800, 85 percent of humanity lived on the equivalent of less than $2 a day. Today it's less than 9 percent.[2]) After tens of thousands of years of grinding, relentless poverty (with only a few rare, brief exceptions), humanity has undergone massive economic growth and global trade, with billions of people lifted into the middle class, and some beyond that. There is much talk today about inequality and distribution of wealth, and these are important issues. But the larger question here is: How was so much wealth created in the first place? "Our riches did not come from piling brick on brick," McCloskey claims, "or bachelor's degree on bachelor's degree, or bank balance on bank balance, but from piling idea on idea."[3] Ideas. Creativity. Resourcefulness. Imagination. Innovation. That is the real secret of our collective success. So how do innovative ideas result in a historically unprecedented upsurge in overall wealth? It comes down to a tacit agreement that would-be entrepreneurs make with society that allows breakthrough ideas to take root and thrive.

It goes something like this: Let me be entrepreneurial, let me innovate, let me create value, let me do it without too much interference from the government, let me disrupt established industries in the process, let me keep the profit from it, and, yes, I may (hopefully) get rich in the short run. Entrenched interests may temporarily suffer. Wealth will initially flow to me and to the capital invested in my idea. But as the "deal" plays itself out over time, and others rush in to capitalize on this new innovation, the benefits will start to expand rapidly. The innovation reaches more and more while becoming cheaper and cheaper. The benefits flow out, impacting and improving lives. Little by little, innovation after innovation, life improves, wealth is created, and society moves forward. In the long run, I and millions like me will help you prosper—meaning that we will help make all of us more prosperous—and immeasurably improve all of our lives in the process.

In some respects, "innovationism" would really be a better name for "capitalism." In our opinion, capitalism is at its best when we deeply appreciate that it's more about the application of human creativity than about the allocation of financial capital. That's why the successful innovator, entrepreneur, and even executive needs to focus on creating value rather than simply creating profits. By "value" we simply mean the quality of product or service that encourages someone else to want to do business with you. Yes, value is tested in the marketplace, in the crucible of actual trade. But always remember that profits are downstream from created value, not the other way around.

The ability to innovate and create value for your fellow human beings (and sometimes for other secondary stakeholders, like animals or the environment) is a fundamental element of conscious leadership. Most of the world's great companies started with some new, game-changing form of value creation. It can be dramatic and revolutionary—like the steam engine, electricity, or the internet. It can be unheralded but transformational, like better plumbing or the washing machine. It can be unexpected but timely, like Ray Kroc inventing a new way of selling hamburgers and franchising stores, or Whole Foods providing natural and organic food to a nation that hadn't yet realized there was a massive new business opportunity in healthier eating. Fast-forward a few decades and those innovations have changed the entire food industry.

Innovation can take innumerable forms, but at its heart it's about creating life-enhancing value and sharing it with others. In the magic of that exchange lives the DNA of our collective rise, and a fundamental engine of growth for our economy. *Innovate and create value.* In a continually evolving, dynamic environment, one must innovate or be left behind. To sit still is to be copied and then out-competed and eventually made irrelevant. *Innovate and create value.* It's the impetus of the entrepreneur, the target of the venture investor, and the ongoing challenge for any established company, big or small. In Joseph Campbell's formulation, it's the "call to adventure" stage of the hero's journey—an active, engaged, dynamic virtue that directly connects the conscious leader to the life-improving, wealth-generating core of Conscious Capitalism. *Innovate and create value.* Rinse. Repeat.

In case you're feeling intimidated by such lofty pronouncements, and wondering if you have what it takes to continue this proud tradition, let us be clear: A conscious leader does not necessarily have to be a novelty-producing genius. Indeed, few leaders are ever going to personally have the creative chops of great innovators like Thomas Edison, Steve Jobs, Bill Gates, Jeff Bezos, or Elon Musk. We can certainly learn from their examples, and develop our own creative powers to their fullest extent, but for the conscious leader it is equally if not more important to ask: What can I do to help foster a creative spirit in the people around me? How can I create and nurture a culture of innovation? Can I recognize and support innovation when it occurs? And can I facilitate the process of turning a novel idea into genuine value that will be proven in the marketplace? Leaders have an outsize influence, and conscious leaders think carefully about how to use that influence to inculcate innovation and value creation in individuals, teams, and the organizational culture that connects them.

PRACTICING INNOVATION: Contemplate Progress

Every aspiring conscious leader should take some time to reflect upon the tradition of innovation that allowed creative leaps of imagination to take that critical journey from the mind to the marketplace and, ultimately, to impact all of our lives for the better. Start by simply looking around you at the objects you use every single day. How many of them existed a decade ago? Two decades? A half century? Think about your parents' lives, and your grandparents'. What do you take for granted that they couldn't have imagined? You can take this contemplative journey as far back in time as you like. If your imagination falters, turn to the data experts, like the late Hans Rosling, author of *Factfulness*. It's a powerful and inspiring way to get in touch with the impact of innovation in changing our world for the better.

INNOVATION LOVES COMPANY

We often imagine that the path to innovation involves a heroic individual doing a deep dive into their own unique vision and emerging with some incredible novelty—a work of art, a piece of music, a revolutionary software product, or a genius solution to a tricky problem. Certainly, individual creativity is critical to innovation, but the iconic image of the lone creative genius may be oversold. In his book about the beginnings of the personal computing revolution, *From Counterculture to Cyberculture*, Stanford professor Fred Turner made the astute observation that "ideas live less in the minds of individuals than in the interactions of communities."[4] Innovation, creativity, and breakthrough ideas require more than networks of interacting neurons in our brains. They depend on interacting networks of actual people—engaging, refining, inventing, imagining, sharing, and building on one another's work.

In fact, when you take a closer look at many of the real geniuses throughout history, you find that they have been inspired by, and part of, a highly creative culture, group, or "scene." Musician Brian Eno coined the wonderful term "scenius" to describe this collective form of genius. Think of America's Founding Fathers, the English Romantic poets of the early nineteenth century, Paris in the 1920s. Think of London's rock-and-roll scene in the 1960s and '70s, or Silicon Valley from the 1970s through today. Often one or a few brilliant individuals inspired those collectives, but there was something about the scene itself that took on a life of its own, supercharging the creative capacity of the individuals. Such scenes become hotbeds of innovation, and they play an important role in incubating new ideas—in art, philosophy, literature, politics, and business too. In fact, the most innovative companies manage to do just that: they build a creative scene that attracts and inspires talented people and original ideas. Edison himself, as many historians have pointed out, relied on a team of highly talented people—his "muckers" as they were called—to be the critical engine of his innovations. Innovation loves company, and Edison's genius resided as much in his capacity to inspire and encourage other people's commitment and creativity as it did in his solitary brilliance.

So how does a conscious leader not only encourage individual creativity, but build teams that have innovation infused into their DNA? How can we influence organizational culture to be more creative and dynamic? Here are some strategies for your consideration.

Create the right incentives. Humans are social creatures, constantly looking for feedback, affirmation, and cues from our social tribes. As a leader who is helping to set the tone of a business tribe, be aware of the "possibility field" that you are incentivizing and rewarding. Every statement (either explicit or implicit) about what is desirable, what is acceptable, which ideas are interesting, which suggestions are rewarded, which proposals are affirmed, which projects are funded, and which activities are compensated goes into building the cultural DNA. Is that culture full of optimism, free thought, and exploration? Is it notable for its rigor, work ethic, and discipline? Does it encourage experimentation and creativity or incentivize consistency and conformity? In general, cultures are not intrinsically good or bad, but they are distinct, and serve certain purposes. A conscious leader thinks carefully about the written and unwritten agreements that shape their organization's "personality."

In his classic song "Brownsville Girl," Bob Dylan sings, "People don't do what they believe in, they just do what's most convenient, then they repent."[5] We hope things aren't that bad in corporate America, but it is important for a leader to remember that when it comes to creating culture, it's not about what you say you believe in; it's about what you actually do—what you model as a leader and, most important, what you incentivize in the culture every day. There is nothing that will undermine your culture more than saying one thing and rewarding something else. Humans have evolved a highly developed sensitivity to hypocrisy in their social environments.

Incentives can be monetary, but they can also be much more than that. Sometimes just acknowledging the right person at the right time can have a greater impact than showering them with bonuses. One should never underestimate the power of authentic appreciation. If you genuinely reward creativity, new thinking, and innovative ideas, you'll get more of the same over time. If you want a creative, innovative culture, make sure you build that DNA into your incentive system early and often.

Encourage healthy competition. At Whole Foods, one of the reasons our stores have kept pushing the edge in terms of the customer experience is that we allow a great deal of freedom to innovate at the regional and store levels. Each regional and store team brings new ideas to the table, building and improving on what has come before. A healthy competitive dynamic is born, with each team trying to outperform the others and come up with more innovative ideas. The best ones get replicated across the company, and the ones that don't work fade away. I'll give just one of many examples: the mochi bar you often see in our stores—that colorful collection of small ice cream balls encased in mochi (sweet Japanese rice dough)—has been a huge success. That started as the inspiration of team members at one particular location. It took off in that store, and its design was replicated all over the company.

That distributed autonomy inspires the creative spirit of our teams in a manner that never would happen if our corporate headquarters dictated the exact design of every new store. This practice has played a significant role in making our stores industry leaders in terms of design. Walk into most new conventional grocery stores today and you'll see the Whole Foods influence—imitation being "the sincerest form of flattery."

Competition, as seen in this example, is not antithetical to collaboration. Competition sometimes gets a bad name these days, with pundits decrying the dog-eat-dog culture of what business ethicist Ed Freeman calls "Cowboy Capitalism." But competition doesn't have to be cutthroat. There are very productive, positive forms of competition. Over the years Whole Foods has had many competitors. One of our fiercest rivalries has been with the national chain Trader Joe's. For many years, Doug Rauch was their president, and he and I had gotten to know each other quite well. Trader Joe's was always quick to adopt some of our innovations and had plenty of its own that we copied. But Doug, above all, was an honorable leader, and not only did his competitive drive make Whole Foods better, I think customers all over the nation benefited from the rivalry. Both companies benefited too. Doug retired in 2008, and over the past decade our competition has turned into cooperation, as Doug served for several years as CEO of the Conscious Capitalism organization. When honorable leaders compete, it's not just the businesses that win.

Competition can be a healthy spur to innovation, internally and externally. Just look at what Peter Diamandis is doing with his X Prize Foundation. He's using competition, with significant financial prizes for the winner, to incentivize innovation in areas that will offer great benefit to society. Since the first $10 million X Prize was announced, in 1996 (for the first nongovernmental organization to launch a reusable craft into space twice within two weeks—it was won in 2004), the X Prize Foundation has gone on to offer competitions in areas including health, technology, education, exploration, climate, and more.

Start a conspiracy. John Street, a Colorado technology entrepreneur who has built several successful companies by anticipating IT trends, has an interesting spin on the marriage of creativity and collaboration. He suggests that truly innovative organizations have a certain "conspiratorial element" to their culture. There is a sense that all the team members are in on a secret, an opportunity that the rest of the world doesn't yet appreciate or see. The team or the company feels the sense of creativity and autonomy that comes from breaking the established rules, but the sharing of that "conspiracy" also forges an important bond. This appeals to the positive side of our tribal nature, the need for community, connection, and collaboration. And it adds to the sense of excitement and the feeling that everyone has a stake in the success of a shared mission.

How does Street accomplish this in his companies? Communication is key, he explains: today's team members want context. You can't start a conspiracy if people don't feel in on it. They need to understand more than *how*; they need to know *why*. They need to understand the overall goals of the business and how they fit in. They work more effectively if they have a stake in the enterprise, and, while some of that is financial, it's also social.

In the book *Play Bigger*, the authors echo this point when they point out that the most successful companies tend to be "category kings."[6] They define a new market category and have some sort of strong "point of view" on exactly how they are altering the market space for the better. Whole Foods has a point of view about healthy eating; it's built into every store we create. Salesforce has a strong point of view about software. Airbnb has a strong point of view about travel and hospitality. In other words, conspiracies have a story that creates a shared emotional worldview, an internal set of touchpoints that bind a group together and inspire their work. It even defines a cultural membrane that identifies the tribe of those who are on the inside (and outside) of this exciting project. It's for this reason that successful businesses with strong internal cultures are often described as "cultlike." Of course, that can be taken too far, which is why this advice should be balanced with the kind of autonomy and creative freedom we described above. But when the "conspiracy" of a business is well established, when the "point of view" is strong and clear, and when the leader has been able to bring their team inside the emotional penumbra of that experience, it inspires a kind of directed innovation that can be very creative and powerful.

Embrace the edges. If you're looking for innovation, you probably won't find it at the heart of the establishment. Genuine evolution and novelty creation often happens on the borders, at the boundaries, in the in-between zones. It thrives in those places where different cultural patterns can mix and mingle, where established rules and conventions hold less sway, and where experimentation and invention can take place free of restrictive oversight. That is true for the evolution of life, culture, and business. There is a reason why one of the great American art forms, jazz music, was developed in New Orleans, a city of multiple intermixing cultures and musical styles. Urban environments have always played host to some of the most remarkable innovations in history as cultures, people, and ideas intersect and overlap in a creative and dynamic cauldron of engagement.

As sports fans, one of our favorite examples of "evolution at the edges" is the profound change in NBA basketball over the past several decades to an up-tempo, shoot-the-three, pace-and-space style of play. This innovation didn't emerge fully formed in the heart of basketball orthodoxy, in the locker room of the L.A. Lakers, or on the practice courts of the Boston Celtics. It was first nurtured, cultivated, and developed in the Italian league, where coach Mike D'Antoni experimented with up-tempo styles, far from the center of the basketball universe. Eventually, it came across the pond with D'Antoni to the "seven seconds or less" Phoenix Suns, and finally found its full maturity in the success of teams like the Houston Rockets and the Golden State Warriors. Today, it's become the defining style of the league.

The same principle explains why the peninsula south of San Francisco became such a center of innovation, beginning in the late sixties and early seventies. It was far enough removed from the more staid business institutions of the East Coast, less caught up in the existing traditions, customs, and social hierarchies of the American corporate establishment, but still well positioned to benefit from investment dollars and from Stanford and Berkeley's intellectual capital. On the sunny southwest corner of the Bay, there was room to think more freely, experiment more openly, embrace new organizational attitudes, and reimagine business in a context of technology. Garages, basements, and dorm rooms became the birthplaces of HP, Intel, Google, Apple, and so many others. Almost five decades later, after trillions of dollars has flowed out of a few initial startups, Silicon Valley has become the biggest engine of economic wealth creation in history. The outsiders have become the establishment, the barbarians have stormed the gates and set up shop inside the castle.

Today, money, power, and status flow through the Bay Area like a gusher of never-ending cash. Happy millennials from top colleges stroll through futuristic campuses, stumble upon serendipity, enjoy abundant food courts, and play after-hours Ping-Pong while fellow engineers doodle inspired ideas on wall-size whiteboards. Are the resulting cultures more innovative? Maybe. But looking for innovation in the places where we most expect it has generally been a fool's errand. "The story of innovation has not changed," claims former Google CEO Eric Schmidt. "It has always been a small team of people who have a new idea, typically not understood by people around them and their executives."[7] One wonders where the next great innovative business ecosystem will find its own apocryphal garages, basements, and dorm rooms in which to incubate the future. At the center of institutions—in C-suites, executive offices, or boardrooms—conservatism more naturally reigns. That is not necessarily a bad thing. There are times when institutionalization is critical, periods when centralization should be the primary goal for any business or organization. Just don't expect innovation to thrive in such circumstances.

Innovation starts on the edges and moves inward. Institutionalization starts at the center and moves outward. Both are important. But leaders must understand the difference. It's not enough for conscious leaders to wish, hope, and pray for regular visitation from the muses of novelty; they must actively pay attention to the borders and boundaries of their own business ecosystems, where tomorrow's disruptive ideas, processes, and technologies are incubating the next revolution.

Sometimes companies do more than just pay attention to their disruptors. They work to literally create that disruptive edge themselves, building skunkworks teams that can operate outside of normal institutional parameters to develop new products and ideas. An example of this approach comes from the stock exchange Nasdaq, under former CEO Bob Greifeld. In his book *Market Mover*, Greifeld describes how he recognized the need for a protected space for innovative projects and initiatives that was not subject to the same economic rigors he was applying to the organization as a whole. In general, he consciously rewarded fiscal discipline, cost cutting, and ruthless efficiency. But these incentives, while critical for the organizational turnaround he was undertaking, ran counter to the longer-term spirit of innovation. So he set up what he called the "Gift Council," which functioned similarly to an investment committee at a VC firm. Nasdaq team members would present ideas for innovative projects or initiatives, and those that were deemed promising received funding and were considered independent of the proposers' operational budgets. In other words, their success or failure would not impact the bottom line of the particular department. "That may sound simple," Greifeld reflects, "but for a large company wedded to fiscal discipline, it was like trying to engage another side of the brain. The metrics for Gift Council projects had to be entirely different from our normal operational metrics; otherwise, the fiscal discipline of our culture would eat those nascent projects alive before they could show their true potential."[8] Not all projects succeeded, but the ones that did became the future growth drivers of Nasdaq's business. It's a reminder for conscious leaders to always be mindful of the vast difference between creating new things, new products, new businesses, and new categories and the business of managing those things, products, businesses, and categories in an efficient and productive manner.

Recognize innovation as it happens. "Skate to where the puck is going to be, not where it's been"—a line from hockey star Wayne Gretzky—has become almost a truism in today's innovation industry. In other words, one must anticipate the future, understand where cultural and technological trends are converging, and create products and services that fit into that emerging landscape. (For more on the art of forecasting in an exponentially changing world, see chapter 6.) University College London economist Carlota Perez cautions us to recognize that many innovative solutions "don't come from sheer imagination but from identifying already existing trends in the right direction and accelerating them."[9]

A truly forward-looking company is paying attention not simply to its competitors or the existing market, but to the next market transition or disruptive shift. John Chambers, the celebrated CEO of Cisco Systems, who oversaw the rise of that networking giant into one of the great technology companies of our era, emphasizes this point: "When a transition occurs, you focus on the transition, not your competitor. If you focus on competitors, you are looking backwards."[10] By focusing on where the market was moving—which was a signal of where innovation was headed—Chambers was able to keep Cisco ahead of the curve for many years, avoiding mistakes and the creeping obsolescence that comes from playing in one sandbox for too long.

One of Chambers's talents was recognizing when the company had made mistakes or fallen behind a market transition. Not only did he prefer to restrict Cisco to competing in industries in which he was the number-one or -two player (following the famous advice of Jack Welch), but he was willing to acknowledge a failure and quickly change direction when market signals indicated a rapid shift. A great example of this was when Cisco bought the Flip camera, the popular camcorder that took over the consumer market in 2008. After Cisco paid more than $500 million for the company, the iPhone came along, with its own capable, embedded video camera. Flip cameras quickly became obsolete. In 2011, only a couple of years after buying the business, Cisco shut it down completely, acknowledging their mistake. They didn't pour increasing amounts of money into this initiative or waste more time hoping to recover their considerable sunk costs. They moved on. For any innovative company, risk is part of the equation. That means occasional failure is inevitable. Being able to acknowledge failure, change strategy, move on quickly, and not get entangled in unsuccessful ventures allows more energy to be put into truly innovative, successful initiatives.

While we'd all like to be in possession of a crystal ball, we can't always be the one anticipating or creating the future. Once again, conscious leadership is not just about being innovative ourselves. Sometimes it's just as important to recognize paradigm-changing innovation when it's happening, appreciate it, and bring that value forward to others. Google started out very late in the search engine business, but it had by far the best product. Facebook didn't invent social media, but it recognized its enormous promise and created the best platform. Whole Foods didn't start the natural and organic foods movement, but it saw the potential for a much larger market in a way that almost no one else did.

Legendary venture capitalist Arthur Rock had a knack for this particular aspect of leadership. He didn't found Intel or Apple; he didn't drive the remarkable success of those companies; he didn't invent the microprocessor or the integrated circuit. And yet he played an indispensable role in all of it. His particular genius lay in being able to recognize and appreciate the disruptive innovations happening south of San Francisco in the sixties and facilitate their emergence. He brought East Coast capital and business experience to what was then the Wild West of the business world, acting as a "boundary spanner"—a person who is able to function on the border between two worlds and often create something greater in the interaction. He was not a brilliant inventor or technological visionary, but in his own way, he had an enormous impact on the companies that were central to the emergence of Silicon Valley. He was surrounded by many bright stars, individuals like Gordon Moore, the father of the semiconductor industry; Robert Noyce, co-founder of Intel and one of the great visionary businessmen; and Andy Grove, Intel's long-serving and hard-driving CEO. But Rock was the behind-the-scenes maestro, helping all the parts to work together. Later, he was a key contributor to the rise of Apple, providing two unknown kids named Steve Jobs and Steve Wozniak with one of their first major investments and helping turn Job's visions and Wozniak's engineering talent into a workable, functional company. Rock knew how to recognize creative leaders with purpose and vision. And he knew that great companies have great purposes and that real innovation is far more important to success than the profit motive on its own. "If you're interested in building a business to make money, forget it. You won't," Rock once remarked about his own style of investing. "If you're interested in building a business to make a contribution to society, then let's talk."[11]

PRACTICING INNOVATION: The Great Idea Hunt

Investment company The Motley Fool is known for its innovative and fun-loving culture. One of the ways they keep ideas flowing is a practice they have come to call the Great Idea Hunt. They split into different teams, and each team is tasked with a goal: to visit another business or organization (usually one within a few hours of headquarters) and come back with at least one new idea or practice. Then they make a film of everyone's discoveries and play it for the whole company. It connects people, it gets them out of their familiar surroundings and into a fresh perspective, and it's a fantastic way to source real nuggets of wisdom and discover innovative solutions that other companies may be successfully implementing. The Great Idea Hunt is itself a great idea.

RETHINKING ORGANIZATIONAL DESIGN

When we think of innovation, we often focus on products or services. But innovation can also work its magic in the fundamental design of a company—transforming structure and culture in such a way as to liberate the company's creative capacities to serve its stakeholders. In the past few decades, we've seen a growing wave of experimentation with organizational design and a shift away from traditional structure in favor of more fluid approaches.

For most of human history, standard designs for larger organizations have been heavily bureaucratic, with power concentrated at the top. They have relied on "command and control" hierarchies appropriated from military culture. Command and control is one way to answer the questions: How do we get lots of people to row in the same direction? How do we establish clear, top-down communication and authority within a large, complex organization? This structure helps ensure control, consistency, and standardization, and while it has its downsides, there were many reasons why it was probably the most effective organizational design at a time when the world changed very slowly and innovation was rare. But today, while governmental organizations still tend to retain bureaucratic hierarchy, businesses are evolving rapidly away from this organizational design. New structures are proving necessary to keep up with the unprecedented pace of change in technology and in competitive landscapes. Bureaucratic hierarchy is simply too slow to be successful.

So how do we develop self-organizing, fast-iterating, dynamic cultures? How do we distribute the right kind of intelligent, problem-solving autonomy throughout our organization, even as we all participate in a shared mission and move in a common direction? To answer these questions, we need to do much more than command and control. We need to *create and collaborate*. We need an organization that is designed to give people the freedom to innovate and flourish creatively while also offering a structure within which they can effectively collaborate to institutionalize and operationalize those ideas.

Balancing these two imperatives is no easy feat. Any time humans socially organize in small or large groups, they inevitably form strong cultural patterns, and as those patterns become self-perpetuating and self-replicating, it is easy for a certain type of institutional inertia to set in. The culture, in other words, reinforces itself. Every organization has the equivalent of an immune system that rejects new ideas that don't fit into the dominant organizational paradigm. But real creativity demands the opposite—questioning the "way things are," suggesting new directions, and challenging the status quo. The philosopher Arthur Koestler once called creativity "an act of liberation—the defeat of habit by originality."[12] Creativity and innovation often move at right angles to the prevailing winds. So if creativity is going to thrive in a company culture, beyond the inspiration of a few people at the top, leaders need to rethink the way they structure their organizations to allow autonomy and tolerance for experimentation.

Inspired by methods like lean manufacturing and Agile project management and software development, many companies and business thinkers today have set out to do just that. Rejecting top-down control, they are reinventing organizations to be more "self-managed" or "self-organizing." While they vary enormously, most of these approaches involve some form of networked structure built on self-directed teams.

At Whole Foods Market, for example, we have organized our company around interconnected teams. Everyone who works at Whole Foods is a member of one or more teams. Each of our stores has a variety of teams specializing in different customer service areas, such as produce, meat, seafood, prepared foods, grocery, specialty, whole body, and customer service/front end. While each team has work roles and responsibilities that are specific to them, we encourage all the teams to support and help one another as needed. We believe that cross-training work skills between teams is also important to improve customer service and job satisfaction.

The key to the Whole Foods organizational system is that each team is empowered and largely self-managing, while being closely connected to all the other teams in each store. Each store is a member of one of our twelve regional teams, and all the regional teams are members of our global leadership team. Teams, teams, teams—everywhere! Whole Foods has hierarchy, but so far we have largely escaped being overly bureaucratized, despite now employing more than 100,000 team members. This has enabled us to create a great culture of caring for our team members and customers, while fulfilling our higher purpose as a business and being financially successful.

There are many other fascinating examples of new organizational designs that are working well and delivering both great cultures and innovation. The largest and most innovative technology companies—Apple, Amazon, Google, Microsoft, Netflix, and others—have each in their own way rejected the typical bureaucratic hierarchies that most businesses operated with just fifty years ago.

One of our sister companies at Amazon, Zappos, has one of the most interesting and innovative business designs in the world today. Zappos CEO Tony Hsieh was inspired by Holacracy, created by former software engineer Brian Robertson, which offers companies a comprehensive new "operating system" to replace traditional hierarchy. Zappos has worked closely with Robertson's consulting company, HolacracyOne, to implement the system, but also evolved the ideas of Holacracy to better fit Zappos's unique and special culture. The result has been to minimize bureaucratic hierarchy while creating empowered self-organizing and self-managing teams. This has increased their innovation capabilities while also helping them to double down on their commitment to exceptional customer service.

There is much that a conscious leader can learn from the various approaches to new organizational design, regardless of whether or not you choose to adopt such a system wholesale. Any organization that wants to survive and thrive today and tomorrow will need to find new ways to be adaptive and innovative in its decision-making processes. And any leader who embraces a spirit of service must focus on empowering their teams rather than simply exercising authority over them. A decentralized approach to management can uncover and liberate creativity at all levels in an organization, encouraging people to make decisions and take initiative by removing bureaucracy and management bottlenecks.

While creativity, empowerment, and autonomy are good things, too much of a good thing can occasionally be a problem. There are times in any business when everyone simply has to get on the same page and move forward in sync, when the ability to closely collaborate, take direction, and deliver on a common mission is essential. Remember that hierarchy is not inherently bad; nor is the absence of hierarchy inherently virtuous. Every conscious leader must be attuned to the dynamic sweet spot between creativity and consistency, autonomy and collaboration, hierarchy and empowerment, originality and institutionalization.

As always, the conscious leader's guiding light should be purpose: *How can I structure and lead my organization so that the best decisions will be made in service of our purpose?* Sometimes a clear hierarchy and assertive leader is the best fit. Other times, a highly distributed, team-based approach might be ideal. Whatever the case, we can keep these new approaches in mind and look for appropriate ways to empower people, reduce bureaucracy, streamline processes, and increase organizational agility.

EMBRACE HUMILITY AS A COMPETITIVE ADVANTAGE

The wonderful thing about innovation is that it can come from anywhere—and probably will. You never know where the next breakthrough idea, fantastic new technique, or organizational advance may emerge. If it's not in your office or down the hall, don't ignore it. Many of the most successful companies are not just innovative; they are fast followers. They imitate as well as innovate. (And if they can't do either, they often acquire other firms that can. There is a reason why some of the most important technology companies in the world are serial acquirers; they are not attached to in-house innovation.) Conscious leaders are always on the lookout for the best ideas, wherever they originate.

To do this, we need to get over our own personal and organizational ego. It doesn't matter how smart we are—too much organizational pride can torpedo success in the blink of an eye by interfering with a clear assessment of opportunities and threats. This is often referred to as the "not invented here" syndrome. It can be a subtle but dangerous form of blindness, one that infects even very successful organizations.

In fact, this affliction can be especially difficult to inoculate against in highly creative organizations that are used to being the source of their own innovations. Sometimes the most innovative teams (and leaders) are the most susceptible to organizational ego. They become attached to their own processes and approaches and get lost in their own visions. They lose sight of new directions, fail to connect with customers or market needs, or miss important breakthroughs happening around them. A conscious leader is more concerned about actual innovation and value creation than exactly *who* does it, *where* they do it, or *how* it happens. Stay nimble and flexible. Be ready to pivot. Expect surprises. Humility, in a leader and in an organization, is a powerful competitive edge.

What is true for an organization is doubly true for an individual. Nothing interferes with the creative intelligence of a team more than undue arrogance in a leader. If you want to have a creative team, the first rule is that you have to be able to interact with a group or a team in a way that is relatively free of ego. An arrogant person reacts to criticism and disagreement with the instinctive response "I'm right and you're wrong." They fight for their position from a place of reactivity and defensiveness. A humble person is willing to listen and consider legitimate feedback. As Ray Dalio, former CEO of Bridgewater

Associates, the largest hedge fund in the world, explains, they go from saying "I'm right" to asking "Why do I think I'm right?"[13] A humble person wants to get it right more than they personally want to *be* right. As a leader, one has to model this, encourage it, and even insist upon it. Truth and good ideas come in many packages, some loud and strong, some quiet and unassuming. A conscious leader is always listening for the best approaches, most sensible arguments, and creative ideas.

Humility does not mean you lack confidence or eschew strong opinions. But it's easy for an organizational leader to get comfortable in a bubble and grow accustomed to a constant flow of affirmation. You can get used to hearing the sound of your own ideas reflected back with words of praise. But the old saying is true: "If you're the smartest person in the room, you're in the wrong room." The higher you go on the corporate ladder—in fact, in any ladder or power structure—the more you have to take responsibility for not living in an affirmation bubble.

FOCUS ON CREATING VALUE

If you can implement even a couple of the suggestions above, you can be sure that the wellspring of innovation will begin to flow. But remember, a company cannot live on innovation alone. If it fails to do the extra work to create real value for stakeholders and customers, it is unlikely to truly thrive. That's why we say "innovate *and* create value." A classic example is the cautionary tale of Xerox PARC, the once iconic research lab of the mighty Xerox Corporation that invented some of the foundational technologies of the past fifty years, including the laser printer and the graphical user interface. But they were unable to operationalize their creations into successful businesses. Instead, their outputs became fodder for a grateful generation of startups who happily took advantage and built world-class businesses out of those ideas—companies like Apple, Microsoft, and 3Com.

Don't forget to create value. Too often, innovators fail to take full advantage of their own genius. But as a leader you can do something about that. You can recognize genius, encourage it, stoke it, test it, and, most important, operationalize it. And you can remember that innovation in a business context never exists in a research vacuum. New products and services must always create real value in the marketplace, solve client problems, provide new services, or in some other way add tremendous value in the context of voluntary exchange. That's the essential alchemy that fashions economic and social value out of the raw material of creativity.

In a nonbusiness context—such as a nonprofit or a government organization—one may be focused more on adding social value rather than economic value, but the essential point is no different. Bruce Friedrich was once an activist for the animal rights group PETA, working tirelessly to promote animal welfare, trying to get people to stop eating a meat-based diet. A vegan himself, Friedrich eventually came to the conclusion that his confrontational approach was ineffective. He still believed in the idea, but he wasn't creating much value.

So he took a break, refreshed his thinking, reconsidered his options, and had an insight. Instead of changing people's minds, why not change the food that was available? That would take more than activism; it would take innovation. Today, Friedrich's Good Food Institute is one of the most active organizations supporting the burgeoning business of plant-based alternatives to animal-based food, changing industry practices, connecting investors to food technology startups, starting investment funds, and generally shifting the conversation about what's possible when it comes to changing our relationship to animal agriculture.

When we talk about creating value, it's also important to remember that we mean value for all of the stakeholders in a business, not only the customers. Innovation doesn't always have to be solely about the customer. In fact, some of the most successful and innovative companies, many in the tech space, have found that out the hard way. After experiencing extraordinary growth in the past years, they have come up against enormous pushback from some of their other relevant constituencies—local communities, team members, regulatory bodies, suppliers, etc.—in part because they weren't adequately taking care of all of the stakeholders in their business ecosystem. Now obviously, disruptive companies have societal impact. They change the status quo, put others out of business. They can even change the way we live. They're never going to make everyone happy; that's the inevitable consequence of real innovation. But it's also important to remember that finding ways to truly create value for the many stakeholders in the business, and going out of your way to innovate new methods of doing so, not only is the right thing to do but can pay back enormous dividends over time. If your suppliers appreciate you, they are going to bend over backwards to work with you on favorable terms. If team members have a largely positive experience of their work life, they're going to be your best ambassadors. If your community has felt the positive benefits of your presence, it is going to be more inclined to support you, even when your public relations hits some rough waters (and it will).

INNOVATION CAN HAPPEN ANYWHERE

Sometimes we need reminders that innovation can happen in the least expected areas of the economy. Entrepreneur Miki Agrawal has found inspiration precisely by looking at those areas of life that no one else wants to touch—periods and poo. As she puts it, "If you are going to dive into something and spend all of your time on it, you might as well dive into a really big problem." What struck Agrawal was that the feminine hygiene category hadn't had any real innovation in half a century, and the entire category of products consisted of tampons, pads, and menstrual cups. Moreover, not much has changed in the toilet category for at least a century. So the company she co-founded with her twin sister, Radha, called Thinx, set out to design period-proof underwear for women that was easier to use, more comfortable, and built with modern conceptions of environmental sustainability in mind. Her other venture, Tushy, is attempting to reinvent the toilet category with an inexpensive, environmentally friendly millennial-focused bidet that might just catch on in an American market that has never adopted the European approach.

Not to be outdone by her sister, Radha Agrawal decided she wanted to innovate on the idea of community. In her mid-thirties, she was a regular at a well-known New York nightclub, but one night, while dining on a 4:00 a.m. falafel, she took a long, hard look at her actual experience of the scene—the drugs, the escapism, the lack of joy and connection. Surely she could create something better. For a millennial generation longing for more connection and community, she began to envision "new containers for belonging." Her solution was a movement that turned the traditional idea of nightlife on its head. Instead of late night, it would be early morning. Instead of drug-fueled, it would be sober. Instead of being draining and ending in sleep, it would be energizing and end in work. She called it Daybreaker. Greeting the day with dancing, yoga, poetry, and other forms of interpersonal connection, Daybreaker has been a hit around the world, inspiring hundreds of thousands of people in more than thirty cities to greet the day with an experience of community. She calls the experience a DOSE—meaning a natural hit of dopamine, oxytocin, serotonin, and endorphins. Not a bad cocktail with which to start your day.

A popular contemporary business aphorism states, "Your margin is my opportunity." It's also true that sometimes "your neglected area is my opportunity." Sometimes those areas that have not been touched in years, if ever, are ripe for change. The Agrawal twins are reminders that innovation doesn't necessarily come in the form of a tricked-out new gadget. There is always a space for unique business models and unconventional missions that happen to fit the zeitgeist of the day. The fields of value creation stretch as far as our imagination can follow.

THE CONSCIOUS LEADER'S TOOL KIT

The Adjacent Possible

How are we supposed to anticipate opportunities, respond to trends, invest in the future, and make effective plans in an economic landscape changing with such speed and disruptive power? It's a daunting task for any leader, but there is an important mental tool contained in the work of complexity theorist Stuart Kauffman that helps. It's called the "adjacent possible." Kauffman developed the concept, based on his observation of biological agents, to define a space of possible futures that are "adjacent" to the current reality. What authentically realizable, near-term potentials surround any given situation?

To understand this concept, it can help to consider that which is *not* in the adjacent possible. If you attempt to progress too far into the future, to leap too many steps away from your current position, you have overshot the adjacent possible. For example, bench-pressing 500 pounds is far outside any of the authors' adjacent possible! But perhaps bench-pressing 250 pounds, becoming a scratch golfer, or even thru-hiking the Pacific Crest Trail could be there.

Author Steven Johnson succinctly describes the idea of the adjacent possible in *Where Good Ideas Come From*. "The phrase captures both the limits and the creative potential of change and innovation . . . The adjacent possible is a kind of shadow future, hovering on the edges of the present state of things, a map of all the ways in which the present can reinvent itself."[14]

In a fast-changing environment, where it's hard to see beyond certain event horizons in the economic landscape, the notion of the adjacent possible can be powerfully clarifying. It encourages us to peer into the *possible* future and know which chess moves are immediately available and which need to wait for two or three steps down the line. It helps to distinguish a pragmatic, possible step forward from an unrealistic and foolhardy leap. In fact, great leaders often use this idea instinctively, even if they don't have a name for it.

What is in the adjacent possible of your own team, business, technology, organization? A significant part of leadership is being able to see into the adjacent possible, recognize a desired and achievable future, and create a pathway forward for you or your team to get there. And remember, with every move forward, the adjacent possible shifts as well. Its borders expand even as you pursue them. New potentials become available that were previously hidden from view. In Kauffman's words, each foray into the adjacent possible "increases the diversity of what can happen next."[15]

In a fast-moving, globalizing world where contemplating the future can be overwhelming, this one powerful yet simple tool can ground our attention in what's most important, helping conscious leaders make that critical connection between the realities of today and the possibilities of tomorrow.

THINK LONG TERM

> The signature characteristic of our time is the pace of change. After 13.5 billion years of evolution, change went hypercritical in our lifetime. The world is changing faster than companies can become resilient.
>
> —GARY HAMEL[1]

HALLA TÓMASDÓTTIR WAS growing dissatisfied. Not with her job, exactly—she had a good one. She worked for PepsiCo, climbing the corporate ladder at one of the premier companies in the world. Before Pepsi, she had worked for Mars, a huge private company known for its strong values-driven culture. Both had influenced her leadership style, but as the turn of the millennium approached, neither had been able to satisfy some vague feeling that she wanted more out of her career choices.

Halla had always been independent minded. That's part of what brought her to America in the first place, traveling from Iceland to attend Auburn University. A hardworking young woman, she adjusted well to life in the United States and school in the Deep South. In those days, she recalls, she could "outwork the men in the day and still outdrink them at night." After receiving her MBA, Halla had stayed in the States for the opportunities, which were unlike anything in her home country. Pepsi, after all, had more team members on its corporate roster than Iceland had citizens! She was grateful for the experience, but eventually, like many budding conscious leaders, she began to sense that there was something more meaningful for her to do with her life and career. And selling more cola around the world didn't seem to be the pathway to discovering it. As she pulled on that thread of meaning, her commitment to corporate America began to unravel. It was time to head home.

In Iceland, Halla found the first hints of a higher purpose—not in Iceland's relatively small corporate sector, but in academia. She led a breakthrough initiative at Reykjavik University teaching women's empowerment and entrepreneurial skills. This was a chance to have a real impact, and she relished it. It also gave her a voice in the small country. Soon, Iceland's chamber of commerce asked her to become its CEO, a high-profile job that put her at the heart of the national business community, which at the time was undergoing a massive transformation.

For most of its modern history, Iceland was known for its fishing industry and for aluminum smelting—a power-intensive industry that took advantage of the country's cheap geothermal energy. But in the years leading up to the financial crisis, Iceland underwent the biggest boom-and-bust per capita in the world's entire economic history, driven by a massive bubble in the financial sector. When Halla took over leadership of the chamber of commerce in 2006, the assets of the financial sector totaled more than four times the size of Iceland's GDP. By the time the bust came in 2008, it had ballooned to more than ten times. (For comparison, Switzerland—a country built on banking—had a financial sector with assets totaling only about twice the size of its GDP.) "It was a deal-junkie culture," Halla recalls. "Every company was growing simply through borrowing cheap money and buying other companies." That kind of short-term financialization of the economy felt unsustainable. There was too much debt, too much risk, too much ego. The entire small country seemed a bit drunk with money. Signs of a bubble were hard to miss. International celebrities were being paid exorbitant sums to speak at events. Small Icelandic companies were buying up bigger European counterparts. Iceland's tiny business community—which consisted mostly of men—seemed to have lost its grounding. No one seemed focused on building long-term, sustainable economic value. In her position, Halla had a platform and a voice. She spoke out.

People talk about speaking truth to power, but for Halla it was more like speaking truth to the wind. No one seemed to care or listen. "It was like being at a fantastic party at midnight and trying to get everyone to stop so that we wouldn't be hungover in the morning. No one wants that person at their party!"

As she struggled to be heard amid the get-rich-quick frenzy of the time, she found a receptive ear in a colleague, a female banking executive who shared her concerns. An evening rant over a glass of wine evolved into something more—a plan for an alternative approach. If Iceland was experiencing a rash of unsustainable, growth-obsessed short-termism driven by a largely male-dominated business world, they decided to create a counterpoint: a women-centered, value-oriented, long-term-focused, purpose-rich investment firm, guided by both profit and principle. For Halla, it seemed as if everything in her life—her corporate experience, her time teaching young women, her knowledge of business in Iceland, her care for the country's future—had led to this moment. She was able to highlight a different face of capitalism, one that put purpose first and focused on long-term value creation.

Halla and her colleague didn't change Iceland's boom-and-bust trajectory. When the crash came, it hit hard, and the hangover was disastrous. People lost everything. The social contract was strained to the breaking point. In 2008, the prime minister came on TV and asked God to bless the now bankrupt country. But Halla's clients—many of them the nation's wealthy women—already felt blessed. Their firm was a rare bright spot amid the carnage. Their funds had advised clients to seek safer waters well before the downturn. While everyone else had been obsessed with how to profit today, they had been thinking about how to build for tomorrow.

Now, finally, people were ready to listen to Halla. Her prescience and her values gave her new influence in Iceland's business community, and beyond. She has used it to deliver the message of purposeful business and sustainable long-term value creation, even going as far as to run for president of the island nation, falling short but garnering more than a third of the votes. Her path had not always been straight or well marked, but her once thin thread of purpose had developed into a life thick with meaning.

Not all leaders have the opportunity to play a role in such a stark morality tale, but if we are going to build a business, an economy, and even a nation that creates sustainable prosperity over the long term, then many of the same principles apply. It's imperative that we look to a longer horizon, understand the dynamics of change, and invest with a multi-year—even multi-decade—timeline. To do that, we must resist the always present temptation to maximize short-term gains at the expense of longer-term investment. Of course, the short term is always an important part of the picture—that's never going to go away. But as in Iceland, when we start harvesting tomorrow's potential value and spending it today—in the form of significant debt, environmental unsustainability, or financial sleight of hand—we are constraining and diminishing the prospects of the future. As conscious leaders, our goal should always be the opposite: to enlarge and expand the opportunity set of tomorrow in both economic and social terms. We can accomplish this only by keeping one eye on the long term. And if we don't want to be blindsided by unexpected events that are seemingly beyond our control, we had also better understand something about the dynamics of change in today's economy and, more specifically, the technological forces that are accelerating those dynamics.

AWAKENING A LONG-TERM OUTLOOK

One of the downsides of a fast-moving, quickly changing world is that it invites a short-termism that can be both pernicious and hard to escape. The need for immediate gratification in business, in markets, and in finance can be strong, driven by a 24/7 business news cycle. Investors want results yesterday and expect ever-shorter periods between vision and implementation. In such an environment, it's easy to lose sight of what's most important. The conscious leader must find ways to move at right angles to such injunctions—to escape the allure of momentary matters and raise their vision to consider a deeper, longer, larger timeline. They have to tear themselves away from the spell of this week's urgent crisis or can't-miss opportunity and consider timespans of many years, even decades. They must break out of the tyranny of the quarterly income statement and embrace more expansive metrics for success. They have to carve out time and space in their own minds and in the minds of their teams for another mode of thinking, one more suited to creating value over years, decades, and beyond. And be warned: thinking long term might sound lofty and philosophical, but in today's business context, where the financial markets drive so many of the decisions of leadership, it can be a dangerous, even subversive choice. It could endanger your job, your company, and more. But it's a risk all conscious leaders must take if they are truly dedicated to building a more conscious capitalism.

At Whole Foods, I chafed against the short-term focus of so many in the public markets who were primarily focused on a quick pop in the stock price, not the long-term appreciation of the shares. In particular, I resented the scourge of activist investors, also called shareholder activists—investor groups that take a significant ownership stake in a company and then use it to pressure the board to increase short-term profitability and stock price. As I recounted in chapter 4, it was the actions of one such activist, JANA Partners, that led to our merger with Amazon—a solution I came up with to serve and protect the long-term interests of our company and our stakeholders from JANA's short-term profit-seeking.

Another leader who has repeatedly done battle with shareholder activists is Ron Shaich, founder of the phenomenally successful restaurant chain Panera and a true exemplar of conscious capitalism. Few have been more articulate about the importance of long-term thinking than Ron. When he first resigned from his position as CEO in 2009, it wasn't because he didn't love the work. Rather, it was the demands of the position, which involves a great deal of day-to-day ceremonial activities and public relations. As he puts it, "I was tired of spending 20 percent of my time telling people what I just did, and 20 percent of my time telling them what I'm about to do." All of that energy was detracting from what he felt was most important: focusing on the long-term development of the company. In fact, the competitive advantage of long-term thinking was one of the most important lessons Shaich had learned from his many years running Panera, and Au Bon Pain before that. As he stepped away from day-to-day leadership and into an executive chairman role, he finally had time to more carefully consider longer time horizons.

Panera had long been the poster child of the "fast casual" restaurant revolution, achieving remarkable growth that allowed it to perform as well as or better than close retail cousins Chipotle and Starbucks. But Shaich knew that the secret to that track record had been his willingness to embrace transformative changes and investments that may have required some challenges in the short term but kept the company creating value over the long run. Once again, he felt Panera needed that focus.

As the short-term demands of the CEO role faded, he was able to focus on the larger trends in the restaurant industry, including the accelerating impact of technology. We all sometimes need adequate time and space for such concerns to come to the forefront of our mind. Long-term thinking is not simply a tap that can be turned off and on. You need to make room for it. It's like engaging a different part of the strategic brain. Shaich's thoughts germinated, little by little, until finally, after a trip overseas, he poured out a twenty-page memo about what needed to happen for Panera to be competitive over the next decade: embracing technology, a greater health focus, a transformed loyalty program, clean food, delivery. He sent it out and, after getting buy-in from the executive team, worked on developing a prototype of this new vision.

Soon Shaich was back as CEO (the existing CEO had to step down for personal reasons) with a focus on implementation. But transformations take time, and the "What have you done for me lately?" attitude of Wall Street again reared its head. The stock price temporarily stagnated, and activist investors circled. They even called for him to be removed as CEO. Eventually, Panera's investments paid off, the reinvigorated company found its footing, and, yes, the stock price eventually reflected that success. But Shaich had had enough. He and the board agreed to sell Panera to a private company, where it could continue to incubate a long-term focus.

Shareholder activism is one of the greatest threats to the burgeoning Conscious Capitalism movement. It's like a parasite that has dug its way into the very structure of financial capitalism, and if we don't root it out, it could very well kill its host. Recognizing this, many people have proposed legal and structural changes to the market designed to disincentivize such thinking—from changes to the tax structure to reconsidering the quarterly schedule of reports to rethinking public and private markets altogether. Some businesses have adopted the relatively new but very successful Benefit Corporation (B Corp) certification standard, an alternative corporate organizational form, now legal in thirty-five states and several other countries. B Corps legally require their boards of directors to take into account the interests of multiple stakeholders, including social and environmental impact, and in so doing, they encourage a long-term focus. As Jay Coen Gilbert, founder of B Lab, the nonprofit behind B Corps, puts it, these new organizations have the potential to create a more "durable prosperity" for more people, because they are "inoculated against the virus of short-termism."[2] We believe B Corps are an excellent starting point, but many more such innovations will be required if we are to truly remake financial capitalism. Another new and interesting player is the Long-Term Stock Exchange, founded by Eric Ries, which is creating ways for companies to access public markets without the short-term pressures and incentives that normally accompany such a move. But whatever new incentives and evolved structures we come up with, they will not lessen the need for individual leaders and teams to adopt long-term thinking as a foundation of their own approach to business. Sometimes that comes easy, sometimes it's extraordinarily difficult, but how successful we are at doing it depends to a large degree on how we see the business community and our role as a member of it.

PRACTICING LONG-TERM THINKING: Conduct a "Pre-Mortem"

In business, we often talk about "postmortems," a somewhat morbid shorthand for the retrospective analysis that leaders use to analyze the success or failure of a project. But how about pre-mortems? Panera founder and CEO Ron Shaich says he relies on these to help him more strategically approach the long-term future by bringing clarity to what really matters rather than what temporarily seems important. A pre-mortem, he explains, is the practice of looking at your current self from the perspective of the end of your life. Imagine you were on your deathbed, looking back at yourself today. Ask yourself: *What really matters? What do I really care about? What risks are worth taking? What fears don't actually mean that much? What needs to get created?* It's an amazingly clarifying exercise. Conduct a pre-mortem regularly on your own life trajectory. If you do it honestly, Shaich suggests, the quality of your leadership—and your humanity—will reflect that long-term, life-positive perspective.

GARDENING FOR INFINITY

In our current business environment, it's easy to lose sight of what's necessary to build a resilient company that is focused on long-term success—one that is not just reacting to competitive market demands, but building an innovative, adaptive culture that can thrive over the long haul. That distinction between "winning" in the short term and building for the long term is the difference between what some have called "finite games" and "infinite games." Those terms originally come from religious scholar James Carse, author of *Finite and Infinite Games*. For Carse, an infinite game is an open-ended game in which the purpose is not simply to "win" but to continue the game. It's a long-term endeavor that keeps changing and developing as it moves forward. A finite game, on the other hand, is one more like the win-lose scenario we discussed in chapter 4, with defined boundaries, specific rules, a finish line, and a clear winner and loser.

Drawing on this distinction, Simon Sinek's book *The Infinite Game* points out that business is a great example of an infinite game. It's open-ended, there aren't always clear winners and losers, and the game itself is endlessly being reinvented over the long term. But here is the key point: leaders have to decide how they are going to play. Many business leaders play finite games—they become good at coming out on top in short-term, win-lose competitions. The best leaders and organizations, however, play infinite games, endlessly inventing and creating new arenas of cooperation and competition. As Sinek puts it, "Infinite games have infinite terms . . . To succeed in the infinite game of business, we have to stop thinking about who wins or who's the best, and start thinking about how to build organizations that are strong enough and healthy enough to stay in the game for many generations to come. The benefits of which, ironically, often make companies stronger in the near term also."[3] Innovation over the long term is a hallmark of an "infinite" mindset, as are resilient, successful cultures. One can succeed in finite games and still fail in infinite ones, as exemplified by Iceland before the financial crisis.

Conscious leaders need to wake up to the infinite game they are already playing. Indeed, much of the criticism about business and capitalism today focuses on the ways in which some seek to exploit the system and extract wealth from it for their own short-term interests, often at the expense of other stakeholders. But the answer to extractive, short-term, finite-oriented, win-lose capitalism is not to get rid of business or capitalism as an institution. Rather, it is for the whole institution to evolve, and the way it evolves is through our recognizing more deeply that it is by nature a long-term, even infinite, endeavor. And for that, we need conscious leaders who are willing to become masters of long-term thinking.

Of course, it's also important to recognize that short-term thinking can't be altogether discarded. We all must do it. No one escapes that reality. Business must prosper in the here and now, even as it creates value over decades. We must harvest some crops to live on today, even as we plant for the future. The trick is in finding the right balance. If we merely harvest the energy, innovation, and business investments that have already been created, the business's days will be numbered, however successful it is in the short term.

There's a people element to this challenge as well, which is why succession planning is a critical part of a conscious leader's job. A moment of leadership transition is often a perilous one even for the best companies, because it requires recognizing that the skills required to nurture and tend a business for the long term are different from those required to manage the abundant harvest. Too often, a new CEO comes in after a founder and innovator has created an extraordinary business. They address many important issues: cutting costs, increasing efficiency, and "making the trains run on time." The business may perform better in the short term. In fact, if the business has a long enough runway, that approach can reap rewards for some time. But ultimately, unless those leaders are also able to think long term—or empower others who can—and plant seeds of investment for the future, they'll never be adequate stewards of the business over a longer time frame.

We're inviting conscious leaders to embrace a way of thinking about time, change, and possibility that will affect multiple areas of life and work—from innovation to technology to people development to operations. Thinking long term is about understanding the trajectory of success. When we see dramatic achievements, we easily miss the essential antecedents, the hard work and struggle, the constant investments and small improvements that went into the early stages of that seemingly sudden success. We want the payoff now; we want to get to the good part immediately. We want the "hockey stick" curve without the long trek up the slight incline. We want to start harvesting without ever planting and tending the garden. But success over the long term, today more than ever, means understanding the relationship between early investments and later rewards. And in our era, like none before, thinking long term requires that we do this in the midst of tremendous uncertainty, unpredictability, and accelerating change.

THINKING EXPONENTIALLY

Once upon a time there lived a great king who loved to play chess. In order to entice would-be gamers of the era to play, he offered any person who could best him at his favorite game the chance to "name your own reward." One day, a traveling sage took him up on his offer and managed to achieve victory. As his prize, he requested what seemed a modest compensation: that grains of rice be placed on the chessboard, starting with the first square and doubling on each subsequent one. However many grains of rice ended up on the final square, that would be his payment. The king, thinking he was getting off easy, enthusiastically agreed and instructed his attendant to fetch him a bag of rice. He placed one grain on the first square, two on the second, four on the third, eight on the fourth, and so on. At first, the numbers were small, but soon they ballooned almost beyond measure. You see, what the king failed to realize—and the same is true of many leaders today—was that the tiny initial sums masked a much more important fact: *the growth rate.* That's the number that matters. As any good mathematician can tell you, by the time you get to the back half of the chessboard, there isn't enough rice in the entire world to match the numbers attained. Such is the unexpected nature of exponential growth. Today, exponential growth rates are impacting the entire economy and culture.

Many of the core virtues we champion in this book are ancient. Love, integrity, and purpose, for example, are "evergreen," and their relevance is hardly unique to our era—though we continue to develop in our understanding of how they are expressed in contemporary organizational settings. However, conscious leaders can't just double down on timeless values; they must also embrace new truths. Some of the most important leadership mindsets are specific to our time, and none more so than the ability to "think exponentially." It's a critical subset of long-term thinking. Yes, there has historically been some understanding of compound growth rates (as the story would suggest). Einstein is alleged to have declared compound interest the eighth wonder of the world, and whether he actually said it or not, its wisdom is certainly worthy of him. Still, the importance of thinking exponentially goes deeper than finance—as we have recently seen with the "exponential" growth of the COVID-19 pandemic. Indeed, the mathematical reality behind this obscure term has quickly been brought home by the fast-moving spread of the virus. But it's also important for leaders who aspire to be more conscious as they steward their organizations and people into the future. We're not just suggesting you improve your math, or even your forecasting skills (although those are important). But to better anticipate those potential impacts, we had better stretch our minds to fit this unfamiliar way of thinking and examine some of the ways it's shaping the world around us.

Only in recent decades have we really begun to grasp how the rise of information technology has changed the game of business—and life—fundamentally. In 1965, Gordon Moore, then CEO of Intel, published a paper observing that the number of components on an integrated circuit was doubling every year, an observation that is famously known as Moore's law. Over time, he revised this observation into a prediction that the doubling would continue every two years. And it has more or less done exactly that, right up into the present day. Whole manufacturing blueprints and projections have been based on it for decades.

Like the rice on the chessboard, this doubling results in truly remarkable numbers over time. In the early 1970s, there might have been thousands of transistors on a microprocessor. Today we are headed up into the many billions all in less than a human lifetime. That means that the relatively inexpensive phone in your hand is significantly more powerful than the entire computing setup that took us to the moon in 1968. We've gone from a mainframe that takes up a whole office floor to a personal computer that takes up the top of a desk to a mobile device that fits in a pocket, and onward. This is exponential change in action.

Technology hasn't just changed the game for those in Silicon Valley—it's changed it for all of us, no matter what field we're in. In the decades to come, no company or individual will be left untouched by the tides of exponential growth, and the wise leaders will be the ones who strive to understand these forces and help their people and their organizations navigate them more skillfully.

We evolved to think "linear and local," explains technology pioneer Peter Diamandis, but today we must think "global and exponential."[4] Our minds adapted to be highly concerned about local events, and it's difficult to transcend that particular conditioning and sustain an interest and awareness of larger trends and global concerns. Unfortunately, our localized perspective is inadequate for understanding the increasingly interconnected, rapidly changing, globalized world that we are operating in every day. And our linear intuition will jump to conclusions that misunderstand the nature of change.

PRACTICING EXPONENTIAL THINKING: Do the Math

"If I take thirty steps . . . I get to thirty meters," says Salim Ismail, author of *Exponential Transformation*. "If I take thirty doubling steps . . . I get to a billion meters."[5] No, that's not a typo. But if you doubted, even for a moment, the truth of his statement, you're not alone. Most of us find that the math of exponential growth defies belief, especially at first glance. How about this one: If you fold a piece of paper in half, its thickness doubles. How many times would you need to fold it to make it thick enough to reach the moon? The answer is forty-two. Don't believe it? Do the math! You can test your own grasp of exponential thinking with a simple exercise. Pick a square on the back half of the chessboard—anything between 32 and 64—and try to quickly guess (without resorting to a calculator) how many grains of rice would be on that square in the parable we shared earlier. Write down your estimate, then get a calculator and figure it out. Were you right? Close? If so, it shows you have an unusual intuitive grasp of exponential growth that will serve you well in leadership today and tomorrow. But if you were way off, as many of us are, let it humble and inspire you to open your mind to greater possibilities.

In 1990, the Human Genome Project was launched, an international scientific effort to fully sequence the human genome. It kicked off with high expectations and plans of completion within only fifteen years, which immediately drew criticism. It was too ambitious, some claimed, suggesting it would take decades if not generations. Those doubts seemed to be confirmed when only 1 percent of the genome had been finished at the halfway mark. But to exponential thinkers like theorist Ray Kurzweil, they were right on schedule. After all, the real power of exponential growth is in the back half of the chessboard, when the numbers start to rise dramatically. If you're doubling tiny numbers, initially it doesn't seem like much, until suddenly the growth spurt is massive. One percent, in this case, was actually more than halfway. The project finished ahead of schedule.

It's good to remember that the idea of something progressing or developing over time, in an evolutionary process, is still a historically novel concept. There was a time in history, not so long ago, when we were hardly aware that the world was developing or evolving at all! Of course, we can now look back and see evolution in action, but the speed of change was so much slower that it was hard to appreciate in the course of a lifetime. A cyclical perspective dominated the experience of most people. From generation to generation, there was little change in the *how* of living. There might have been minor, and occasionally major, changes in ruling powers or climate or religious views or geopolitics or health. Such things were always in flux, but fundamental elements of life and work weren't significantly changing. The increasing speed of technological progress has upended that world—opening up a previously unknown universe of change, progress, improvement, newness, and even abundance. As former editor of *Wired* Kevin Kelly puts it, "Newness is such an elemental part of our lives today that we forget how rare it was in ancient days . . . The idea that the future brought improvement was never very popular until recently."[6]

Today, the reality of time-based, developmental processes of rapid change intercedes in our awareness in dramatic ways. But we're still cognitively—and sometimes culturally—wired to an older world. "The truth-is-stranger-than-fiction factor keeps getting jacked up on us on a fairly regular basis, maybe even exponential basis," says science fiction author William Gibson. "I think that's something peculiar to our time. I don't think our grandparents had to live with that."[7] In other words, today we all live on the back half of the chessboard.

Thinking long term requires not only stretching our minds further into the future, but also learning to think "developmentally." That means learning how to cognize change over an arc of time. We don't just see discrete products or services staying the same as time moves ahead, but we see a *process*—from a version 2.0 to a 3.0 to a 5.0. What did transportation industry executives think in 2009 as they looked at the picture of the founders of Google with the silly-looking Toyota Prius self-driving experimental car with its huge, expensive Lidar sensor on top? Did they dismiss it as impractical technology? In that particular moment, it was just that. But was it just an early square on a new chessboard? Where was it headed? What process was it undergoing? What was its evolutionary pathway? How many of them had the developmentally informed foresight to see that only a decade later the technology would be where it is today? Thinking exponentially and developmentally encourages us to explore the trajectory of a given technology over a decade or two, and the perspective we adopt is very different. No longer under the spell of the local and linear, we grasp the *process in time*, not simply the *object in space*. We can trace the antecedents of that product or service (which, in the case of self-driving cars, go back decades) and better predict its pathway into the future. We see the versions that came before and the ones that might come after, understand what's driving the changes, and consider the speed and trajectory.

For business leaders today, there are important insights—about products and services, about growth trends, and even about whole industries—that reveal themselves only when we start to see processes in time instead of objects in space. Incidentally, the cost of self-driving car technology has dropped precipitously over the past decade and is still dropping fast today, even as the technology has improved dramatically—another common feature of exponential growth curves.

PRACTICE: "10X" Your Mindset

Thinking exponentially and thinking long term may sound great in theory, but how do we get ourselves into that mode? How do we internally generate that creative, strategic mental mindset? Dev Patnaik, CEO of the Silicon Valley firm Jump Associates, has a simple strategy that he recommends for strategically jump-starting one's daily routine. When you wake up in the morning, before you get into the rote activities of the day, take a few minutes and think to yourself: *How can I 10X my thinking right now? What would it mean to think much bigger about our work, our organization, about everything we're doing? How can I raise my leadership game to another level? What is the farthest impact of our actions?* In that fresh, creative, open-minded awareness that exists just after waking, and before the demands of your daily schedule come rushing into awareness, can you bring a heightened level of consciousness to your leadership approach? Can you take a creative mental leap? Consider starting the day by 10X-ing your mind.

WHAT BUSINESS ARE YOU IN?

In a world of accelerating change, long-term thinkers must be resolutely attuned to the question *What business am I in?* This is true for the simple reason that business categories are changing much faster than they did in previous decades. Define the answer to the question too narrowly and you may miss opportunities or fail to see important disruptive developments. A decade ago, if you had asked this question of Netflix, you might have expected to get the answer "We're in the mail-order DVD rental business." After all, they practically invented that sector. Luckily for Netflix, however, founder Reed Hastings had a different answer. He knew that Netflix was in the entertainment business. That's why he was able to pivot his company to online streaming and eventually to content creation as technology rendered its previous business model obsolete. The future of the company depended on that broad and flexible understanding of the company's mission.

The shifting landscape of business for companies like Netflix has been exacerbated by a particular tendency in technological evolution called *convergence*. At times, a group of new technologies will converge together to create a robust *platform*—think of the PC, the iPhone, the internet, or even the internal combustion engine. A platform, in this sense, is a virtual or physical "habitat" for a host of other technologies to thrive in. It supercharges innovation and disruption, quickly rendering earlier platforms obsolete. Within the entertainment industry, the delivery platform for video content has undergone several massive shifts in the past few decades—from theaters to VHS to DVD to internet-based streaming. Only a company with the vision to decouple its value-creating activity from the shifting methods of delivery could continue to thrive through such changes.

In many respects, this changing of the platforms is not just a tendency of technological evolution, but of evolution itself. "Everything that rises must converge," wrote the Jesuit mystic and evolutionary philosopher Pierre Teilhard de Chardin[8] back in the early twentieth century. He is often credited with being one of the first theorists whose writings anticipate the internet. He wasn't talking about technology but rather about biology, yet in some respects, biological evolution and technological evolution exhibit similar characteristics. Cell division, for example, exhibits exponential growth. Biological evolution also tends to produce new "platforms" upon which evolution can continue to operate and accelerate. DNA was once an incredible new platform for the acceleration of biological diversity, the Cambrian explosion being the fossilized record of that historical quickening. The human mind could also be considered an extraordinary platform of evolution, and it has fostered the emergence and accelerating evolution of culture.

Coming back to technology, let's consider the internet itself, a magnificent example of convergence (as well as an accelerant to human cultural evolution in all kinds of ways) and a platform for thousands of new businesses. Some thrived, like Amazon, and some failed (like our aborted WholePeople.com business, described in the introduction). In fact, the early days of an emerging platform often provide unique "gold rush" opportunities. Microsoft built its business on the word-processing and spreadsheet capabilities that were implicit in the newly created personal computing platform (the operating system of which it also owned). Whole suites of new businesses are often implicit in emerging platforms. For example, consider a more recent platform, the smartphone operating system, of which iOS and Android are the two most prominent players. Ridesharing apps like Uber and Lyft are among the many businesses that are implicit in the smartphone—a device that tracks exactly where you are, with mechanisms to handle mapping and transactions. So are thousands of other applications, some yet to be realized. Just as it does in biological evolution, the platform speeds up and makes possible all types of emergent breakthroughs and disruptive innovations.

Leaders today, in all fields, must be attentive to convergence, the power of platforms and their evolutionary potentials and, by extension, the business potentials that are implicit in them. In such a world, it is necessary to be agile, stay light on your feet, play the long game (or infinite game), and beware of thinking too narrowly about your industry. If you are in the business of selling cars, the future is highly uncertain. If you are in the transportation business, you have great opportunities ahead of you.

It's natural to have some concern, even fear, about the potential impact of technological disruption on your business. But ultimately, a healthier response is to be inspired by the future that technological change is making possible. Conscious leaders don't fundamentally fear the future; they're too interested in being a part of it, building it, and shaping it. They are more focused on creating that future than in strategically defending their own businesses against change. The future is part of that infinite game, and conscious leaders and long-term thinkers express a natural "faith in the future" by planting seeds that will bear fruit in that extended time frame.

FORECASTING DOS AND DON'TS

"It's difficult to make predictions, especially about the future," says an old Danish proverb. This is even truer in an accelerating world. In

1980, AT&T asked the top consulting company, McKinsey and Co., to advise them on the future of the mobile phone business. How many mobile phones would there be by the year 2000? After a careful study of that issue, McKinsey concluded there would be no more than 300,000—a market opportunity hardly worth pursuing for the huge phone company. But when the year 2000 arrived, companies were selling 300,000 mobile phones *every three days*.

But don't blame McKinsey. At that point, everyone was just beginning to grapple with the nature of these exponential growth curves that enable and create entirely new categories of economic possibilities. In 1980, few realized that communication technology was undergoing an incredible exponential price/performance growth rate driven by information technology. But today's leaders have fewer excuses.

That being said, the goal of this chapter is not to turn leaders into unerring forecasters—if such a thing were even possible. Exponential change and unexpected innovations will always take us by surprise, at least to some degree. Disruption in markets is a phenomenon that's never easy to deal with, and it's ten times harder if it's being driven by accelerating technology. We may always be caught off guard by innovations that change our lives, and growth curves with hockey-stick-like properties. But if you want to be Netflix rather than Blockbuster, Apple rather than Nokia, or Uber rather than your local taxi service, it's critical to be able to look at the chessboard, see a few handfuls of rice in the middle, and appreciate the mountain that is coming, even if you can't see it clearly.

Still, becoming better-informed prognosticators, while important, has limited utility. Even the most innovative, technologically sophisticated companies make plenty of mistakes when it comes to predicting the future of technology. It's perhaps a truism today that "no plan survives first contact with the enemy," or, to put it in Mike Tyson's more blunt style, "everybody has a plan until they get punched in the face." That is always true when markets undergo transition, especially ones under the influence of exponential changes. Therefore, the capacity to pivot on the fly, to change direction, and to change one's conclusions is one of the most important yet most difficult qualities of both organizations and individuals. The most important benefit of learning to think exponentially is that it can help you to not double down on a poor decision, and to acknowledge your own fallibility. As Mark Twain is said to have observed, "What gets us into trouble is not what we don't know. It's what we know for sure that just ain't so."[9] The same could be said for forecasting.

Thinking long term is a way to not make the obvious mistakes, to learn from what we've collectively come to understand regarding both the advance of technology and human cognition and its biases. It gives you the *opportunity* to succeed—or at least to make new mistakes. We speak a lot about humility in this book, and here again it's worth a mention. Remember that humility does not necessarily have anything to do with an absence of confidence or conviction. One can have tremendous self-confidence and still be humble. One of the world's top experts on forecasting, Philip Tetlock, explained in his recent book *Superforecasting* that when it comes to peering into the future, a very particular kind of self-reflection is required for good judgment:

> The humility required for good judgment is not self-doubt—the sense that you are untalented, unintelligent, or unworthy. It is *intellectual* humility. It is a recognition that reality is profoundly complex, that seeing things clearly is a constant struggle, when it can be done at all, and that human judgment must therefore be riddled with mistakes. This is true for fools and geniuses alike. So it's quite possible to think highly of yourself and be intellectually humble. In fact, this combination can be wonderfully fruitful. Intellectual humility compels the careful reflection necessary for good judgment; confidence in one's abilities inspires determined action.[10]

A HEALTHY OPTIMISM

"A leader is a dealer in hope," Napoleon Bonaparte is said to have declared.[11] We're not suggesting you should emulate the world-dominating ambition of the nineteenth-century French general, but in this respect he was onto something. A significant element in the practice of long-term thinking is the exercise of hope. To plan and build for the long term, we have to believe in it. That also means believing that the future can be impacted, changed, and improved through our creative activities. In a world whose mood leans so heavily toward pessimism, a conscious leader must be able to convey to others a unique combination of faith and foresight. That doesn't mean being naive, arrogant, or boastful. It simply means that one believes that the trajectory of the future can, in some small way, bend around one's commitment, work, and intention. However strong our vision, dreams of the future are always risky: they're often not shared by others, and reality never gives any guarantees. The economist Deirdre McCloskey once described entrepreneurs as those who possess "the virtue of courage combined with prudence and a pinch of hope."[12] Hope is not sufficient for creative leaps forward, but it is indispensable.

Perhaps the most important leadership lesson to be gained from a deep dive into the exponential nature of technological growth trends is a simple one: a healthy optimism. By that, we don't mean a Pollyannaish techno-positivity, or a pseudo-faith that technological evolution is the simple answer to every complex question. No, we're talking about a highly rational optimism, a realism infused with idealism, based not on faith but on the trends of history. It's hard to look at some of these trend lines and not be inspired about the possibilities of the future. There will be disruption, yes, and plenty of unintended consequences, no doubt. There will be steps back even in the midst of larger leaps forward. There will be more than enough hype and disillusionment to go around. Such is the nature of progress and development in just about any form. But despite it all, we are now living during the healthiest, most prosperous and peaceful time in history.[13] Even with all of our challenges, the rise of technology has massively improved the human condition. Whatever our complaints about current realities, few would want to return to the world of a couple hundred years ago, much less several thousand. And, more important, the exponential future will provide breakthroughs and opportunities we can scarcely imagine today—for businesses, for organizations, for entrepreneurs, for leaders of all kinds. Technology will provide opportunities to improve the human condition that dwarf our current tools. Genetics, robotics, self-driving cars, quantum computing, AR, VR, 3D printing, an abundance of cheap energy, biotech, nanotech, and many other as-yet-unrecognized breakthroughs. Some are already languishing on the front half of the chessboard. Don't be fooled: soon they might change everything. Or, more specifically, they might inspire the businesses, products, services, and processes that will provide the *opportunity* to change everything. They won't do it alone. Ultimately, those tools will need human guidance from conscious leaders with long-term perspectives to reach their true potential. That will take more than technology; it will take wisdom and insight. Some from the past, but plenty from the present and future as well.

THE CONSCIOUS LEADER'S TOOL KIT

The Hope and the Hype

Have you ever noticed that many predictions of societal or planetary doom seem to be about ten years away? It's close enough to grab attention but far enough away to seem like it just might be possible (and that people will forget it if it fails to materialize). Author Gregg Easterbrook even coined a term for this tendency in his book *A Moment on Earth*: "the Law of Doomsaying." When it comes to predicting the future, there are more than a few cognitive traps that most fall prey to. Another common one is thinking that a new, exciting technology is just around the corner. For example, the hype around self-driving cars has been playing havoc with crystal balls for the past decade. Everyone knows this disruptive technology is coming soon, but predicting its arrival date has been a difficult dance, with experts constantly revising the timeline. Finally, J.D. Power conducted a survey of consumers, asking when they expected this new technology to debut. Their answer: ten years.[14]

"We tend to overestimate the effect of a technology in the short run and underestimate the effect in the long run" is a phrase that has become known as Amara's law, attributed to Roy Amara, an American futurist. Indeed, just because something is overhyped doesn't mean it is unremarkable.

When a radical new technology first hits the cultural radar, people naturally tend to go a bit crazy speculating about all of the incredible uses and possibilities about to arrive on our doorsteps. But its rapid adoption is often overstated—at first. Over the longer term, as the exponential curve spikes, the changes may be more dramatic than we ever could have expected. This waxing and waning of hype over new technologies has led the research firm Gartner to create something called Gartner's Hype Cycle. It tracks technologies from the initial trigger that brings them to our collective attention to their widespread adoption.

The Hype Cycle

1. **Innovation Trigger**: A new technology hits public awareness through research results or media interest.
2. **Peak of Inflated Expectations**: Expectations of a new technology are outsize and overdone.
3. **Trough of Disillusionment**: A new technology fails to immediately transform our lives and struggles to fulfill high expectations.
4. **Slope of Enlightenment**: The technology begins to improve and work its way into our lives.
5. **Plateau of Productivity**: As the technology hits the mainstream, it scales and spreads.

Just like a sports star, no technology should get caught up in reading its own press clippings—and no leader should, either. Understanding the adoption path of new technologies allows us to appreciate their impact without becoming transfixed by the initial hype, or fooled by a period of media disillusionment. Keeping clear eyes and a balanced perspective amid today's techno-transformations is critical for making good decisions. Understanding Amara's law and the Gartner Hype Cycle can steady our hands.

PART III

PEOPLE & CULTURE

CONSTANTLY EVOLVE THE TEAM

None of us, including me, ever do great things. But we can all do small things, with great love, and together we can do something wonderful.

—MOTHER TERESA

THERE IS A PERVASIVE MYTH about leadership—a falsehood often fed by the media, which portrays entrepreneurs and CEOs as larger-than-life geniuses who single-handedly create breakthrough technologies and great companies that change the world. We are led to believe that all of these great business accomplishments are achieved by almost superhuman individuals such as Steve Jobs, Jeff Bezos, Elon Musk, Bill Gates, Mark Zuckerberg, Sara Blakely, Larry Page and Sergey Brin, Reed Hastings, Meg Whitman, Michael Dell, Anne Wojcicki, and Jack Ma. While each of these leaders is undoubtedly a brilliant and exceptionally talented entrepreneur, let's be clear—they wouldn't survive an audition for the Avengers or the Justice League. So how do they accomplish so much? At least part of the answer involves an important, underappreciated secret to transcending our individual talent level: a fantastic team. Working alongside each of these successful individuals is an amazing, talented group of people who both complement the strengths of the leader and compensate for their weaknesses.

In the real world, everything we accomplish is done with and through other people. As leaders, we are only as good as our teams. That may be a cliché, but it's no less true because of it. While the leader of the team often gets too much credit for successes and too much blame for failures, it is the results of the collective that are ultimately being judged. Given that truth, attracting, hiring, inspiring, developing, and retaining the very best team possible is critical for the success of an organization and its leaders. For conscious leaders, the necessity to invest in and constantly evolve our teams is a priority that far outweighs the need to individually shine. A growing organization that creates great opportunities for talented people to excel has potential far beyond the genius, real or media-hyped, of any one person. Its opportunity set is larger, its runway is longer, its culture is healthier, and its future is brighter.

For a conscious leader, the health of the team around them is a never-ending project, a living, three-dimensional, ever-evolving puzzle that they are always working to complete. They know that the development of the team is not simply something they can outsource to the HR department. Yes, it may take help and support from others, but it also takes care and real engagement. When we say that a conscious leader is constantly evolving the team, we mean that they are living with that imperative—working to ensure that growth, positivity, synergy, and expansion are the primary experiences of the people around them, regardless of external circumstances. *Is it healthy? Is it thriving? What does it need? Is it productive? How can I help it develop?*

PRACTICING TEAM LEADERSHIP: Chemistry Checks

A leader should always be asking their team about internal chemistry, to better know if there are any relationship challenges they need to try to help solve. Ask questions such as: *How are people getting along? How high is the trust between people on the team? Is there anyone on the team who is disrupting morale? What can and should I do about that disruption?* You're responsible. You're the leader and the coach. Take responsibility and do something about it if the chemistry of the team is off.

HIRING, FIRING, AND THE SPACES IN BETWEEN

It sounds like a simple project: create a great team of smart, capable individuals and provide a culture in which they can develop and thrive. Okay, but how? This chapter is all about that question. And let's start with a clarification: it's not fundamentally about hiring and firing. If a leader thinks all of the answers to team performance are to be found in the realm of recruitment, the chances of a truly conscious culture developing in that organization are probably minimal. Nevertheless, it's also true that the journey of a great team begins with good hiring decisions.

The crucial importance of good hiring decisions is well understood by Steve Hall, founder of the highly successful car dealership company Driversselect. In the process of building his business, Hall learned that the key to creating a thriving organizational culture is to invest significant time up front in the hiring process. Even when interviewing for entry-level positions, he now seeks to hire people who can eventually do jobs that are two or three positions up on the organization chart. For example, when hiring a receptionist, he looks for someone who could eventually become an office manager. When hiring a car lot attendant, he looks for someone who might one day become assistant controller. Then, once a new hire is brought on board, Hall invests in leadership training to develop his entry-level people. Even though this training is costly, his turnover rate is one-third the industry average, which more than compensates for the extra training expense.

When it comes to hiring, leaders have two options: they can seek new talent from outside the organization or they can promote existing talent from within. When weighing these choices, leaders should be aware that businesses are very similar to complex ecosystems. They have multiple interdependencies that coexist to create dynamic and evolving organizations. When one part of that system is disrupted, it can cause a chain reaction that impacts the entire system's ability to thrive. Hiring new team members from outside the organization is one of those activities with tremendous disruptive potential—in both positive and negative directions.

Creating the right ratio of internal to external talent within an organization is a delicate exercise. Overdoing it on either side can have far-reaching consequences for a business and its culture. We need to strike a balance by providing our best people with opportunities for promotions while simultaneously recruiting top candidates from outside the organization to elevate the whole team's potential. The continuity and stability of the team are critical, but so is occasionally shaking things up by bringing in an outside perspective. A leader must always be looking several steps ahead and asking: *Does our internal talent line up? Do we need to add specific roles?* These are the delicate decisions to evaluate.

Inevitably, there will be times when a leader needs to reach outside the organization to find new talent. Just don't make that your default. It's easy to fall in love with the shiny new hire who appears to be full of upside potential, with no obvious downsides. In that workplace romance, as with any infatuation, we can get caught up in our fantasy of what a new team member will be like—the ideal skill set, the perfect synergies, the imagined impact. But as in romance, fantasy is not a healthy basis on which to pursue a long-term relationship. It's much better if we live in reality, and in reality, the best person for a role is often already working in the organization. He or she has already proven to be a good leader, earned the trust of the team, fits into the culture well, has developed the professional experience and skill set needed for the new role, and is ready to take on more responsibilities. Growing our internal talent by rewarding high-performers creates more opportunities for the next generation of leaders to step into new roles. Research has shown that internal hires tend to be more successful. And it creates tremendous internal goodwill. It shows how the company recognizes and appreciates hard work, commitment, competence, and potential.

Rewarding productive team members with promotions and a clear path upward in the organization is not just a practice for the executive suites. For example, one of the great things about Whole Foods is that a college degree isn't a requirement for becoming an effective leader in the company. More than 90 percent of our store team leaders have been promoted to their positions from within the company. We have many people who have been with the company for twenty or more years, starting their career in one of our stores and working their way up to become a regional president or senior vice president. Every industry has different dynamics and career paths, but never underestimate the power of smart, effective internal leaders who already know your company and are committed to its success.

In order to better reap the rewards of promoting from within, a company needs to be willing to invest in training. In 2019, Amazon committed to providing skills training to 100,000 team members over six years, through a $700 million investment. Some companies skimp on training, afraid that they'll simply be training their people to go and get a better job elsewhere. The computer service outfit Geek Squad turned this fear on its head. Understanding that most of their young technicians saw their job as a stepping-stone to further career achievement elsewhere, they set up an outplacement service for their senior team members. Geek Squad found that the payoff in trust and loyalty was well worth the investment.

So what is the best ratio for internal versus external hires? Every situation is different. At Whole Foods, we strive to fill about 75 percent of our leadership roles with internal candidates. If we dip too far below that ratio, our morale dips, too. At the same time, we also need to be careful about making too few external leadership hires, because it not only limits our intellectual capital, it also hinders our potential to revitalize the organizational culture with fresh perspectives. For many years, we tended not to hire leaders from the outside. In retrospect, I think that bias toward internal promotions ultimately meant that we were not always evolving our team as effectively as we could have been. It took a couple of decades to really learn that sometimes the very best people weren't working for the company yet. Today we consciously work to keep the level of outside leadership hires from falling below 20 percent.

COMPENSATION CONSIDERATIONS

"Show me the money!" screams Cuba Gooding Jr. to Tom Cruise in a famous scene from the iconic 1996 movie *Jerry Maguire.*[1] That phrase has gone on to become a signature cultural meme when it comes to negotiations of all types. It even became the name of a short-lived American game show. But despite the ascendancy of that phrase in the cultural lexicon, money is often overrated when it comes to compensation. Of course, paying a competitive market rate for talented leaders is important; nobody wants to feel like they're being cheated or that their experience is being undervalued. But people who view financial compensation as their driving motivator—instead of more meaningful factors such as purpose and cultural fit—often don't last long. More often than not, they'll be looking for the next, higher-paid gig rather than staying around to really make a long-term contribution to the organization. There's always going to be someone else willing to pay more if a person has a good résumé and track record, so we must look carefully at whether someone is passing through our organization just to upgrade their résumé until a better opportunity in the future comes along.

As we look at compensation, it is essential that internal and external compensation be both competitive in the marketplace and widely seen as fair. If we are paying external hires below the market rate, we're probably going to have trouble recruiting the best people, because their reaction is likely to be "I like the company, but I can't justify that kind of pay cut." At the same time, if we pay people from outside the organization more than we are paying our existing team members, that's going to create resentment. That's why both internal and external pay equity is so critical.

One of the ways Whole Foods tries to achieve this is through wage transparency. This has been a hot topic for many years now, particularly when it comes to executive pay ratios and gender pay gaps, but it's something we've practiced for decades. Total compensation for all team members companywide, including the company's leadership team, is available to everyone in our company through our wage disclosure report. We want team members to have a clear line of sight into pay equity. It also empowers people to consult with leadership if they feel there is a lack of fairness. This, in turn, gives the company an opportunity to change and evolve potential inconsistencies, creates a sense of solidarity throughout the organization, and helps keep resentment and gossip about pay low.

DON'T HIRE FOR PRESENTATION SKILLS

Have you ever been "wowed" by someone in an interview because he or she had amazing charisma and an ability to captivate their audience? It's a true gift. However, the reality is that often the most talented candidates don't have it. That doesn't mean that they won't become a fantastic team member. Never overselect for presentation skills. Remember, you're not hiring for the position of "good interviewee." Go beyond your gut instinct. Take the time you need to get to know someone more deeply than initial impressions. In fact, that's one of the many reasons we're great believers in the power of multiple interviews, particularly a series of group interviews, when hiring and promoting. Finding the right fit can take time, reflection, conversation, and extended consideration. It might be easy for a candidate to charm one person with a blast of charisma during the hiring process, but that becomes far more difficult when there's a group involved. We all have conscious and unconscious biases, but the collective wisdom and varied perspective that comes with a conscientious interview group makes it much harder for a candidate who isn't a good fit to convince multiple people otherwise.

The person who's responsible for the overall performance of the team should have the authority to make the final decision on who is hired, but it's a consultative process that accounts for the collective feedback from the entire group. The worst decisions that people have made in hiring at Whole Foods have occurred when a leader made a unilateral decision by either avoiding doing a final group interview or disregarding concerns and feedback raised by the group.

There are several things we look for when considering the best candidate. Obviously being smart and having a high IQ is important, particularly if the role involves intellectually demanding work. But that's not enough anymore. We also need to carefully evaluate:

- ***Emotional intelligence:*** This is a characteristic that's increasingly important, particularly in more complex organizational environments that are organized into teams. Team members need to be able to connect with people, listen well, and empathize with what others are feeling. Communication, brainstorming, collaboration, and sharing ideas is a day-to-day necessity, so people without this quality can prevent teams from fully flourishing and damage morale.
- ***Character:*** Does this person have good ethical character? Are they fundamentally going to act with integrity? If not, it doesn't matter how brilliant and capable someone is. The always wise Warren Buffett has said, "We look for three things when we hire people. We look for intelligence, we look for initiative or energy, and we look for integrity. And if they don't have the latter, the first two will kill you, because if you're going to get someone without integrity, you want them lazy and dumb."[2] He may have been partly joking, but there's a lot of truth in his words! Integrity is not always easy to determine in a few interviews, but we should always be aware of its importance as we make decisions about new hires.

- *Cultural fit:* Every organization has a culture, and many teams within an organization have subcultures. Don't underestimate their power. If we hire someone who fundamentally is not aligned with and open to our culture, he or she will eventually fail. Just because someone has the relevant experience and was successful in another company in the same role doesn't mean those skills will translate across the cultural divide. A team reacts to a bad cultural fit the way the body's immune system reacts to what it perceives as harmful bacteria or viruses—it creates an immune response to repel the foreign invader. Of the sixteen senior executives that Whole Foods Market has hired from outside the company, only 50 percent were ultimately successful. Each, without exception, had a high IQ, an excellent résumé, strong references, and great work experience. The reason for the failure, in every instance, was poor cultural fit.

DEVELOPING A CONSCIOUS CULTURE

Once we've hired the right people for the team, the next challenge is to continue to develop a culture in which individuals and teams can grow and thrive. It's hard to overestimate the power of culture in the success of the organization. One of our goals as conscious leaders is to create the absolute healthiest culture we can possibly create. "Healthy cultures everywhere" should be our motto, because we know creating a wholesome culture will help the business to flourish and help team members to reach their highest potentials. We'll have lower turnover rates, lower training costs, and greater loyalty. Our customers will develop a true affection for the business and become its best marketers. Our stakeholders will benefit in all kinds of ways. When our culture is flourishing, the business synergizes at a much higher level. Everything functions better.

How, then, do we make our organizational culture healthy? It sounds obvious, but the most important first step is to make it a high priority. Too often, leaders take their organizational culture for granted and don't focus much time or attention on it. An organizational culture is a bit like a garden—it takes careful tending to turn a patch of soil into an abundant, verdant, flowering, productive ecosystem. And if we neglect it, all kinds of toxic weeds will begin growing, which will eventually crowd out the healthy fruits and vegetables we want to harvest. A healthy culture doesn't get built overnight, but the long-term rewards of cultivating one are enormous. We need to be vigilant in weeding out unhealthy aspects, while also making sure to implement processes and structures that lead to team member satisfaction, growth, and happiness. Our goal should be to build a culture of enjoyment, appreciation, and satisfaction, but also of hard work and productivity, one in which the values of development and growth become widely shared across the organization.

Of course, every team experiences highs and lows. An effective leader uses their emotional and cultural intelligence to understand the right decisions they need to make. At one moment, that might mean nudges, pushes, or even big changes; at another it might simply mean a supportive and appreciative "job well done." The art of leading a team, like many things in life, involves interdependent polarities. (See "The Conscious Leader's Tool Kit: The Art and Science of Polarities," page 22, for more on this concept.) And one of the most important polarities for conscious leaders to keep in mind is *challenge and support*. Because challenging and supporting are both important modes of leadership, if we focus on only one side of this polarity, we will create a problematic imbalance. While the *support* side of this equation is anchored in patience and nurturing care for team members and their needs, the *challenge* side often involves pushing and pressing team members and even other stakeholders to put in the extra effort necessary to achieve the organization's higher purpose.

Conscious leaders, in other words, must integrate concerns for both people *and* purpose so that both of these aspects of the organization can realize their full potential. Ruthlessly pursuing the purpose at all costs may temporarily lead to progress, but at the expense of people's needs. Pampering team members without regard for external results may yield short-term gains in culture and satisfaction, but the purpose may languish. Conscious leadership entails the harmonization of this polarity. A conscious culture strides forward on the two legs of challenge and support. We must strive to act both as nurturing servants of our people and as courageous champions of our higher purpose.

Here are some suggested leadership practices for developing a truly conscious culture.

Make team member happiness a core value. Team members are not a "human resource" for the organization to exploit as it sees fit. Rather, they are "sources" of innovation, creativity, and productivity that need to be respected and supported. They are participants in the organization's shared mission. When you make that shift in thinking, you start reimagining the kind of environment that you create. For example, conscious businesses such as Southwest Airlines and The Motley Fool make sure that their cultures are fun and enjoyable every day. That can mean many different things—it doesn't have to be the conventional perks and foosball tables of millennial tech campuses. The most important thing is to put on your creative hat and consciously design happiness, fun, and goodwill into your work culture. Cultures that are fun have lower turnover rates and higher levels of productivity. Everyone benefits.

We have said this before, but it doesn't hurt to repeat it: team members want to know that they are valued, cared about, and appreciated. As conscious leaders focused on creating as healthy a culture as we possibly can, it is essential that we demonstrate our care and gratitude for the people we work with every single day.

PRACTICING TEAM LEADERSHIP:
Be Mindful of Those You Lead

Much like a parent thinks about his or her children daily, a leader needs to think about their team every single day in similar ways. You are their leader and their coach, and you have responsibilities to help them as best you can. Ask yourself: *How can my team best flourish? What opportunities can I provide to develop each team member to their highest potential? How do I ensure they have the tools they need to be successful? What are their strengths and weaknesses? Do they need outside leadership development? Are they stuck? Maybe they need an external coach of some type?* Perhaps you can keep a journal or a file that tracks their challenges and their progress. Are you caring enough about your team that you're monitoring it, following it, and giving it your very best attention?

Practice what you preach. Once we accept and embrace our role as leader, one of the most important things we can do is to always lead by example. People pay a lot more attention to what we do than to what we say. Whether we want to or not, we are going to be a role model, and everything we do will be observed by our team. Our actions will have an impact and ripple out far beyond us, first to the team and then to the larger organization. A good leader doesn't shrink from that reality. Be respectful and caring to your team every day. If you disparage people, how can you possibly think you'll maintain positive morale? Ultimately, we each get the team that we deserve. The quality of our character, our integrity, our sense of purpose, and our capacity to lead with love will all shape and impact our team. They will evolve and grow under our leadership, or the lack of those qualities will hold back their development.

At the same time, don't let the need to lead by example encourage any kind of leadership pretense. Authenticity is especially important when it comes to leadership today. People can sniff out pretense quickly.

As leaders, it is very difficult to develop any team beyond our own level of consciousness. Our own level of development can provide an upward pull on those around us, but it can also act as a ceiling. This is one more reason why it is important that we practice the virtue of continuously learning and growing (see chapter 9).

Leader, know thyself. It's no secret that the initial culture of an organization is usually created, unconsciously, by the original founders. Their strengths and weaknesses become the default character of the organizational culture. But over time, through greater self-awareness and by directly soliciting feedback from our team, we can come to better understand these dynamics. The more we're aware of those things, the more effectively we're able to build a team that compensates for those weaknesses, and that can make a huge difference in overall productivity.

When I look at Whole Foods Market, I see my strengths as a person and leader well represented, but the organization also mirrors back to me my weaknesses and the qualities I don't love about myself. For example, I tend to be a very creative person who's good at brainstorming and coming up with innovative solutions and new ideas. The shadow side of that strength, however, is that I frequently don't pay enough attention to the details. One of the consequences is that Whole Foods has been highly innovative but too often hasn't paid enough attention to all the operational details—especially in our first twenty years as a business. Over time, as I became more and more conscious of both my strengths and my weaknesses as a leader, I slowly but steadily developed a team that could compensate for my weaknesses. My executive team today is extremely good at thinking through structure and complex details while maintaining the innovative, entrepreneurial culture of Whole Foods. Over the years, this team has included many exceptional people, such as Glenda Flanagan, A. C. Gallo, Walter Robb, Jason Buechel, Sonya Gafsi Oblisk, Jim Sud, and Keith Manbeck.

Create an environment of safety and trust. "Google is not a conventional company. We don't intend to become one."[3] This phrase appeared in the founders' original letter to investors when the tech giant went public back in 2004. And Google has been true to its word. One of the characteristics of that independence is that when it wants to know the answer to a conundrum, it doesn't rely on other people's work or opinions. In 2012, when Google's executives decided they needed to understand the most important attributes that make a team really work, they didn't call up McKinsey or some other consulting firm for research or advice. No, they pursued the question themselves. Dubbed Project Aristotle—in recognition of the great philosopher's phrase "The whole is greater than the sum of the parts"—the company's research included an exhaustive study of 180 internal teams, along with all of the relevant internal research material and survey data they could find. They subjected that data to rigorous statistical models to determine the most critical factors for producing positive outcomes—measured both quantitatively and qualitatively.

Several of the key results were not exactly surprising. For example, we should hardly be shocked that they found that teams should have clear structure and transparent roles, responsibilities, and goals. Or that teams work best when there is a sense of being able to rely on the contributions of fellow team members. Still, several other findings don't exactly jump off the page of your average MBA textbook. For example, the research found that two of the top five qualities that create successful teams were the ability to do work that is meaningful and the knowledge that that work has an impact. Meaning matters. Of course, not all work is meaningful, and not every form of meaningful work has a clear path to impact in the world. But combining those two is a powerful cocktail that inspires real team performance.

The number-one finding from Project Aristotle was particularly fascinating. The most important attribute of team performance was "psychological safety." By that they meant a team culture in which people feel they can be vulnerable, take risks, ask questions, ask for help, bring up difficult issues, even make mistakes, and generally trust that the other members of the team will have their best interests at heart. That environment of real trust and mutual care is delicate, but it's the fount of great performance. A leader's job is to nurture that environment of trust and model it themselves by being willing to take risks, ask tough questions, acknowledge mistakes, and put the wellbeing of the team above their own.

Provide clear goals and reviews. It's critical to respect people's ambition and desire to develop. What do they need to learn? What do they need to do to be promoted? If they are promoted, what would that next role be? What skills and attributes do they need to improve to better perform at that next level as the marketplace changes and evolves? Providing clearly defined career paths gives people something to strive for and an outlet for their ambitions and goals. If we don't show our teams that we are invested in their professional development, we run the risk of losing our best people because they will become frustrated and see no future, ultimately leaving us with a pool of less talented people.

Job reviews are extremely important, yet many smaller organizations don't do them. People need to receive consistent and candid feedback to know where they stand, where they are excelling, and which areas they need to further develop to become more successful. If we don't have constructive and direct dialogue with our teams as part of job reviews, then we are doing members of the team and the organization a disservice. There's frequently a disconnect between how a person perceives his or her work, leadership, and contribution and how colleagues and other leaders view those same things—hence the value of 360 reviews (which include feedback from their team, their peers, and their team leaders). Thanks to the holistic feedback loop these create, leaders conducting a 360 review are less likely to overlook issues and challenges, because consistent themes and feedback will become apparent.

360 reviews are also valuable in helping underperformers see that their struggles are often not with their leader but with the larger

team. In other words, let's say a team leader is providing candid, constructive feedback to a team member. That person might just rationalize it away: "I'm doing okay. They just don't like me. It's personal." People begin to create a victim narrative about how they're being misunderstood and unfairly treated. The 360 review can be a very powerful way to wake underperformers up, because the feedback comes from many directions. It can't simply be rationalized away as one person's prejudice. Over the years we've seen 360 reviews wake up many people who otherwise were content to stay asleep.

One of the best ways to create clear goals and inspire people to meet them is to use other successful organizations as benchmarks for excellence. Tom Gardner, CEO of The Motley Fool investment firm, a company that prides itself on having a lively, fun, and healthy culture, is a firm believer in "cultural benchmarking." The Motley Fool employs a full-time team member whose job is to reach out to other companies to ask them what they've learned that they'd be willing to share. And as it turns out, leaders from other organizations are often eager to share their insights and best practices. Motley Fool is not hesitant to implement those ideas that fit.

PRACTICING TEAM LEADERSHIP: Develop Your Feedback Skills

Some people have a natural gift for providing direct and honest feedback to people, but most of us need to work at developing this skill. As with any skill, the more we practice, the better we will become at it. A leader can start by telling their team that they want to become more skilled at providing candid feedback, but they need help and encouragement to do it well. Now the team begins to be invested in helping the leader to develop their own coaching skills. They are helping to coach their coach! This helps humanize the leader by making them more open and vulnerable. It also invites patience and understanding from the team if the leader is less skillful initially.

Instigate a coaching culture. Hiring external coaches for the highest potential leaders in an organization is a growing trend, particularly in the tech industry. It can be an expensive investment, but in a large organization where the quality of the leadership can make a huge economic difference, it can be a worthwhile investment. Whole Foods only discovered the value of external leadership development programs in the past few years, and we have seen great success using the Stagen Leadership Academy, founded by Rand Stagen in Dallas. For some of our leaders who have struggled in specific areas, such as self-awareness, emotional intelligence, and communication skills, the improvement has been outstanding.

Anyone who wants to hear firsthand accounts of the power of this kind of coaching, involving some of the most respected leaders and companies of our time, should consider reading *Trillion Dollar Coach: The Leadership Playbook of Silicon Valley's Bill Campbell.* A legendary executive coach who passed away in 2016, Campbell counseled some of the most brilliant minds in business, including Larry Page, Sergey Brin, Eric Schmidt, Jonathan Rosenberg, and Sundar Pichai at Google; Steve Jobs at Apple; Brad Smith at Intuit; John Donahoe at eBay; Marissa Mayer at Yahoo; Dick Costolo at Twitter; Sheryl Sandberg at Facebook; and other well-known tech leaders. Even at the pinnacles of their careers, these legends were mentored and guided by Campbell, who built trusting relationships, helped inspire courage, and fostered personal growth in the best and most challenging times.

While external coaches can be invaluable, the focus on coaching need not be limited to that format. In fact, conscious leaders recognize that it is part of their own role to be a coach, and they work to encourage that recognition in every leader and team member within the organization. As executive coach and founder of Bluepoint Leadership Development Gregg Thompson writes in his insightful book *The Master Coach*, "Coaching is everyone's business. The beauty of coaching is that it is not a role that is reserved for those with specialist knowledge or in positions of power . . . Any person in the organization can sit with another person and challenge them to lift their game, encourage them to see new possibilities, confront them with their own potential, affirm their many talents and remind them of how great it feels to do extraordinary work."[4] Thompson makes the crucial point that coaching is not about solving problems for other people; it is about creating a context in which people can solve their own problems. He advocates the creation of a "coaching culture" that transcends scheduled sessions and becomes an everyday feature of organizational life.

Value mentorship. Beyond any team leader's responsibility to be a coach, there's also tremendous value in formal mentorship programs. Amazon's Technical Advisor (TA) program is a great example. Essentially, senior leaders in the company each take on a TA, who shadows them in everything they do for a year or more. Given an unprecedented amount of exposure to the day-to-day responsibilities of Amazon's current executive leaders, TAs are Amazonians who are identified as having high potential as future leaders within the company. After their stint as a TA is completed, they are usually placed in an important leadership role somewhere else in the company.

At Whole Foods, I had an incredible mentor from age twenty-four to forty: my father, Bill Mackey. When I co-founded the company back in 1978, I had almost no experience in business, and I'd taken zero business classes in college. Fortunately for me, my father was a former professor of accounting at Rice University and had left teaching to work in business. He eventually became CEO of a public hospital management company, Lifemark, until it was sold in 1984 to a larger corporation. There is no doubt in my mind that Whole Foods would have failed in its earliest days if not for the mentorship of my father. For sixteen years, I never made an important business decision without consulting with him first. However, by the time I turned forty, I was ready to end the close mentorship with him and lead the company on my own. It was a difficult separation, and there was pain on both sides. However, it has ultimately proven to be a win-win-win solution—good for me, good for him, and good for Whole Foods. Mentorship from an older and more knowledgeable leader can prove to be an invaluable experience, but there also comes a point when it is time to move past the mentorship and step fully into one's own power as a leader.

Former Campbell Soup Company CEO Denise Morrison credits her early success to finding the right mentors. Working at Nestlé in the 1980s, she sought out the company's CEO, Alan MacDonald, to share the direct customer feedback she was hearing every day. And as she helped MacDonald connect with Nestlé's customers, she also sought his advice on how she could excel. Cultivating this mentor relationship eventually resulted in MacDonald's recommending Morrison for the promotion that transformed her career. Grateful for the mentors who had helped her along the way, when she became CEO Morrison "paid it forward" by regularly meeting with her female colleagues to help them manage their careers. As she explains, "I started the Camp Campbell program to mentor the next generation of female leaders and entrepreneurs to inspire thought leadership and foster creative collaboration . . . Everyone needs mentors and sponsors to achieve their goals and advance their careers."[5]

Manage underperformers. No matter how well we hire, no matter how well we coach, no matter how much we invest in leadership development, every team is going to have people who underperform. The question is: What are we going to do about it?

First, it's essential that clear and candid feedback be provided, both when people are doing well and when they're challenged. People do far better with positive feedback, praise, and appreciation, so that should be the emphasis, but if we're not also giving the necessary tough but constructive feedback, then we'll be doing a disservice to our team and to the team members. People need to know if they are falling short and receive guidance on how to do better. Rand Stagen says it well:

"When you withhold feedback, you are sabotaging the other person's ability to succeed."[6] One of the mistakes that many leaders make is to sit on such feedback, avoiding a potentially unpleasant conversation while making silent judgments. Too often, they wait until the grievances and dissatisfaction grow to a breaking point and then they lose their temper.

After giving clear feedback, the second thing we need to do is give opportunities for the person to course-correct and help him or her to learn and grow. Some patience is required in these situations, because we need to give people a chance to act on what we've discussed. However, while patience is a virtue, such situations should never be an excuse for the leader to simply procrastinate in making a difficult decision about the team member's future. Setting a deadline can be helpful. While it's never easy, part of constantly evolving our team is removing people who are underperforming and holding the collective team back.

Removing someone from the team doesn't necessarily mean firing them from the company. There can be other alternatives, depending on the reasons for the underperformance. A conscious leader takes the time to figure out what went wrong. Frequently, a person is underperforming because they've been promoted to a position that is simply beyond their abilities. They were successful and performing well in their previous role, which is why they were promoted in the first place. It is a terrible waste to terminate hardworking and loyal team members just because they were unsuccessfully promoted. It is far better to recycle them back to their previous position or a different one that's a horizontal move. Give them a new opportunity to start fresh under a different leader and they may just flourish. One story illustrating this really stands out in my mind.

Way back in 1988, Mark Dixon was store team leader when we opened our Richardson store in Dallas—our seventh location. We knew that this new market was going to be a stretch for the company. Richardson was an affluent suburban location, but one with very little consciousness of natural or organic foods. The store started at an incredibly low sales volume—the lowest of any store we had ever opened—and it looked as though it was going to be a big mistake. Mark was really struggling. We gave him a couple of years to grow the store sales, but ultimately he was unsuccessful as store team leader, and the morale of the team members was poor. After two years of frustration, we made the decision to bring in a new leader with fresh ideas and high energy. However, we did not fire Mark from the company. Instead, he was demoted back to the same role he had occupied prior to his promotion. He took his demotion with the right attitude, which was "I understand that I wasn't ready. What do I need to learn to get back to that next level?" He listened carefully to the feedback we gave him and learned from his failure.

The person who replaced Mark did a tremendous job, and sales at the Richardson store grew by more than 25 percent for ten consecutive years. It went from having the lowest sales in the company to becoming one of our top performers.

Mark, meanwhile, took all the necessary steps to grow as a leader. Not only did he become a store team leader again, but he became one of the very best that the company has ever had, and eventually successfully led three other stores. Within just a few years he was promoted to regional vice president and eventually president of our Southwest Region. Mark served in that role for more than ten years and was an incredibly valuable member of Whole Foods Market's leadership team before he retired in 2017. He was inducted into the Whole Foods Hall of Fame in 2020, which is a very rare and greatly coveted honor within the company.

Of course, not every story has such a happy ending. Not everyone has the strength and humility to be demoted, learn from their mistakes, and go on to greater success in the future. Sometimes we need to remove people not only from their team but from the company.

Tough personnel decisions are a part of leadership that can't be avoided. We must constantly evolve our team through how we hire, how we coach, how we develop our team, and also through how we remove people who cannot perform to our high standards. If we're unwilling to do that, then we're probably not going to reach our potential as leaders.

So how do we let people go? First, it should never be a surprise. If somebody is surprised they're getting fired, then the leader has done a bad job giving feedback. Second, it should never come suddenly (unless there's been some type of integrity breach or ethics violation).* Third, it should be done with compassion and encouragement for the future. In my personal experience, hardly anyone who has been failing and been given candid feedback is ever surprised. They knew it was coming. They are grateful for the opportunity, and we wish them well in their next job, wherever it is. It may be too much to hope that we'll remain friends, but I've fired a number of people over the years with whom I have been able to stay on good terms. Panera founder and CEO Ron Shaich says he's received thank-you notes over the years from people he's fired. It may have been tough at the time, but in hindsight they learned from the hard truths and became better for it.

Build community. Humans thrive in community. We are tribal creatures, and there is nothing that soothes our souls like healthy connection. In today's world, for better or worse, the organizations in which we work are a huge part of what passes for community. So let's make them the best that we can! Of course, we can't meet every human emotional need in a corporate or nonprofit setting, but we can create real forms of community. And to help facilitate the creation of closer bonds between colleagues, sometimes we need to get outside of our normal work settings. Perhaps it's an outdoor activity, a leadership retreat, an off-site gathering, volunteering as a team to do community service, or even just spending time cooking and sharing a meal together. There's something about being out in the world, away from the workplace—

---

* The poor performance should be transparently documented, and obviously we need to follow all legal and HR guidelines for our company, regardless of how small or large the organization. In today's complex world, we put ourselves at risk if we don't follow the rules regarding due process and severance consistently.

for example, sleeping in the same hotel, waking up, hiking, and then having breakfast together—that helps knit the bonds of community.

Brett Hurt, founder of the fast-growing Data.world, a B-Corp, encourages his team members to form interest groups within the company. These groups, which Data.world team members create spontaneously, without official permission, are known as "tribes." Data.world's "wakeboarding tribe" meets in the morning before work, their "cooking tribe" meets at lunch, and their "yoga tribe" gets together after work. There is a reason why the company has been rated one of the top places to work in the local region: the experience of community.

The most important thing to remember about building community is that it doesn't have to take a lot of intensive control or effort. Humans have been doing it naturally for thousands of years! Just provide the right nudges and opportunities, and watch it begin to happen all by itself.

THE CONSCIOUS LEADER'S TOOL KIT

Personality Types

Humans love putting things into categories, including ourselves. We've categorized the physical world in great detail—from every species we've discovered on the planet to every star in the night sky—and we've made numerous attempts to categorize the less tangible, more mysterious aspects of the world as well. One enduring focus of this endeavor is mapping the various manifestations of the human personality. After all, people are not exactly the same. We know this intuitively, but is there a method to the madness? Do our personality differences fall into a distinct set of patterns, like our blood types or our ethnic makeup? Ever since ancient Greece, some of humanity's brightest minds have theorized that the human personality can be divided into types. Hippocrates proposed that four "humors" of the body were influential in shaping personalities, and both Aristotle and Plato came up with their own personality categorization systems.

Today, the fascination with personality types continues. Many business leaders and consultants have adopted modern-day personality-type systems as part of their organizational development tool kit. Leaders know that the hardest part of their job is often the delicate balancing act of working with diverse personalities—figuring out how to motivate people, how to spark their creativity, how to help them get along, and how to prevent or manage conflict. In all of these endeavors, it can be helpful to have a system for understanding how and why people respond so differently.

Are you an introvert or an extrovert? Thinking-driven or feeling-driven? Group-oriented or self-reliant? Contemporary personality systems map things like how we communicate, how we interact with others and with groups, how we lead, how we handle conflict, how we solve problems. These are not good/bad value judgments or moral evaluations, but simply differences that may require distinct kinds of leadership to bring out an individual's full potential. If you treat everyone as if they're fundamentally the same, you'll cheat your organization out of the richness of human diversity.

When it comes to specific personality-type systems, they can be both useful and problematic. Critics complain that they lack scientific evidence and are little better than astrology. It's true that none of these systems have clear, empirical backing, and some derive their distinctions from quite esoteric sources. Still, advocates insist that they are highly valuable and accurately describe at least some features of the landscape of human personality. Whatever the ultimate verdict, many companies have adopted their insights and are already putting them to use. Conscious leaders should be aware of them and appreciate what they have to offer without becoming ideologically attached.

Linda Berens, president of the Association for Psychological Type International, says that "typology frameworks give us a language to understand themes of behaviors, deep motivations and drives, talents and more."[7] They can help us to break free, she explains, of our "be like me" bias: the tendency to assume that others do—or should—relate to the world just like we do.

The Myers-Briggs Type Indicator is the best-known personality typology. Other popular systems include the Keirsey Temperament

Sorter (KTS), the Enneagram, the Big Five personality traits, and the Sixteen Personality Factors (16PF). Rather than focus on one as being the "way things are," we encourage you to recognize the important truth these systems are conveying. The understanding that there are distinct personality types can help a leader recognize, motivate, and employ diverse talents on any given team. At their best, personality-type systems allow leaders to respect and honor real differences in people's fundamental approaches to life. But we must remember to always hold them lightly. Types are, as Berens says, "a language to understand differences not labels to tattoo on the forehead."[8]

REGULARLY REVITALIZE

Almost everything will work again if you unplug it
for a few minutes, including you.

—ANNE LAMOTT

IN THE FIRST FLUSH OF the new millennium, one of the world's best investors, Stanley Druckenmiller, made one of the greatest trades of his life. He accurately predicted that the direction of Treasury bonds in late 2000 and early 2001 would be contrary to conventional wisdom. He was able to see the reality of the economic situation, trade heavily against the market trend, and reap the rewards. That insight netted him a nice payday, and he acknowledges that it only happened for one simple reason: he took a break.

Before making that huge and ultimately successful trade, Druckenmiller had taken four months away from Wall Street. He had stepped out of the noise of the financial news and rested his body and his mind. He relaxed and recharged. When he finally returned many months later, he could suddenly see the big picture with fresh eyes. And what he saw changed his life.

"I will go to my grave believing that if I hadn't taken that sabbatical, I would have never made that bet," Druckenmiller reflected in an interview years later. "It's because I was freed up . . . my mind was clear and fresh."[1] In a business where everything depends on clear thinking and good decision-making, a little rest and relaxation made all of the difference.

For leaders in any field or area of expertise, the power of rest, repose, relaxation, and rejuvenation should never be underestimated. It might seem counterintuitive to suggest that such passive, quiescent activities can be the fount of dynamism and creativity, but that's exactly the point. Indeed, there may be few things that spur productivity more than those behaviors that allow us to empty our mind of prosaic mental clutter. That might mean meditation, sleep, a long run, or just a walk in the woods. In those moments of relative stillness, the superficial concerns that usually fill our waking mind leave our attention like water flowing out of an overturned vase, and the deeper cognitive algorithms and higher intuitive functions of our mental apparatus can begin to work their own magic on the issues of the moment. Often, the result will be the pleasant surprise of creative insight, or a newly affirmed conviction in the right way forward.

"The problem is never how to get new, innovative thoughts into your mind, but how to get old ones out," writes the co-founder of Visa, Dee Hock. "Clean out a corner of your mind and creativity will instantly fill it."[2]

A recent survey of American workers suggested that more than 60 percent are burned out or highly stressed.[3] *Harvard Business Review* reports that job burnout accounts for an estimated $125 to $190 billion in healthcare spending annually, and contributes to a number of chronic diseases.[4] And among executives, one study conducted by Harvard Medical School found that a stunning 96 percent of senior leaders reported feeling burned out to some degree, and a third of these described their burnout as extreme.[5] While we may be tempted to blame our stress on the pressures of the job, the culture of the workplace, the expectations of stakeholders, the balance sheet, and so on, the reality is that every human being has a significant degree of power over their own states of being. No, we may not be able to remove all those sources of stress, but we can do a tremendous amount to improve our resilience.

Too often, it takes a crisis to force the most driven among us to take a pause. Jay Coen Gilbert, one of the visionaries behind the B

Corp movement, shares how a diagnosis of non-Hodgkin's lymphoma, in late 2016, forced him to change the pace of his life dramatically. He recovered, but he's trying hard not to forget the gift hidden in that difficult episode. "When I have taken time to slow down it has always been rewarded with better decision making, more trust, and deeper relationships—both personally and vocationally,"[6] he says.

Ideally, conscious leaders shouldn't wait for a health scare or other crisis to force them to change their habits. The ability to revitalize ourselves is one of the lowest-hanging, sweetest fruits that any of us can pick off the tree of life. Finding the rhythm of deep engagement and quality disengagement, activity and stillness, passionate focus and restful detachment is one of the most important skills for sustaining leadership over the long term. While we all may have different set points, tipping points, and breaking points, no one escapes the need to recharge. A few minutes, a few hours, a few days, a few weeks, or even a few months—everyone needs the time and space to properly revitalize and reinvigorate the self. Those who do it well give themselves a powerful physical and mental edge—not to mention a superior quality of life.

WHO'S YOUR CHIEF ENERGY OFFICER?

At its core, revitalization is all about energy—how we use it, how we can have more of it available, how we understand it, and how we manage it. For high-performance leaders in most fields, these are essential issues. How can they keep their drive alive and maintain the strong level of motivation necessary to meet the rigorous demands of conscious leadership? These were the questions Tony Schwartz sought to answer when he founded The Energy Project consulting firm. Tony has helped many of the world's most prominent leaders achieve sustainable high performance by more skillfully managing their own energy, as well as the energy of their teams. The path to sustainable, higher energy is not simply a personal path. As we know, authentic vitality can be infectious. Schwartz counsels the leaders he works with to see themselves as their organization's "chief energy officer."

Schwartz's deep dive into human energy has its roots in his love of sports, and specifically tennis. It began with the work of a colleague, sports psychologist Jim Loehr. While watching professional tennis matches, Loehr noticed that the best players were deliberately resting—not just between matches or games, but even between points. Rather than move around or bounce the ball, they took a moment to be completely still or to consciously breathe deeply. As Loehr studied these champion athletes, discovered a remarkable fact. Some were actually conserving just a little bit of extra energy between points and games, and the edge that their superior energy management gave them in long, intensive matches provided a demonstrable boost in their results. These players had learned a secret that is relevant far beyond the tennis court: if energy is the ability to do work, as physicists tell us, then *resting is part of the work*. This insight led Schwartz and Loehr to the realization that personal energy is something that not only can be conserved, by using the right techniques, but can also be actively expanded and multiplied. It was upon this epiphany that Schwartz built his business.

As the turn of the millennium came and went, Schwartz recognized how the steadily growing influence of technology was making ever-increasing demands on people's time, requiring more and more attention and intruding deeper into all areas of life. In response to this challenge, he realized that even though time is a finite resource, personal energy can be effectively expanded. But doing so was going to require a fundamentally different approach to energy management. Too often, it seemed to Schwartz, individuals and organizations were behaving as if humans were machines, designed to run steadily and consistently without stopping. Schwartz's work took a stand for a fundamentally different truth—that humans are actually designed to operate in natural cycles, and we need periods of time to regenerate and renew our energy levels. In other words, humans are not computers. We have natural energetic peaks and valleys, and denial of this fact is a sure way to end up in a serious energy deficit. We need to respect our cycles during the course of a year or a month, but we also need to appreciate them during the course of a day.

For example, consider an average workday. Schwartz's research suggested that humans naturally work in roughly ninety-minute increments. After that, we need a mental break—maybe we need to go for a walk or a run, eat a snack, stretch, or have some other temporary period of renewal before diving into another work cycle. Again, it's that brief but critical period of rest that keeps both the tennis player at peak performance during their match and the executive at the top of their leadership game during the day. *To truly do more, we sometimes have to get better at doing less.* Generally, Schwartz realized, we can expect to be operating at our peak for about three intensive work cycles in a day. That's around four and a half hours where we are functioning at our highest level of overall energy. That doesn't mean we should never work eight-hour days; it simply means that outside of those three ninety-minute periods of highest performance, we should be focusing on less mentally demanding tasks. Again, this is just a general rule of thumb, but it gives you a sense of how thinking about humans as working in cycles—periods of focused energy expenditure followed by interludes of renewal and revitalization—can transform how we manage our daily activities. It brings much greater self-awareness to our energy levels and shows how we can work with them instead of trying to override them or wishing them away. With these insights at hand, Schwartz began to recognize that our "capacity to do work," individually and organizationally, can be increased significantly. Soon, The Energy Project was born.

Schwartz's firm identified and carefully analyzed four essential kinds of personal energy: physical, emotional, mental, and spiritual. While these forms of energy are closely related, they are also distinct in the sense that working to increase each type requires its own specific set of practices. Schwartz's model offers a powerful holistic lens for managing and cultivating both one's own energy and the energy of one's team. Let's briefly look at the key distinctions that inform his work.

- ***Physical energy***—the energy of your body—needs to be continuously renewed and replenished through adequate sleep, healthy nutrition, and regular exercise. We wholeheartedly concur with Schwartz's emphasis on these foundational but too often overlooked components of physical well-being, and we'll return to them in greater depth later in the chapter.

- ***Emotional energy***, in Schwartz's model, refers to the quality of our energy. Learning to take more control of our emotions, he explains, will improve our ability to be positive and resilient amid whatever challenges we face. Leadership can sometimes be frustrating, and it's inevitable that we encounter moments when our emotional energy fails us, for whatever reasons. Learning how to release the inevitable negativity that arises in the course of a day is therefore another important aspect of a personal energy practice.

- ***Mental energy*** is required for numerous leadership abilities, including curiosity, creativity, and detailed memory. But among all the demands of leadership, the ability to concentrate and focus—the skill of sustaining attention over extended periods—is the leadership capacity that consumes the most mental energy. The ability to pay attention is like a muscle, so it must be regularly "worked out" to keep it strong and flexible. Just as critically, it must be given time to recover and renew, using the ninety-minute-cycle approach mentioned above.

- ***Spiritual energy***, in Schwartz's model, is the energy of meaning and purpose—the surge of inspiration and vitality that comes from having one's everyday activities aligned with one's core values and knowing that you're making a meaningful difference in people's lives. There is no denying the spiritually energizing power of an authentic higher purpose. To access this energy, Schwartz recommends that people clarify their priorities and use their time consciously for the things that truly matter, whether at work or in other areas of life.

PRACTICING EMOTIONAL REVITALIZATION: Releasing Negativity

Check in with yourself regularly and notice how you feel. If negative emotions are dominant, try this four-step method from Tony Schwartz. (1) Calm your physiology with some deep breaths, feel your feet touching the ground, and center your awareness in your body. (2) Now consider the circumstance of your discontent. Distinguish between the facts of those circumstances and the story you're attaching to those facts. (3) If there is another person involved in your frustration, take a moment to disconnect from your story and imagine the same situation from their perspective. How would the circumstances seem or feel from their point of view? (4) Change the story in your own mind. Ask yourself if there is a more optimistic story that can be told about those same facts. By working to uncover the fears, blind spots, and confirmation biases that drive negative emotions, you can master the "inner game" of staying positive. Positive energy is contagious, so remember to smile and be cheerful (or at least not cranky). And in those inevitable times when you do become angry or discouraged, affirm your role as chief energy officer and try to keep those negative emotions to yourself. Distinguish between the genuine experience of frustration or negativity, which may be outside of your control, and the choice you always have to affirm a positive relationship to the various circumstances of life.

SLEEP, REVISITED

Breathe in; breathe out. Night and day. Activity and passivity. As humans, we are rhythmic, cyclical creatures, and the most fundamental cycle of all—this side of life and death, at least—is the circadian rhythm of sleep and waking. That's why the foundation of any path of deep revitalization begins with sleep. No doubt many of us have been told or perhaps read that we should be getting more sleep. But too often, those words have little power. They simply go in one ear and out the other, in part because we don't directly experience the necessity. Sure, we might have a hard time dragging ourselves out of bed in the morning, and find ourselves nodding off after lunch, but our nocturnal shortfall doesn't always appear to have an immediate cost. Sleep is universal, yes, and we all need it, but for a leader in the middle of a demanding daily routine, with 24/7 incoming, high-stakes decisions to make, and an endless to-do list, there can be a strong tendency to simply do the best we can with as little sleep as possible and tell ourselves we'll make it up at a later date.

That's a bad idea. That's not how sleep works, as we've come to find out. In recent years, research has uncovered a treasure trove of new insights into why we sleep and how it impacts our brain and body. And while there is still much that we don't know, the basic message is quite stark. We absolutely need good, consistent sleep, and not getting it fundamentally compromises the self in ways that science is only just beginning to measure. In fact, trying to be a conscious leader without getting adequate, consistent sleep is like trying to win a football game with an injured defensive line. It makes everything else that much harder. We might score an occasional touchdown, but who would bet on a victory?

In his recent book *Why We Sleep*, Matthew Walker, professor of neuroscience at UC Berkeley, makes a startling claim: "The physical and mental impairments caused by one night of bad sleep dwarf those caused by an equivalent absence of food or exercise. It is difficult to imagine any other state—natural or medically manipulated—that affords a more powerful redressing of physical and mental health at every level of analysis."[7] And in case that wasn't definitive enough, he goes on to say, "Sleep is the single most effective thing we can do to reset our brain and body health each day."[8]

Seven to nine hours. That's what experts are recommending. If you are part of the "I can get by on five or six hours" crowd, consider this interesting statistic: in a recent analysis of thirty-five thousand leaders, *Harvard Business Review* found that the more senior a person was in a given organization, the more sleep that person managed to get on a nightly basis.[9] Now, one could interpret that as meaning that once they achieved a higher spot in leadership, they stopped pulling all-nighters and finally started sleeping well. But that wasn't the conclusion of the researchers. They suspected that those senior executives might have achieved higher performance in part *because* they had the tailwind of healthy sleep habits behind them. Whatever the case, the beneficial power of sleep shouldn't be underestimated. Research continues to establish its remarkable impact on all kinds of critical leadership skills, like problem-solving, memory, and quality of attention. And lack of adequate, consistent sleep raises red flags across the board. It has been associated with suppressed immune function, higher blood pressure, greater risk of chronic diseases such as heart disease and stroke, and several kinds of degenerative brain diseases like dementia and Alzheimer's.[10]

In other words, the days of a workaholic CEO bragging about how little sleep they need while they knock back a triple espresso should be relegated to the dustbin of bad ideas. The highest forms of leadership are always about quality, not quantity, and for that, we need to be at our healthy, rested, engaged, attentive, revitalized best.

DEMYSTIFYING NOURISHMENT

In French, the word for food is *nourriture.* It comes from the same root as our English word *nourishment.* Yet how often do we forget that food, at its most basic level, should be truly nourishing? Unfortunately, the busier we are, and the more chaotic our lives, the further we seem to distance ourselves from this basic truth. We go for the quick and easy over the healthy and satisfying. Temporarily, we might not notice the impact. But sustainable leadership means taking care of our physical selves. And food—*nourishment*—is a key piece of that puzzle.

At Whole Foods Market, we always consider healthy eating to be the first line of defense against sickness, burnout, fatigue, and so many other physical difficulties that can lead to unhappy team members and underlie poor performance. That is why we incentivize healthy behaviors—for example, we offer a discount on in-store food purchases that increases as team members reach certain health markers and adopt good health practices, such as not smoking. And we offer free "Total Health Immersions" that help our least healthy team members reboot their health and learn how to develop better habits. Those are win-win-win programs that benefit the company, help our team members, and support the communities we operate in. In my decades leading the company, I have watched with great pride and gratitude as thousands of people have transformed their health through the insights they gained in these programs. There are few things that can transform our day-to-day experience of both life and work like going from chronic disease and physical deficit to real nourishment and true health.

Never forget the simple choices that make a profound difference.

That can be more difficult in a world where biohacking bros and the technorati are enamored of the health promises of science and technology. The questions on their minds are largely focused on performance. *How can I reach peak performance? How can I raise my level of energy? How can I hack my biology to get better results? What substance, supplement, practice, food, drink, workout, or technology can catapult me into higher states of flow and self-mastery?* From Dave Asprey's Bulletproof Executive to Tim Ferriss's Tools of Titans, the search is on for a demonstrable performance edge in today's high-tech work culture. There is certainly nothing wrong with using the latest, greatest app, supplement, or wearable biofeedback device to maximize your leadership mojo, as long as you remember at least two fundamental points when it comes to health and wellness.

First, for all the hundreds of thousands hanging on the wisdom of the latest peak performance podcast, there are tens of millions who wake up every day with diabetes, heart disease, and other chronic conditions. Unfortunately, this includes many leaders in companies around the world who might otherwise make real contributions but whose impact is compromised by these debilitating conditions. These are slow-moving plagues, and we need to continue to recognize how much more needs to be done to nudge the majority in this country and others toward better basic health choices. As a leader, you may find yourself in a position to make a difference. If that involves exploring the edges of peak performance, good for you. But it may also involve helping yourself and others negotiate basic but lifesaving health choices. Which brings us to the second point about health and wellness, and perhaps the most important: sometimes the best advice is not the latest, the trendiest, or the sexiest.

The author and poet Andrei Codrescu once insightfully described American culture as "an uninterrupted anthology of fads chasing each other faster and faster across shorter and shorter time spans."[11] And perhaps nowhere is this more true than in the area of diet. South Beach, low-carb, Atkins, Zone, gluten-free, blood type, blood sugar, vegan, paleo, low-glycemic, DASH, pegan, and ketogenic are just a few popular diets to capture the culture in recent years. But amid all of our efforts to radically upgrade our eating habits, we should never forget that the basic healthy dietary pattern is not some massive mystery that requires the virtuous efforts of a bestselling self-help author to untangle. Experts don't know everything about diet and health, but neither are they groping in the dark. As Yale physician David Katz, one of the leading diet experts in the country, writes, "We are not, absolutely not, emphatically NOT clueless about the basic care and feeding of Homo sapiens . . . The fundamental lifestyle formula, including diet, conducive to the addition of years to our lives, and life to our years, is reliably clear and a product of science, sense, and global consensus. Really. You can be confused about it if you want to be, but I advise against it. You will be procrastinating, and missing out—because healthy people have more fun."[12]

What is that formula? Michael Pollan put it most simply, in his famous and carefully researched nugget of dietary wisdom: "Eat food. Mostly plants. Not too much."[13] Each of this book's authors strongly subscribes to that advice. And while this is not a diet book, and it would be beyond its scope to delve deeply into the subject, we could expand it to say: Eat real food. Eat whole foods whenever possible. Eat mostly whole grains, legumes, vegetables, leafy greens, fruits, nuts, and seeds. Limit your intake of animal products, added sugars, refined grains, and processed food. If you follow these guidelines, whatever the details, health and wellness will be your long-term companions. Still not sure? Consider that this basic dietary pattern is found in every one of the world's "Blue Zones"—the areas of the planet that are home to humanity's longest-lived populations.[14]

Speaking of the Blue Zones, another thing their populations all do is *move*. Movement is critical not just to physical health and well-being, but to emotional, mental, and spiritual vitality as well. That doesn't mean you have to be pumping iron in the gym seven days a week or training for an ultramarathon, but it does mean taking the time to figure out: *What truly gets me energized physically?* Is it dancing, yoga, a walk, a run, or a bike ride? Is it the get-out-in-nature pleasure of mountain biking or hiking? Is it the thrill of competition, maybe a tennis match or a basketball game? Is it the intensity of strength training or the sweat of a spin class? Is it the satisfaction of breaking limits in endurance sports like running or triathlon? It is the contemplative beauty of the golf course? Or is it simply an extended walk around the neighborhood, connecting with friends and local community? Physical exercise can come in so many forms, and perhaps the important element to making it sustainable over the long run is to figure out what inspires you to get up off the metaphorical or actual couch and come alive.

DON'T JUST DO SOMETHING, SIT THERE

What if we told you there was an underappreciated shortcut to better leadership skills—a powerful technique that takes only a few minutes a day, can be done by anyone, and has been shown to help you become a more focused, creative, capable leader? As a bonus, this particular activity has a highly beneficial effect on health outcomes—it improves insomnia, helps chronic pain, and lowers blood pressure. Finally, what if we mentioned that individuals like Bill Ford (chairman of Ford), Marc Benioff (CEO of Salesforce), Jack Dorsey (CEO of Twitter), Jeff Weiner (CEO of LinkedIn), Ray Dalio (founder of Bridgewater), Russell Simmons (CEO of Rush Communications), and even the Super Bowl–winning Seattle Seahawks football team embrace this technique?

Welcome to the ancient, yet very modern, practice of meditation. For millennia, it's been the muse of monks and mystics. Fifty years ago it was the province, in the West at least, of hippies and seekers exploring the practices of Buddhism, Hinduism, and other Eastern traditions. In a few short decades, it's traveled from the counterculture to corporate culture and, in truth, just about everywhere else. And why not? This side of sleep, there are very few activities that offer the same degree of relaxation and recharge for the time invested.

In the same way that sleep relaxes the body and empties the mind of the detritus of daily life, allowing us to wake up renewed and refreshed, so does meditation shed and discard layers of habitual mental activity, allowing deeper layers of attention and intention to emerge. But while sleep involves being unconscious, meditation involves being extra-conscious.

Meditation offers an unpredictable, hard-to-quantify experience of refreshment at the level of *being* itself. Amid a life of constant *doing*, it provides balance. For a period of time, we are able to withdraw from a busy, buzzing chaotic mental world into a deeper stillness and silence. Amid the intensity of life and work, we put aside the "cult of busyness" that so many of us follow with great devotion and remember that there is more to existence than what passes across our mental windshield on any given day.

It should be noted that the term *meditation* is broad, and beneath its banner are a great variety of practices and techniques. All of the world's great wisdom traditions have their variations on the theme, as do most forms of contemporary spirituality. There are also many other types of spiritual practice, prayer, and religious ritual that offer similar benefits. You may already have discovered the practices for spiritual renewal and growth that speak to your own soul.

Broadly speaking, meditative practices fall into two categories: those that emphasize concentration and those that emphasize letting go. Experiment and see what works for you. Both can be extremely powerful and revitalizing.

PRACTICING MEDITATION: Concentration

Practices of concentration involve an object of focus—for example, a mantra practice, where you train your attention on a certain specific set of words—in this case, particular Sanskrit words—and deeply concentrate on that higher thought form, withdrawing from all other mental activities for a temporary period. Sometimes it is not a mantra but an affirmation—a positive statement that we repeat to ourselves again and again, imprinting that injunction very deeply in our consciousness. Perhaps there is a certain prayer, whose focused recitation brings about a deep sense of spiritual renewal. Sometimes, such as in Vipassana, the focus is not on words but simply on the breath, carefully following the inhalation and exhalation of our own rhythmic breathing. Practices of concentration can be very powerful in focusing and releasing our spiritual energy, but the exact form they take will depend upon your own spiritual predilections.

PRACTICING MEDITATION: Letting Go

The practices that focus on letting go involve, well, exactly that. It is extremely simple but notoriously difficult. Can you sit quietly for twenty or thirty minutes, or even an hour, and withdraw your attention from the busy, buzzing activity of your own mind? Can you let go of a whole layer of mental activity and let yourself sink to a deeper layer of being, while remaining alert? The meditation practice of letting go means not attaching yourself to any of the thought streams or emotions that arise in your mind. As thousands of "thought bubbles" come and go in your inner universe—as endless forms, both base and beautiful, arise and pass away in the infinite space of your mind—can you let go of it all? Imagine that your mind is a computer screen. Headlines jump out, demanding your attention. Pop-up windows suddenly invade your vision. Notifications appear and fade away. Calendar alerts buzz. Can you let it all simply *be*, resisting the temptation to click on anything? And if you do find yourself lost in the stream of thought, you need only let go and return to a meditative state of nonattachment and presence.

For all the benefits that have been attributed to meditation, there is a small catch. You can't always draw a direct line of cause and effect between the practice of a type of mindfulness or meditation and a particular outcome. It doesn't work like that. Your mileage may vary. Meditation is one of those practices that you have to do for its own sake, setting aside the desire to quantify the results—even while knowing that it is likely to be fruitful. There is some degree of surrender of control involved, a letting go of the tendency to measure the ROI of every activity. This can be a challenge for many leaders, who owe some degree of their success to that very tendency. In fact, an important part of many forms of meditation is the injunction to let go of the need for any particular outcome!

There's certainly nothing wrong with engaging in meditative practice for its many more prosaic and tangible benefits. But it's also wise to approach the meditative experience with a certain humility and respect for its history and significance. Meditation can put you in touch with deeper layers of self that are rarely accessed except during a spiritual or religious experience or under the influence of mind-altering substances. As twentieth-century Indian sage Nisargadatta Maharaj explained it, "The primary purpose of meditation is to become conscious of, and familiar with, our inner life."[15] Getting in touch with those deeper layers can bring greater self-knowledge, confidence, and inspiration, and that is a huge positive. But delving into the depths of consciousness is never a fully controlled experiment.

PUT PURPOSE ASIDE

Revitalization comes in many forms. Sometimes it entails a vacation far away from it all—a lake, a beach, a mountaintop, a beautiful vista, a walk in the woods, or a cabin in the wilderness. Sometimes it involves a luxurious retreat or spa where you can pamper the senses. We all have our preferred forms of mini breaks and longer vacations that help rejuvenate body and soul. They may involve rest and relaxation, travel and new experiences, sports and physical challenges, friends and family—or all of the above. What makes vacations so refreshing is that they lift us out of the scheduled, purposeful, task-oriented routine of our daily lives. But there are also ways of recharging that are a little closer to home. For conscious leaders who put purpose first, who are driven to make an impact in the world, it's critical to carve out time to put purpose aside and engage in activities we love for their own sake. In a world where it sometimes seems that everything has to have a rhyme and reason, we can too easily forget the sheer joy of following our natural interests and passions in unexpected directions. Hobbies, curiosities, play, sport, leisure activities, aesthetic pursuits, arts, crafts—those directions may have no particular purpose, other than that they are immensely satisfying. They may not lead to anything other than wonderful wasted hours, but those hours can have a positive effect on our psychology and physiology. In fact, studies have suggested that there is a link between health outcomes and cultivation of hobbies. All of those hours spent tinkering or dabbling or reading offer protection for the brain, as researchers have noted that individuals who love hobbies tend to have less dementia and more functionality later in life. Others have found more immediate benefits; it's been suggested, for example, that scientists who cultivate more hobbies tend to be more successful in their chosen careers.

In fact, a wide range of interests can itself be a sign of an agile, creative, insightful mind. In his book *Where Good Ideas Come From*, Steven Johnson writes that "legendary innovators like Franklin, Snow, and Darwin all possess some common intellectual qualities—a certain quickness of mind, unbounded curiosity—but they also share one other defining attribute. They have a lot of hobbies."[16] Another such example is a great innovator in our own time, Bill Gates, who loves to read widely in many fields, and each year takes one week away from everything and designates it as his "Think Week." In those hours and days of relative seclusion, he reads, has time alone, and pursues his interests without the day-to-day demands of his normal life. Important creative insights, strategic directions, and even innovative ideas for Microsoft products have emerged from these weeks of quiet, focused, and free contemplation.

In the end, we don't need social science or anecdotal evidence to convince us of things that we can see in our own experience. Not everyone may be equally suited to a reading vacation, like Gates, or to a serious game of backgammon, as Charles Darwin apparently was. You might not feel inclined to master Beethoven's piano concertos or learn the art of basket weaving. But whatever your passion or curiosity, however seemingly trivial or purposeless, have the courage to follow it. And do it for its own sake. Resist the temptation to turn every hobby into a side hustle. It may not lead in a straight line to any particular destination, but in that winding, meandering journey, conscious leaders may very well discover unexpected perspectives, unbidden insight, and the joy of mental refreshment.

PRACTICING REVITALIZATION: Go to Ground

Sometimes it's the simple things that make all the difference—daily ways of grounding ourselves. For example, if your work is mentally demanding, a grounding activity might be to work with your hands—gardening, cooking, building something, even cleaning. Walter Robb, former co-CEO of Whole Foods, says that whenever he needed a mental break to get away from the grind, he would just go down to the store and bag groceries for an hour. Such grounding breaks can reset our brain and nervous system, making a huge difference in the flow of our day. For many, interacting with animals can have the same effect. Play with a cat, walk a dog—and watch your nervous system relax. When you need to reset and revitalize, find ways to go to ground.

RECHARGE IN NATURE

Have you ever noticed how different you feel after you spend time in the natural world? Immersing yourself in nature—whether by visiting a park, gardening, getting out on the water, or simply gazing at the sky for extended moments—is a powerful way to recharge and refresh, physically, mentally, emotionally, and spiritually. Hike in the wildernesses, visit an undeveloped seashore, take in a panoramic view, or stroll in a forest and "nature's peace will flow into you,"[17] as John Muir put it.

When interacting with nature, try to do more than simply walking or observing the view. Use all your senses. Be sure to touch things—brush your hand against the bark of a tree, feel the smoothness of ancient stone, and, when you stop for a rest, take off your shoes and let your bare feet touch the earth. Feel the breeze on your face. Listen to birdsong. Bend down to inhale the delicate fragrance of a flower, the aroma of fresh-cut grass, or the rich smells of the forest floor. Notice the exquisite geometry of plants and the symmetry of their blossoms. Tune in to the music of water and watch the dappled play of light and shadow.

We instinctively know that it feels good to spend time outdoors. But it turns out that interacting with nature is a proven way to improve your health and increase your sense of well-being. As Florence Williams, author of *The Nature Fix*, writes, "Science is proving what we've always known intuitively: nature does good things to the human brain—it makes us healthier, happier, and smarter."[18]

THE CONSCIOUS LEADER'S TOOL KIT

Digital Fasting

In our digital age, unplugging may be more important than ever, precisely because we are so plugged in. With smartphones, social media, and seemingly universal internet and mobile access, it's hard to find a moment of time or a square inch of the earth in which we are *not* connected to an onslaught of information, communication, and, along with it, distraction. Any leader today is acutely aware that their attention is one of their most valuable assets, and so it's imperative that we think carefully about our relationship with our devices and the digital universe to which they connect us. Although the digital revolution has brought us tremendous benefits—personally and as a society—it has also left many addicted to the relentless need to be always on and ever connected. According to several studies by Nielsen, the Pew Research Center, and Smart Insights, in 2018 people spent an average of four hours per day on their phones!

This increase in "screen time" is having a significant impact on everything from our ability to communicate to our cognitive capacity and mental health. A Microsoft study in Canada, for example, found that the average human attention span has decreased from twelve to eight seconds since 2000.[19] More important, this decreased bandwidth gets in the way of our ability to concentrate and make decisions. A 2017 study by the *Journal of Consumer Research* found that even when a smartphone is turned off, its mere presence takes up a significant amount of attention and reduces our cognitive capacity.[20]

Technology isn't going away anytime soon, so as leaders we are confronted with a critical question: How can we enact a more conscious relationship with these ever-present devices? Whether it's being mindful about how much screen time you're engaged in on a daily or weekly basis or taking the time to periodically unplug by going on a "digital fast," there are many ways to reconsider the posture of infinite availability that is the unwritten rule of the information revolution. There is nothing inherently wrong with being connected, of course, but we each must consider how best to enact a more powerful relationship with our digital worlds, so that they won't, by default, have undue power over us. Some leaders, the authors included, engage in digital fasting by spending extended periods of time in the wilderness, where cellphone reception is limited. Hiking on the Appalachian Trail or the Pacific Crest Trail has afforded us much-needed respite. In the midst of all the pressures and urgent decisions that come with significant leadership roles, this can be a critical way to step outside the fray and refresh. Joyeeta Das, CEO of the big-data startup Gyana, makes sure to take two extended "digital detoxes" per year—one a silent retreat and the other a deep-sea diving mission. She says, "That's where I'm at the mercy of water and faith in the universe, and this recharges me every time."[21]

Of course, the "cold turkey" method of detoxification doesn't work for everyone. And there are a wide variety of practices you can use to decrease your addiction even in the midst of your normal workdays. Tom Patterson, CEO of the clothing company Tommy John, checks his email only before and after the workday and abstains in the hours in between. Arianna Huffington puts her phone to bed at night by keeping it out of her bedroom and never checks it first thing in the morning when she wakes up.

The key to an effective digital fasting strategy isn't doing something specific—it's just doing something. Simply being willing to confront your own digital addiction—to have a more conscious, deliberate relationship to the always-on information revolution—is the first step toward liberating your precious attention from technology's addictive grasp.

CONTINUOUSLY LEARN AND GROW

To exist is to change, to change is to mature, to mature
is to go on creating oneself endlessly.

—HENRI BERGSON

IN THE YEAR 1716, in the city of Boston, a ten-year-old boy was pulled out of school and told he would now be working full-time in the family business. He'd been in school for only two years and had shown great promise, but it was little surprise that his father, a soap- and candlemaker, could not afford the luxury of an education for the fifteenth of his seventeen children. Two years later, the boy was sent to work at his brother's printing press as an indentured apprentice. You might think that was the end of this young man's education—that, like so many of his peers, he became a career tradesman, getting by on basic reading, writing, and arithmetic skills. But no. An unusual passion for learning had awakened in his young mind, and he spent every penny he earned on books, even forgoing meals so he could buy new ones. He taught himself to compose articles and essays through rigorous study and practice. This young man would grow up to become one of the most renowned polymaths in American history, despite less than two years of formal education. His name? Benjamin Franklin.

Franklin, one of the greatest conscious leaders of all time, provides an excellent example of what can be achieved through a lifelong commitment to continuous learning and self-improvement. Most readers are familiar with Franklin's outstanding achievements: Founding Father of the United States, groundbreaking scientist and inventor, accomplished diplomat, successful businessman, inspirational writer, and veritable Renaissance man. Franklin built this remarkable list of accomplishments by conscientiously working throughout his life to develop his knowledge, his writing skills, his leadership capacity, and his personal character.

In 1726, at the age of twenty, he established a foundation for his own self-improvement by formulating a system of thirteen virtues that he vowed to live by. He then methodically charted his personal progress in these virtues, working to strengthen each one on his list before moving on to the next. Franklin also shared his enthusiasm for self-improvement with his local community by founding a mutual improvement club among his peers that met weekly to share knowledge and discuss current events.

Franklin's pioneering work in the field of self-improvement helped him steadily grow in his leadership capacity. He continually broke out of old forms, growing into larger versions of himself throughout his life—first as a businessman and author, then as a scientist and philosopher, and finally as a revolutionary founder of a great nation.

One of the most significant lessons from Franklin's lifetime of personal betterment is the need to be self-critical and focus on incremental gains. Commenting on the difficulty he encountered, Franklin wrote that he "was surprised to find myself so much fuller of faults than I had imagined."[1] But he gradually overcame his shortcomings by working to make small marginal improvements, which compounded throughout his life to create the towering leader to whom we remain indebted. His journey of continuous growth from an uneducated, unknown apprentice to an unlikely genius reminds us of the undiscovered potentials that often lie within the human character, awaiting the right intention, mindset, commitment, and spirit to be set free.

The very essence of conscious leadership is the willingness to follow in the footsteps of individuals like Franklin, and to embark on a journey of never-ending learning and growth. There comes a time in each of our lives when we need to confront our own limitations and recognize that if we are going to evolve further as individuals, it's going to come down to our own intention, effort, and engagement. A universal creative spirit may have reached down and touched our souls; good genetics may have blessed our bodies and minds; and our parents may have loved and raised us into adulthood with great wisdom and beneficence; but that work is done. From here forward, how far we will go and who we will become is up to us.

PRACTICING LEARNING AND GROWTH:
Form a Mutual Improvement Club

One of the best ways to stay inspired and motivated to learn and grow is to spend time with others who are doing the same. Take a leaf out of Franklin's book and form a mutual improvement club with friends or colleagues. These kinds of peer support groups—sometimes dubbed "mastermind groups," a term from self-help legend Napoleon Hill—can be invaluable when it comes to getting helpful feedback, tools, and encouragement for the journey.

DO GROWN-UPS GROW?

Learning. Growth. Development. Until relatively recently, these ideas were more commonly associated with children than adults. As any parent will tell you, the amount of change that occurs for a child from year to year and even from month to month is quite astonishing. Physically, mentally, emotionally, and socially, a child is in a constant state of development—much of which is visible to the observant eye.

However, perhaps because adult development is less evident than childhood development, both biologists and psychologists used to think that not much could or would change after a person had "come of age." Now that idea is being challenged from within the field of psychology itself. In the past few decades, a growing movement known as developmental psychology has begun to recognize and shed light on the fact that adults, too, can and do develop as they age.

This may seem obvious to you. Perhaps you've been involved in some form of personal growth work. Maybe your company encourages lifelong learning, or you've taken adult education classes. Some HR departments have been rebranded as "people development," and offer a whole suite of opportunities for improving both hard and soft skills. But it's worth stopping for a moment to consider that this idea—*adult development*—is still quite new, at least from a scientific standpoint, and is not yet well understood. "The great glory within my own field," says Harvard developmental psychologist Robert Kegan, "has been the recognition that there are these qualitatively more complex psychological, mental, and spiritual landscapes that await us and that we are called to after the first twenty years of life."[2]

Of course, despite psychology's relatively recent embrace of adult development as a field worthy of study, humans have been trying to better themselves since well before Marcus Aurelius penned his *Meditations*, Aristotle was teaching at the Lyceum, or Confucius was exhorting early Chinese culture to embrace a regimen of self-improvement. In more recent times, America itself has nurtured robust cultural movements that encouraged citizens to invest in and commit to their own development—like the Chautauqua movement of the late nineteenth century, the transcendentalists, and the human potential movement of the sixties and seventies. Modern science, psychology, neuroscience, and self-help have added important new elements to this conversation, but the call to growth and maturity is also ancient, encompassing a plethora of philosophical, spiritual, and religious practices. As leaders who wish to follow in those footsteps of history's inspirational learners and growers, we stand on mighty shoulders. But we also have a unique advantage. Just imagine what Franklin would have given to have even a fraction of the wealth of information that exists at the touch of our fingers.

On the time-honored path of learning and growing, one thing is sure: we will inevitably have moments when our feet slip out from under us, when we feel lost, unmoored, thrown into unfamiliar territory. Temporary insecurity is the emotional price of change. But the rewards are rich and fruitful. On the far side of that less traveled road, we are renewed and remade, and we encounter the best parts of ourselves. In those open, untrammeled fields are possibilities—of maturity, of wisdom, of leadership—that we can scarcely now imagine.

THE LIBERATION OF LIFELONG LEARNING

What does it mean to learn, grow, and develop as an adult? Learning is perhaps the simplest of those concepts, although science is now discovering that there is more to it than meets the eye. Simply put, learning is the acquisition of new information and skills. Of course, that includes professional development and keeping up with the changing technological, occupational, and informational terrain in which you're working. Such pursuits are critical to staying at the forefront of a field, but a conscious leader does not limit their learning to the immediate demands of their job or industry. Many of the greatest leaders are voracious learners, reading and studying widely in fields that are seemingly unrelated to their own. They read literature, history, science fiction, biographies, comic books, philosophy, and more. As the saying (often attributed to Harry Truman) goes, "Not all readers are leaders, but all leaders are readers." Legendary investor and Berkshire Hathaway chairman Charlie Munger has put it even more bluntly: "In my whole life, I have known no wise people over a broad subject matter area who didn't read all the time—none, zero."[3]

Every day is an opportunity to wake up and be excited not just about what we're going to accomplish, but about what we're going to learn. While the obvious outcome of learning is increased knowledge, expertise, or proficiency, there are other, less visible results as well. Thanks to breakthroughs in neuroscience, we now know that the brain remains *plastic*—i.e., changeable—throughout the human life cycle. It doesn't simply stop developing once we reach adulthood. In fact, scientists have shown that even people in their seventies can produce brand-new neurons. What changes the brain? One of the primary factors is your mental activity, or lack thereof. When you apply focused attention to a topic, learn a new skill, grapple with a new language, or wrestle with mental puzzles, your brain changes on a physical, chemical level. This has profound implications. We are not just growing as people; we are growing our gray matter. As Dr. Michael Merzenich, one of the leading experts in neuroplasticity, says, people "don't realize that they've been given this great gift. That they could be better and stronger next month as compared to now. It's not just a downhill passage in life. You're not stuck . . . We've actually been constructed in a way that allows for continuous self-improvement."[4]

You might not be able to feel your neurons growing, but there are a host of other positive effects of learning that you're probably more familiar with. If you've ever tried to learn a new skill later in life—like skiing, speaking French, coding, or playing the piano—you are probably familiar with the strange combination of discomfort and exhilaration that accompanies such attempts. Being a beginner again means enduring the myriad small humiliations and triumphs that are part and parcel of the learning experience. For leaders who have risen to the top of their game, who have grown accustomed to being the expert in the room, this is a healthy practice. It can throw you off balance in a positive sense, preventing you from becoming self-satisfied, complacent, or stuck in familiar habits of mind. It can serve as a reminder of what Zen Buddhists call *shoshin*, or "beginner's mind"—an attitude of open-mindedness, free from preconceptions—and help you to bring that fresh approach even to subjects in which you are well versed. And it can set a powerful example for all those who work with you. When a leader does not hesitate to learn, when a leader is demonstrably curious and unafraid to make mistakes in pursuit of new skills and knowledge, it liberates everyone else to do the same.

PRACTICING LEARNING AND GROWTH: Find a Mentor, Teacher, or Coach

Wherever you are on your career path and your journey of personal growth, there are almost certainly people who can help you, support you, coach you, or teach you. That might mean investing in a professional leadership coach or executive coach who can help you learn and grow by identifying strengths to build on, weaknesses that need work, and practices that address both. It might mean seeking out a mentor—someone you respect for their wisdom and life experience. It might mean engaging with teachers who can impart specific skills, growth techniques, or insights. Even leaders at the top of their game should never be too proud to seek the guidance of others.

BREADTH: THE PATH OF A GENERALIST

A specialist, goes the old joke, knows more and more about less and less until eventually they know everything about nothing. Well, today our society must know one heck of a lot about nothing, because specialists dominate. We live in a world that is hewing more and more each day toward hyper-specialization. It is for that reason that it's worth affirming and appreciating the opposite approach to knowledge: being a generalist. Arguably, this less popular intellectual bent is more important than ever—especially for those in positions of leadership. One of the goals of learning and growing is integration—the capacity to better integrate insights from a wide range of ideas and disciplines in sensible, thoughtful ways. That capacity is more needed than ever. The ability to allow one's intellect to range widely across fields, to cross-pollinate diverse ideas, to find patterns across disciplines, and to "see the forest" is crucial in our data-saturated age. If you are at the helm of a company, team, project, or group of people, you need to know a little—even more than a little—about a lot.

It's precisely because of today's intensive focus on specialization that being a generalist is such a powerful advantage for conscious leaders. In his 2019 book *Range: Why Generalists Triumph in a Specialized World*, journalist David Epstein surveyed a broad range of disciplines, from sports to science to the military, exploring the question of whether it was better to be a specialist or a generalist. He found example after example of how generalists, in the long run, tend to be more successful. At the core of his thesis is the fact that having narrow expertise becomes less and less relevant as the complexity of your endeavor increases. "Modern work demands knowledge transfer: the ability to apply knowledge to new situations and different domains,"[5] he writes. Being a generalist, Epstein says, enables you to be more agile and adaptive to changing environments. You aren't stuck in a particular discipline or a narrow mindset and you can draw upon a wide array of knowledge when making decisions, solving problems, or charting the future. Instead of memorizing facts and processes, you are cultivating a more foundational approach to thinking itself. "You have people walking around with all the knowledge of humanity on their phone, but they have no idea how to integrate it," he points out. "We don't train people in thinking or reasoning."[6]

Deep expertise should never be undervalued. But integration is an extraordinarily important capacity for leaders today. And the best integrators manage to achieve a quality that is really the goal of the entire project of learning and growing: wisdom.

DEPTH: THE ACHIEVEMENT OF WISDOM

Settlers along the Platte River in Colorado, Wyoming, and Nebraska used to say, "It's a mile wide and an inch deep, but you can still drown in it." The same could well be said of our data-rich, news-saturated, social-media-enabled age. We live in a time when the sheer deluge of information can be overwhelming, and it's easy to find ourselves lost in the surface churn of that river of digital detritus, struggling for intellectual air against the current of our curated content feeds. If we truly want to learn, in all the many dimensions of what that word means, we need to occasionally set aside quantity for quality. We must dive more deeply into the long-form article, the absorbing book, the engaging documentary, the enriching dialogue, the inspiring inquiry, the edifying conversation. It means committing to *depth*—going beyond the superficial and seeking out the substantive.

It is not always easy to be a person of substance in a world that always want us to move quickly on to the next thing. But when we make that authentic commitment to dive beyond the shallows, the quality of our learning does, in fact, deepen. And, most important, our "leadership ceiling," for lack of a better phrase, is raised significantly. As smart as any of us may naturally be, leadership requires something more. When, through our own curiosity and interest to learn, we draw in new perspectives from a higher quality of intellectual sources, our innate intelligence is tempered and enriched. And the reservoir of knowledge informing our decision-making is upgraded. The hard truth is that there is nothing rote or predictable about conscious leadership, demonstrated at a high level. No matter how many books on leadership we may read, it's never plug-and-play. The moment you think you can just apply last month's insight to today's issues is the moment your decision-making suffers. The context, the situation, and the particulars always show up in new ways, and in order to respond to the ever-shifting, complex needs of any business or organization, our own decision-making must be contextual, adaptive, creative, and highly dynamic.

Our culture tends to idolize youth, and youth certainly has many advantages: the risk-taking, the adventurousness, the mental freshness, the freedom from the burden of history. Business and society have benefited enormously from the boldness of youthful passion. How many times have you heard entrepreneurs say, "If I'd known how much was truly involved, I probably would never have started the company in the first place"? And yet the world is better because they did. In some business cultures today, there is even a mistrust of middle-aged and older leaders, as if they were inevitably lacking the necessary enthusiasm and intensity of commitment. Yet the achievement of real wisdom, and the boon to leadership that goes with it, is rarely the province of the young. Leaders, even brilliant ones, often need time to take that journey "from smart to wise," as authors Prasad Kaipa and Navi Radjou describe it in their book of the same name. Wise leadership entails more than operational or even strategic brilliance. As the authors describe, it means "leveraging our smartness for the greater good by balancing action with reflection and introspection . . . helping us shift from using our smartness for our own benefit—often with a zero-sum mind-set—to using it for creating new value for a higher purpose."[7]

Wisdom may seem a somewhat intangible quality in our world today; it is also a consistently undervalued asset when it comes to leadership of all kinds. It's more than intelligence and smarts; it's more than knowledge; and it's even more than experience. It's the ever-ripening fruit of a long-term commitment to learning and growing.

THE INNER WORK OF GROWTH

Learning, in the tradition of Franklin, should be a lifelong commitment for a conscious leader. But our journey must encompass not only the acquisition of new skills, expertise, and information, but also the inner work of personal growth and self-development. As leadership development consultant Barrett Brown observes, "*How we know* is at least if not more important than *what we know*."[0] And how we know, he explains, depends on the development of our mental, emotional, and relational capacities—the transformation of how we think, feel, and make sense of the world—not just the acquisition of new knowledge or competencies. It's the journey into those new "psychological, mental, and spiritual" landscapes that Robert Kegan heralds. This journey may, to some extent, unfold naturally over a human lifetime, but as Brown points out, leaders today have an unprecedented opportunity to accelerate it. To fully appreciate the rich opportunities that this field presents to leaders today, it's worth taking a short journey back in time and visiting one of the most beautiful spots in the nation.

If the Big Sur coast of Central California were easier to reach, no doubt it would already resemble the great Rivieras of Europe, with all of the glitz, glamour, and luxury that so often accompany seaside beauty. But even today, the winding roads and cliffs that snake down the California coastline, as beautiful and stunning as they are, have a blustery, rugged remoteness that still resists colonization from the jet set. In a previous chapter, we pointed out that evolution—in nature, society, and business—so often happens on the geographical and cultural edges, and there are few more dramatic edges than the Big Sur coast. Perhaps that's why it has long drawn artists, poets, writers, and bohemians of all stripes. So it's fitting that it was here, on a remote clifftop, that a revolution was started, one that was very much in the tradition of previous American cultural experiments but that would ultimately have its own unique flair. It is called Esalen.

The primary instigator of the revolution was a young man from Salinas, California, named Michael Murphy, who had been inspired by Stanford professor of religions Frederic Speigleberg. Speigleberg had studied with Tillich, Heidegger, and Jung but had fled Germany for Stanford to escape Hitler. At Stanford in the late fifties, he encouraged a young Murphy to take up the study of Eastern philosophy and spend time in the ashrams of India, where he met the great sage and revolutionary Sri Aurobindo. All of this was prelude to Murphy's decision to head down the coastal highway and open up his family's clifftop property to a burgeoning countercultural movement seeking new forms of learning and growth and a place to incubate them.

Esalen long ago entered into American lore, and the colorful and amazing cast of characters that passed through—Abraham Maslow, Carl Rogers, Fritz Perls, Aldous Huxley, Alan Watts, Henry Miller, Carlos Castaneda, Arnold Toynbee, Ken Kesey, Linus Pauling, Paul Tillich, Ida Rolf, Werner Erhard, and endless others—are a testament to its remarkable influence. Along with other like-minded communities around the country, it helped seed into our culture something both old and new: the idea that humans had higher potentials, that growth and evolution were possible. And Murphy, along with his fellow founder Dick Price, oversaw all of it. Now in his late eighties, he has held aloft that torch for decades—as an author, marathoner, scholar, researcher, think tank founder, golfer, diplomat, and meditator, to name a few of his titles and talents. Simply put, he has been an example of integral human learning and growth with few equals.

As longtime spiritual practitioners, we have watched with fascination and amusement as the tools, modalities, and practices for growth and transformation, which were cultivated in places like Esalen, have migrated into business over the past couple of decades. Ideas and processes that once flourished in countercultural communities can now regularly be found in typical corporate leadership retreats. Meditation guides now take their place alongside management manuals on HR department bookshelves, and a small army of coaches, consultants, and speakers have found gainful employment sharing these once fringe ideas with the establishment.

But perhaps we should be less surprised. Business is by its nature highly aspirational, pragmatic, and non-ideological. *Show me, don't tell me. Does it work or not?* As a new generation of executives have sought a leadership edge, they have naturally looked to those cultural spaces that are focused on the expansion of human potential. Along the way, those practices and methods have evolved—changed their old clothing, become more secularized, and adapted to a more conventional business audience. But the goal remains similar—growth, development, change, higher levels of flow and performance, and occasionally transcendence. When authentically engaged, they still lead us beyond who we know ourselves to be.

Growth always involves both the discovery of new vistas and the shedding of old shibboleths. We must leave aside what Murphy calls the "inherited orthodoxies"[9] of our lives and travel on new paths, search for new truths, seek new teachers and mentors. Growth and development point us to fundamental transformations of who we are and the ways that we interact with the world. How can you *become* a more excellent person—more mature, evolved, and self-aware? How can you actualize more of your potential? How can you deepen your own self-awareness and expand your interior life? How can you improve, as a human being and a leader? How can you explore the furthest edges of what humans are able to experience and express?

In some sense, this entire book is devoted to these questions. Developing your capacity to love or to serve, for example, will take you on a powerful journey of inner growth. Striving for integrity or pursuing a higher purpose will likewise challenge you to rise up and become a more evolved person. Humans are complex creatures, so our trajectory of growth does not follow one single path; it progresses along many parallel and sometimes intersecting routes. There are, as the mystics have told us, many paths to the mountaintop. In the end, the specific approach to development is less important than the heartfelt commitment to develop. In this realm, intention really matters. The particular structure and method of each journey are much less important than the focus of the individual traveler. We can rarely see the most direct route to growth or the exact series of milestones that will get us where we want to go. What matters is being on the journey.

SUBJECTS, OBJECTS, AND VIDEOTAPE

If growth or development is difficult to pin down, it is even trickier to operationalize in a corporate setting. Yet that is the job description of Adam Leonard, a people development leader at Google. He's responsible for taking the latest insights from developmental psychology, the best practices of the human potential movement, the ancient techniques of the mystics, and the new revelations of neuroscience and turning them into leadership development programs for some of Silicon Valley's best and brightest. And there are few people better suited for such a role. Adam—who also traces his journey back to the Esalen Institute and has worked at the Integral Institute with philosopher Ken Wilber (with whom he co-authored the book *Integral Life Practice*) and at the Stagen Leadership Academy—is a connoisseur of personal growth practices, with an infectious passion for experimentation and learning. Like a consummate mixologist, he knows when to add a dash of this or a splash of that to create a powerful transformational cocktail—whether that means teaching engineering teams about the virtues of vulnerability or taking top leaders to war-torn regions of the world for an immersive experience of systems thinking. When asked about the most powerful leadership tools he's discovered, Adam always has a ready list, but high on that list is a concept that can seem at once obvious and obscure: the subject-object relationship.

It's hard to be objective about yourself. How often do we hear variations on that theme? It's almost a truism. We tend to see other people much more clearly and dispassionately than we see ourselves, because our own experience is inherently subjective. Yet, as developmental psychologist Robert Kegan has observed, the ability to become more objective about subjective matters—emotions, personality traits, biases, beliefs, triggers, prejudices, strengths, wounds, and more—is one key measure of that elusive thing called *growth*. Indeed, if the goal of our developmental journey is to become a more conscious leader, what could be more critical than taking that which is subjective—and therefore often subconscious or unconscious—and making it objective, bringing it into the light of consciousness?

As a simple example, consider an emotion like anger. An immature person might experience the arising of anger as an uncontrollable state that is almost entirely subjective. "I *am* angry"—it's a statement about the self. There is little to no distance between the experience of anger and acting *as* that anger. A more mature person, on the other hand, has developed the capacity to observe the arising of anger more objectively. The experience shifts from "I am angry" to "I can see anger arising." That powerful emotion has become an object in consciousness, not intrinsically part of the self. It's a small but extremely powerful change of perspective, because when something moves from subject to object, we have much more space to make a choice about how to act. We may still experience the same intensity of feeling, but it no longer controls us. We can apply this same principle of *making subject object* to more subtle aspects of our inner world as well.

When something is largely subjective, it's hard to see it directly, so we must often start by looking at the impacts we have on others, then tracing them back to the invisible impulse or trigger. If we repeatedly overreact to certain people or situations, for example, we may uncover a blind spot or deeply buried belief that's causing us to unconsciously conflate a current reality with past experiences or trauma. By seeing this more objectively, we can separate impulse from action and respond more appropriately in the moment.

Adam, who turns to Kegan's wisdom repeatedly in his work at Google, has zeroed in on this foundational idea of *making subject object* as a powerful lever for leadership development. If leaders can learn to see themselves more objectively, they'll make better decisions, improve their relationships with their teams, and be more able to effectively develop themselves. But, because seeing oneself objectively is easier said than done, Adam has employed the help of technology. Taking a page out of the book of professional athletes, who routinely "watch tape" after a game or a match, he films leaders role-playing difficult interpersonal scenarios and then watches the video with them, offering coaching and helping them connect the dots between their external responses and the subjective world they may not be aware of in the moment. The experience has proven to be excruciating—and invaluable. "Everyone hates being videoed," he admits, "but there's nothing like actually seeing yourself on a screen to bring greater objectivity. It's sticky—people remember it. And they get better." Becoming more conscious may sound great, but it's often quite an uncomfortable experience. Discomfort can be a hallmark of growth, so it's something that aspiring conscious leaders must learn to tolerate. Even if you don't want to break out the video camera, we encourage you to practice making subject object—whether in personal contemplative practice, in supportive coaching relationships, or in trusted peer groups.

The most transformative leaders, often without knowing it, enact this subject-object transformation repeatedly—in themselves and in the teams they lead. It is a remarkable quality of human cognition that we have the ability to become aware of the many peaks and valleys of our interior worlds—as well as the gnarly roots and caves—so that our self-awareness continues to deepen, and our own sphere of freedom continues to expand.

THE MANY WAYS THAT PEOPLE CAN BE SMART

"As human beings, we have many different ways of representing meaning, many kinds of intelligence," declares psychologist Howard Gardner, considered by many to be the father of multiple intelligence theory.[10] In his groundbreaking 1983 book *Frames of Mind*, Gardner argued that analytical intelligence, or IQ, was just one of the many ways that people express intelligence.

The idea of multiple intelligences is a helpful way to think about the multifaceted journey of personal growth. The fact that people are born with differing natural talents has been recognized since antiquity. Yet for much of the twentieth century, competence in business was thought to be roughly equivalent to a person's measurable IQ. In the past few decades, however, the field of professional development has been transformed by the empirical recognition of multiple kinds of personal competence, which can actually be more important to overall leadership than IQ. This has led to an expansion of the very concept of "intelligence" to include forms of excellence that transcend cognitive ability alone.

Analytical intelligence is ultimately table stakes when it comes to leadership. In fact, IQ can be an inhibition if it gives you a false or arrogant sense of your overall talents and capacities. As Charlie Munger, chairman of Berkshire Hathaway, famously explained, it's better to "hire a person with an IQ of 130 but who thinks it's 120, as opposed to someone who thinks he has a 170 IQ, when he actually just has an IQ of 150."[11] Luckily, it is eminently possible for conscious leaders to become significantly more intelligent in multiple ways that go well beyond IQ.

Today, multiple intelligence theory is increasingly embraced, both in popular culture and in business, as a way of representing the reality that there are so many ways in which human beings can be smart. Search for books that include "intelligence" in the title and you'll find dozens of examples, from visual intelligence to financial intelligence to moral intelligence to physical intelligence. Some base their claims on more rigorous and empirical research, others are more speculative, but together they are part of a larger sea change in how we understand intelligence and, by extension, what it means to learn and grow. Gardner himself initially posited seven intelligences and suggested a couple more in later writings. Some are more relevant to business and leadership than others, but perhaps the most well-established and important one for conscious leaders to understand is the one that has taken leadership and business circles by storm in the past two decades: *emotional intelligence*.

While Michael Murphy was hosting California's most interesting conversations while overlooking the Pacific Ocean, another young man on the East Coast, also a seeker, was exploring pathways of human development that would eventually send reverberations through the business world. In 1967, Harvard professor Richard Alpert traveled to India, where he encountered the holy man Neem Karoli Baba, who would become his teacher. Richard took the name Ram Dass, and that journey would become the basis of the classic book *Be Here Now*, which inspired a generation to follow in his footsteps. On his return to America in 1968, Ram Dass happened to meet Daniel Goleman, a young postdoc at Harvard. Determined to see for himself the land and people that had wrought such a transformation in his new acquaintance, Goleman set off on his own journey to the East. He, too, came back to Harvard inspired by the possibilities contained within human consciousness. He developed a course, "The Psychology of Consciousness," which became a hit among Harvard students in the seventies, and his first book, *The Varieties of Meditative Experience*, was published in 1977. Several more would follow. But the one that would catapult him to prominence and forever alter our cultural lexicon was not published until 1995. It was titled *Emotional Intelligence: Why It Can Matter More than IQ*, and it has gone on to sell well over five million copies in dozens of languages.

Emotional intelligence, put simply, is the ability to better perceive and understand your own emotions, motivations, and impulses, as well as have greater empathy for and understanding of other people. The capacity to be emotionally intelligent is grounded in self-knowledge and self-awareness. By becoming more conscious of our own emotions and inner life, we gain the ability to manage and align our emotions with our larger leadership goals. We can take more responsibility for our own emotional experience and appreciate how it impacts others. We all know what it's like to be around someone who seems to be out of touch with their own inner turmoil, unable to contain their reactions or feelings, which spill out and affect their work, relationships, and more. We've probably all been that person at different times in our lives. In the stress of work environments, it's certainly common to encounter people who are highly trained in technical skills and good at their jobs but seem almost childlike when it comes to managing their feelings.

By increasing our awareness of our own emotional life, we naturally become more attuned to the emotions of other people. Too often, unwittingly, we relate to others through the filter of our own ideas and conceptions. That filter often betrays and obscures the truth of who they are. The greater our emotional intelligence, the more we are able to authentically attune to other people, and in the process our empathy increases by leaps and bounds. As we develop this capacity, we are better able to interpret a whole host of emotional signals—facial expression, body language, tone of voice—and the interior emotional qualities that undergird them. At its best, authentic emotional intelligence also creates trust and loyalty among colleagues by building bonds of sincere personal connection and care. And it helps leaders to better anticipate and appreciate the ways in which their team members will be emotionally impacted by external events.

As much as its impacts may be felt in the social sphere, the essence of emotional intelligence is really an inner matter. According to Robin Stern of the Yale Center for Emotional Intelligence, "Some people think of emotional intelligence as a soft skill or the ability or the tendency to be nice. It's really about understanding what is going on for you in the moment so that you can make conscious choices about how you want to use your emotions and how you want to manage yourself and how you want to be seen in the world."[12]

PRACTICING EMOTIONAL INTELLIGENCE: Name Your Emotions

There are many methods for measuring, developing, and practicing emotional intelligence, but the starting point is almost always the deceptively simple practice of emotional self-awareness. Can you recognize and identify your own emotions? That may seem like a basic task, but it can be illuminating to sincerely attempt to be aware of and name the many emotions that arise and pass away in your inner experience in the course of an hour or a day. For example, in the midst of a difficult executive team meeting where things are not going the way you'd hoped, you might notice a vague feeling of depression. When you take a closer look, however, you realize that a more precise way to describe the feeling is one of disempowerment. Correctly identifying the feeling allows you to respond to it more authentically. You don't just need a pick-me-up, you need to find a way to come to terms with the decisions that were made and maintain your sense of empowered leadership. The development of emotional awareness—also called emotional literacy or emotional fluency—is a surprisingly powerful path of growth, and one that continually reveals new levels of nuance and subtlety.

While some people conflate emotional intelligence with the closely related notion of social intelligence, Goleman, who has researched and written on both, makes a useful distinction. Social intelligence is more outwardly focused, he explains. When focusing on this aspect of the human character, "the spotlight shifts to those ephemeral moments that emerge as we interact. These take on deep consequence as we realize how, through their sum total, we create one another."[13]

Any leader who works with a team—be it two people or two hundred—will resonate with the importance of this statement. *We create one another.* Human beings are social creatures by nature, deeply attuned to and influenced by each other—not just at the perceptible level of words and actions but at the imperceptible level of emotions, attitudes, and beliefs. Developing your emotional and social intelligence allows you to be more effective in interacting with a wide range of people and understanding and managing the interpersonal and cultural dynamics that operate in any human community, including businesses.

While it's a much newer concept than some of the other intelligences discussed above, we'd suggest one more critical avenue of development that conscious leaders might consider pursuing. We call it *cultural intelligence*. In order to skillfully navigate the controversies that are increasingly roiling the internal cultures at some of America's biggest organizations today, conscious leaders need a sophisticated understanding of values and the larger cultural worldviews that are their source. These conflicts can be felt in every corner of the marketplace. Familiar examples include Google's firing of an engineer over a contentious memo and internal pushback over its government business; Starbuck's nationwide shutdown for emergency diversity training; and the boycott of Chick-fil-A because of its CEO's conservative Christian views. When it comes to issues of values and personal identity, business leaders face a potential minefield, and it sometimes seems as if even the most sophisticated contemporary psychological know-how and personal empathy cannot adequately equip us to deal with these matters. Why? Because the roots of these conflicts lie not simply in individual attitudes, beliefs, or pathologies, or even in institutional structures, but in broader cultural value systems that are changing, evolving, and sometimes clashing.

While there are many ways to be "culturally intelligent," we define cultural intelligence as a newly emerging integrative perspective that can sympathetically harmonize and integrate a wide range of conflicting values. As leaders, can we recognize when traditional values like duty, faith, and self-sacrifice are clashing with values that are more modernist in nature, like personal liberty? Can we appreciate how values like diversity, sustainability, and social justice that have flourished over the past few decades (sometimes called postmodern values) are now significantly influencing business and upending established ways of working together? Can we empathize with the disruption this creates for some people, even as we champion the values we may personally hold dear? Can we honor the positive contributions of multiple value systems, even as we reject their pathologies? These are some of the skills and capacities that will distinguish conscious leaders in the workplace of today and tomorrow. (For a more detailed discussion of the various value systems or worldviews that are active in our country and our world today, please see the appendix, "On Cultivating Cultural Intelligence," page 229.)

PRACTICING LEARNING AND GROWTH:
Build a Learning Organization

Besides the personal practices we've shared in this chapter, we can also recommend the practice of turning your team, or even your entire company, into a "learning organization" (a term originated by Peter Senge in his book *The Fifth Discipline*). A learning organization is one that actively facilitates the growth of its members and thereby continually transforms itself in response to competitive pressures. The notion that an organization itself can learn has led to the widespread practice of team learning, wherein people work together to improve both their individual and collective capacities simultaneously. Many business schools have now integrated team learning into their course structures, especially in their MBA programs. Robert Kegan has also contributed to this field with his research on what he calls Deliberately Developmental Organizations.

THE SPIRIT OF CONSCIOUS LEADERSHIP

A discussion of the many ways and methods through which human beings grow and flourish sooner or later leads us to the threshold of spirituality. What does it mean to grow spiritually? And how can you tell whether you've progressed in your spiritual development? These are questions that have been pondered for thousands of years by some of humanity's greatest leaders and teachers. And while such matters were once seen as being far removed from the worldly concerns of business, today it's not uncommon for leaders to speak openly about their pursuit of spiritual paths and practices, whether or not they use that specific terminology. Spiritual growth is a deep and complex subject, however, filled with potential conundrums, and doesn't readily lend itself to being smoothly conceptualized as merely one among many leadership skills.

Some people describe spiritual development as another kind of intelligence, which is accurate, but it's also much more than that. Inevitably, it means different things to different people. In fact, each of the authors of this book has had a lifelong commitment to spiritual practice and growth, but each of our paths is distinctive and has a unique flavor. We're sure that's true for many of our readers as well. But regardless of how you define it, working to develop yourself spiritually is a crucial aspect of authentic conscious leadership. Spiritual growth has always been intimately related to the quest to become *more conscious*, which of course is the central theme of this book.

Spiritual development is like an internal lever. The more we can develop spiritually, the more powerful an impact we are able to have on all other aspects of our lives, and the greater our ability to effectively and consciously lead. As leadership expert Stephen Covey puts it: "Spiritual intelligence is the central and most fundamental of all the intelligences, because it becomes the source of guidance for the other[s]."[14]

It would be foolish to pretend that we could, in these few pages, even begin to capture the breadth and depth of what it means for humans to develop themselves as spiritual beings. But on the journey of conscious leadership, neither can we avoid the more profound questions of existence. Who are we, in the deepest sense? How do we reach higher in our own individual and collective lives, to better embody the true, the good, and the beautiful? How do we pursue our own higher purpose? How do we contribute to the further evolution of human culture? How do we best serve our fellow people and our planet? Part of coming to terms with our role in this brief sojourn of earthly existence is asking the biggest questions of life, seeking authentic answers, and, when we find those answers, living up to them to the best of our ability.

There are innumerable approaches to spiritual growth, both in the world's great wisdom traditions and in the melting pot of contemporary spirituality. In some sense, they each lead us beyond the narrow construct of a personal, localized self—expanding our consciousness and broadening our horizons.

Some focus on the inner realms—the journey deep into Being, the contemplative exploration of interior worlds, the pursuit of deeper and higher levels of consciousness that expand and transcend the personality. The meditator on the mountaintop, the hermit in the cave, and even today's practitioners who attend retreats that emphasize self-awareness and solitude—all of these seekers are following the well-trodden path that leads within.

Then there are approaches that turn the focus outward, seeing spirit expressed in acts of service and devotion, love for our fellow humans, care and selflessness. The great saints and healers have walked this path, as do many in today's world who find spiritual succor and deep meaning in service. Albert Schweitzer, one of the exemplars of this form of spirituality, expressed it well in his immortal words "The only ones among you who will be really happy are those who have sought and found how to serve."[15]

There are also spiritual paths that emphasize the power of a higher calling, the surrender or commitment to a transcendent purpose. Giving oneself over to something greater than oneself—whether that is conceived as God, a great contribution to the world, or a role in the evolution or our consciousness and culture—is a powerful path for expressing our spiritual convictions. Some of the greatest heroes of history chose purpose as their spiritual path, and we believe the notion is worthy of many of today's purpose-driven leaders as well, in business and beyond.

Purpose, love, integrity—the three virtues we explored in part I of this book—are each, in a sense, a doorway for spiritual growth, and to some extent conscious leaders must engage with each of them. But as individuals, we are naturally inclined to pursue what truly matters in a way that resonates with the particular tenor of our own souls. Ultimately, our intention in this book has been to spark and inspire readers to consider some of these deeper questions and find their own answers. We hope we provided some relevant, important wisdom as well.

Wherever we end up on that journey of learning and growth, a life of conscious leadership demands that we find ways to express our deepest convictions and highest calling in the actions we take every day. Of course, not every mundane moment can be infused with the sublime. The prosaic realities of our businesses and organizations can never be left behind, and there are hundreds of choices that we each make, every day, that remain untroubled by deeper or higher aspirations. But if we walk this path with integrity, purpose, and love; if we're in it for the long haul and we approach the journey with a great spirit of creativity and mutual benefit; and if we care deeply for ourselves and the teams we share the journey with, we will discover the essential spirit of conscious leadership. Our lives, our organizations, and our world will be better for it.

APPENDIX

On Cultivating Cultural Intelligence

In the final chapter we introduced the idea of "cultural intelligence," which we defined as an emerging perspective that can sympathetically harmonize and integrate a wide range of conflicting values. This new kind of intelligence gives conscious leaders the ability to skillfully navigate the culture war that currently afflicts much of the developed world. Cultural intelligence, however, does not seek an impossible neutrality, nor is it inevitably politically centrist. The expanded perspective that is the basis for cultural intelligence is effectively positioned "outside and above" the warring factions that are attempting to use the world of business as their battleground.

The leadership ability of cultural intelligence is founded on a clear recognition of the three main worldviews, or cultural value frames, that are now vying for dominance in the developed world. These three worldviews, either singularly or in some combination, provide the values for the vast majority of the population in North America, Europe, and Australia. However, to keep this discussion from becoming unwieldy, we will confine our analysis to American culture, where we obviously have the most knowledge and experience.

Worldviews, as we understand them, are coherent sets of values and ideals that persist across multiple generations. These large-scale value agreements give meaning to reality and provide people with a sense of identity. Worldviews are arguably the basic units of culture, so the cultural intelligence that conscious leaders need in today's complex social milieu requires knowledge of these dynamic systems of values. The cultural significance of worldviews is readily apparent in the well-recognized difference between the worldview of *modernity* and the traditional religious worldview that preceded modernity in history, and which continues to prevail in large segments of American culture.

The values of modernity (or "modernism") include progress, prosperity, individual liberty, and scientific rationality. By contrast, the values of the traditional worldview include faith, family, duty, honor, and patriotism. There is, of course, considerable overlap between these sets of values, but the cultural distinction between the worldview of modernity and the contrasting worldview of traditionalism is generally accepted within mainstream discourse. However, America's third major cultural block—the progressive worldview—remains inadequately understood. While progressive concerns such as environmentalism and social justice are plainly obvious to the mainstream, the fact that progressivism now represents a third major worldview in its own right is often lost on establishment commentators. Figure A.1 shows some examples of America's three major worldviews, which we generally refer to as modernism, traditionalism, and progressivism.

In terms of demographic size, modernism remains the majority worldview in America today, holding the allegiance of approximately 50 percent of the population, followed by traditionalism, with approximately 30 percent, and then by the progressive worldview, with perhaps as much as 20 percent.[1] But even though the progressive worldview is the smallest, it dominates academia and most of America's media and entertainment industries, so its growing influence cannot be discounted or ignored. For the next few decades at least, the ongoing contest between these three major worldviews will continue to define

	Examples of the Traditional Worldview	Examples of the Modernist Worldview	Examples of the Progressive Worldview
The Good	Faith, family, and country Self-sacrifice for the good of the whole Duty and honor Law and order God's will	Economic and scientific progress Liberty and the rule of law Personal achievement, prosperity and wealth Social status and higher education	Social and environmental justice Diversity and multiculturalism Natural lifestyle and localism Planetary healing
The True	Scripture Rules and norms of the religious community Directives of rightful authority	Science Reason and objectivity Facts, evidence, and proof Literature and philosophy	Subjective perspectives, "whatever is true for you" "Woke" sensibilities The unmasking of power structures
Potential Pathologies	Bigotry, racism, sexism, homophobia Religious fundamentalism and anti-science Resists moral evolution and greater inclusion Authoritarian, xenophobic	Indifferent elitism and selfish exploitation Captured by special interests Can be scientistic and hostile to religion Crony capitalism and self-dealing	Anti-modernism and reverse patriotism Identarian divisiveness Self-righteous scolding and authoritarian demands Magical thinking and narcissism
Some of Their Heroes	Ronald Reagan Winston Churchill Edmund Burke Pope John Paul II Billy Graham William Buckley Phyllis Schlafly Antonin Scalia	Thomas Jefferson John F. Kennedy Franklin D. Roosevelt Albert Einstein Thomas Edison Adam Smith Carl Sagan Milton Friedman Frank Lloyd Wright	Mahatma Gandhi Nelson Mandela John Lennon John Muir Margaret Mead Betty Friedan Joan Baez Oprah Winfrey
Contemporary Figures	Ross Douthat Patrick Deneen Rod Dreher Rick Warren Tucker Carlson	Hillary Clinton Steven Pinker Thomas Friedman Bill Gates Sheryl Sandberg	Bernie Sanders Ta-Nehisi Coates Marianne Williamson Naomi Klein Bill McKibben

Figure A.1. Examples of America's three major worldviews

the contours of American culture as a whole, and organizational culture in particular.

Most businesses operate in an environment that contains stakeholders from every worldview. These stakeholders, for instance, can include progressive millennial team members, modernist investors, and a demographically diverse group of customers that encompass all three.

There is no love lost between these worldviews. But we don't have to get caught in the crossfire. We can learn to rise above and integrate these otherwise conflicting sets of values. This practice of integrating values begins in the recognition that each of these worldviews has healthy upsides and unhealthy downsides. They all contain constructive and enduring values, along with negative shortcomings and pathologies. How do we affirm the good and discard the bad? That is the work of cultural intelligence. (Figure A.1 lists some of the potential pathologies that are closely associated with the positive values of each major worldview.)

Cultural intelligence clearly distinguishes each worldview's positives from its accompanying negatives. Separating the "dignities" from the "disasters" of each worldview allows us to affirm and use the positive and enduring values that each worldview continues to bring to our larger culture. For example, conscious leaders can use traditional values to invoke the defiant spirit of Winston Churchill to steel their backbones in the face of villainy. And in situations where they need to be more inclusive, conscious leaders can use Mahatma Gandhi's progressive spirit of nonviolent resistance to overcome opposition. It is by learning to appreciate and integrate the positive values of all three major worldviews that conscious leaders can expand the scope of what they are able to personally value, and thereby evolve their own consciousness in the process.

To use cultural intelligence, however, we don't have to disregard our loyalties to the specific worldview that informs our own identity. Culturally intelligent conscious leadership can be practiced from within the purview of each of these major worldviews. In the field of business

Emerging Characteristics of the Integral Worldview			
The Good	**The True**	**Potential Pathologies**	**Some of Their Heroes**
Worldcentric morality The evolution of consciousness and culture The positive values of all major worldviews Taking personal responsibility for problem-solving	Dialectical development Inclusive evaluation Harmonization of science and spirituality	Can be insensitive or impatient Can seem elitist or aloof	Pierre Teilhard de Chardin Alfred North Whitehead Sri Aurobindo Jean Gebser Clare Graves

Figure A.2. Characteristics of the emerging integral worldview

books, for example, we can see conscious leadership expressed from a socially conservative traditional perspective in the book *Everybody Matters,* by Bob Chapman and Raj Sisodia. Conversely, conscious leadership from a progressive, postmodern perspective can be seen in Paul Hawken's *Natural Capitalism.* And conscious leadership from a mainstream modernist perspective can be recognized in Ray Dalio's influential book *Principles.* Each author expresses an authentic version of conscious leadership. Yet while conscious leadership can be effectively practiced from within the value frame of each major worldview, the increasing intensity of the culture war puts a premium on those leaders who can sympathetically integrate the full range of positive American values.

Yet even though leaders from each of these existing worldviews can effectively use cultural intelligence, the perspective of cultural intelligence itself is grounded in a fourth worldview—a newly emerging cultural perspective that is essentially *post-progressive.* This post-progressive, or "integral," worldview honors and includes many progressive values, but it is post-progressive in the sense that it is able to do what the progressive worldview cannot: it fully recognizes the legitimacy and ongoing necessity of the positive values of all previous worldviews. This integral worldview thus grows up by reaching down.[2]

The integral worldview also has its own relatively unique values, such as the aspiration to harmonize science and spirituality, an enhanced sense of personal responsibility for the problems of the world, an enlarged appreciation of conflicting truths and dialectic reasoning, and a new appreciation of the significance of evolution in general and cultural evolution in particular. Figure A.2 shows some of the characteristics of this emerging integral worldview, which is the ultimate source of the new leadership skill of cultural intelligence.

Cultural intelligence is not yet fully appreciated as a needed leadership skill set. But as increasing cultural strife impacts American business, the demand for highly effective leaders who can negotiate these three conflicting worldviews grows more and more urgent.

FURTHER READING ON CULTURAL INTELLIGENCE

Inglehart, Ronald. *Cultural Evolution: People's Motivations Are Changing, and Reshaping the World.* Cambridge, UK: Cambridge University Press, 2018.

McIntosh, Steve. *Developmental Politics: How America Can Grow into a Better Version of Itself.* St. Paul, MN: Paragon House, 2020.

Phipps, Carter. *Evolutionaries: Unlocking the Spiritual and Cultural Potential of Science's Greatest Idea.* New York: Harper Perennial, 2012.

Wade, Jenny. *Changes of Mind: A Holonomic Theory of the Evolution of Consciousness.* Albany: State University of New York Press, 1996.

Welzel, Christian. *Freedom Rising: Human Empowerment and the Quest for Emancipation.* New York: Cambridge University Press, 2013.

Wilber, Ken. *Trump and a Post-Truth World.* Boulder, CO: Shambhala, 2017.

ACKNOWLEDGMENTS

As we have said many times in these pages, innovation loves company. Significant achievements are rarely the product of a single mind, but rather spring from the "scenius" of a creative community. This book is no exception.

The authors' goal in these pages was to capture our deeply felt vision of leadership, but that vision is also the expression of an inspired community of trailblazers and entrepreneurs whose conviction in the ethical power of business has helped light the path on which we have traveled. Indeed, we owe an intellectual debt to the many pioneers of Conscious Capitalism and enlightened leadership who have put their mark on this field. There are far more than we have space to list here, but we want to mention a few whose work and example have been indispensable: Stephen Covey, Don Davis, Ed Freeman, Daniel Goleman, Clare Graves, Howard Gardner, Robert Greenleaf, Stuart Kauffman, Robert Kegan, Fred Kofman, Deirdre McCloskey, Doug Rauch, Jeff Salzman, Peter Senge, Robert C. Solomon, Roy Spence, and many others whose worthy contributions have escaped this list.

We would like to thank the knowledgeable, dedicated team at Portfolio; in particular, Trish Daly for her continuous creative support, steady vision, and thoughtful editing; and Adrian Zackheim for his publishing wisdom and deep commitment to this project.

Our agent, Rafe Sagalyn, was instrumental in helping us see the importance and potential of this book, and we appreciate his consistent support throughout the entire process. In addition, Keith Urbahn and the team at Javelin were patient and helpful in the early discussions that led to this project.

This book would not have come to fruition without the editorial mastery of Ellen Daly. We are grateful for her ability to help structure the manuscript, and mold three distinct styles into a single, lucid voice.

Raj Sisodia deserves special mention as an important champion of Conscious Capitalism. His tireless efforts in promoting a more ethical approach to business have helped make this book and many more like it possible. We would also like to extend a note of appreciation to Alexander McCobin and his team at Conscious Capitalism Inc. who do amazing work every day to further elevate humanity through business.

Many people gave generously of their time and wisdom to discuss business and leadership with us. We deeply appreciate their important contributions to this material. These include: Miki Agrawal, Radha Agrawal, Pauline Brown, Mary Ellen Coe, Andy Eby, David Gardner, Tom Gardner, Steve Hall, Brett Hurt, Jonathan Keyser, Adam Leonard, Ramón Mendiola, Dev Patnaik, Jenna Powers, Walter Robb, Cheryl Rosner, Brian Schultz, Tony Schwartz, Ron Shaich, Rand Stagen, Robert Stephens, John Street, Halla Tómasdóttir, and Jeff Wilkie.

NOTES

INTRODUCTION

1. "Business Roundtable Redefines the Purpose of a Corporation to Promote 'An Economy That Serves All Americans,'" Business Roundtable, August 19, 2019, https://www.businessroundtable.org/business-roundtable-redefines-the-purpose-of-a-corporation-to-promote-an-economy-that-serves-all-americans.

CHAPTER 1: PUT PURPOSE FIRST

1. Roy Spence, "We Don't Have to Have Legs to Fly," Conscious Capitalism CEO Summit, Austin, TX, 2017, https://www.youtube.com/watch?v=gDGU5WUNiAY.
2. Richard Branson, "Setting Goals with Virgin Media at Southampton FC," Virgin.com, May 20, 2019, https://www.virgin.com/richard-branson/setting-goals-virgin-media-southampton-fc.
3. William McDonough and Michael Braungart, *The Upcycle: Beyond Sustainability—Designing for Abundance* (New York: North Point Press, 2013), 7.
4. Lydia Denworth, "Debate Arises over Teaching 'Growth Mindsets' to Motivate Students," *Scientific American,* August 12, 2019, https://www.scientificamerican.com/article/debate-arises-over-teaching-growth-mindsets-to-motivate-students/.
5. Kristin Kloberdanz, "Ideas to Action San Francisco: UVA Darden Professors Tell the 'New Story of Business,'" Darden Report, University of Virginia, July 23, 2018, https://news.darden.virginia.edu/2018/07/23/ideas-to-action-san-francisco-uva-darden-professors-tell-the-new-story-of-business/.
6. John Mackey and Raj Sisodia, *Conscious Capitalism: Liberating the Heroic Spirit of Business* (Boston: Harvard Business Review Press, 2014), 52.
7. Nancy Atkinson, *Eight Years to the Moon: The History of the Apollo Missions* (Salem, MA: Page Street Publications, 2019), 41.
8. Bert Parlee, "Polarity Management," Bert Parlee (website), http://bertparlee.com/training/polarity-management/.
9. Barry Johnson, *Polarity Management* (Amherst, MA: HRD Press, 1996), xviii.
10. Quoted in Max Delbrück, *Mind from Matter? An Essay on Evolutionary Epistemology* (Palo Alto, CA: Blackwell Scientific Publications, 1986), 167.

CHAPTER 2: LEAD WITH LOVE

1. Steve Farber, *Love Is Just Damn Good Business* (New York: McGraw-Hill Education, 2019).
2. Andrew S. Grove, *Only the Paranoid Survive: How to Exploit the Crisis Points That Challenge Every Company* (New York: Currency, 1999).

3. This quote is often misattributed to Vince Lombardi. According to Wikipedia, it comes from "UCLA Bruins football coach Henry Russell ('Red') Sanders, who spoke two different versions of the quotation. In 1950, at a Cal Poly San Luis Obispo physical education workshop, Sanders told his group: 'Men, I'll be honest. Winning isn't everything,' then following a long pause, 'Men, it's the only thing!' In a three-part article, December 7, 1953, on Red Sanders, by Bud Furillo of the *Los Angeles Herald and Express*, the phrase is quoted in the sub head. Furillo said in his unpublished memoirs Sanders first made the statement to him after UCLA's loss to USC in 1949." Wikipedia, s.v. "Winning isn't everything; it's the only thing," https://en.wiki pedia.org/wiki/Winning_isn%27t_everything;_it%27s_the_only_thing, last modified Febru ary 10, 2020.
4. Game of Thrones, season 1, episode 7, "You Win or You Die," directed by Daniel Minahan, aired May 29, 2011, on HBO.
5. Game of Thrones, season 5, episode 7, "The Gift," directed by Miguel Sapochnik, aired May 24, 2015, on HBO.
6. Jonathan Keyser, *You Don't Have to Be Ruthless to Win* (Lioncrest Publishing, 2019), 50.
7. Keyser, *You Don't Have to Be Ruthless to Win*, 14.
8. D. H. Lawrence, *Apocalypse* (New York: Viking, 1966), 149.
9. Krystal Knapp, "George Will to Princeton Graduates: The Antidote to the Overabundance of Anger in America Is Praise," Planet Princeton, June 3, 2019, https://planetprinceton.com /2019/06/03/george-will-to-princeton-graduates-the-antidote-to-the-overabundance-of -anger-in-america-is-praise/.
10. Molly Rubin, "Full transcript: Tim Cook delivers MIT'S 2017 Commencement Speech," Quartz, June 9, 2017, https://qz.com/1002570/watch-live-apple-ceo-tim-cook-delivers-mits -2017-commencement-speech/.
11. Sri Mata Amritanandamayi Devi, *May Your Hearts Blossom: An Address to the Parliament of World's Religions, Chicago, September 1993*, trans. Swami Amritaswarupananda (1993; Kerala: Mata Amritanandamayi Mission Trust, 2014), 54.
12. Lewis B. Smedes, *Forgive and Forget: Healing the Hurts We Don't Deserve* (1984; New York: Plus/HarperOne, 2007), x.
13. Edward Freeman, "What Is Stakeholder Theory?" Business Roundtable Institute for Corporate Ethics, Darden School of Business, University of Virginia, October 1, 2009, https://www .youtube.com/watch?v=bIRUaLcvPe8.

CHAPTER 3: ALWAYS ACT WITH INTEGRITY

1. Thomas Jefferson to Nathaniel Macon, January 12, 1819, Manuscript Division, Thomas Jefferson Papers, Library of Congress.
2. Bill George, "Truth, Transparency & Trust: The 3 Ts of True North Leaders," Bill George (website), July 8, 2019, https://www.billgeorge.org/articles/truth-transparency-trust-the-3-ts-of -true-north-leaders/.
3. Elizabeth Haas Edersheim, "Alan Mulally, Ford, and the 6Cs," Brookings Institute blog, June 28, 2016, https://www.brookings.edu/blog/education-plus-development/2016/06/28/alan-mu lally-ford-and-the-6cs/.
4. S. Cook, R. Davis, D. Shockley, J. Strimling, and J. Wilke, eds., *Do the Right Thing: Real Life Stories of Leaders Facing Tough Choices* (Create Space, 2015), xxvii.
5. Stephen M. R. Covey, *The Speed of Trust* (Free Press, 2006), 247.
6. Zach Hrynowski, "What Percentage of Americans Are Vegetarian?" Gallup, September 27, 2019, https://news.gallup.com/poll/267074/percentage-americans-vegetarian.aspx.
7. Robert Solomon, *A Better Way to Think About Business: How Personal Integrity Leads to Corporate Success* (Oxford and New York: Oxford University Press, 2003), 42.
8. Solomon, *A Better Way to Think About Business*, 41.

9. Ken Wilber, Terry Patten, Adam Leonard, and Marco Morelli, *Integral Life Practice: A 21st-Century Blueprint for Physical Health, Emotional Balance, Mental Clarity, and Spiritual Awakening* (Boston: Integral Books, 2008), 43.

CHAPTER 4: FIND WIN-WIN-WIN SOLUTIONS

1. *Glengarry Glen Ross*, directed by James Foley, screenplay by David Mamet.
2. *Shark Tank*, season 1, episode 1, directed by Craig Spirko, starring Kevin O'Leary, aired August 8, 2009, on ABC.
3. Alexander McCobin, "Listening to Adam Smith, Gordon Gekko, and Dilbert: A Human Approach to Capitalism," *The Catalyst: A Journal of Ideas from the Bush Institute* no. 16 (Fall 2019), https://www.bushcenter.org/catalyst/capitalism/mccobin-conscious-capitalism.html.
4. "Declining Global Poverty: Share of People Living in Extreme Poverty, 1820–2015," Our World in Data, https://ourworldindata.org/grapher/declining-global-poverty-share-1820-2015.
5. Stephen Covey, *The 7 Habits of Highly Effective People* (New York: Simon & Schuster, 2013), 213–16.
6. Peter Senge, *The Fifth Discipline: The Art and Practice of the Learning Organization* (New York: Doubleday, 1990), 6–7.

CHAPTER 5: INNOVATE AND CREATE VALUE

1. Deirdre McCloskey, *Why Liberalism Works: How True Liberal Values Produce a Freer, More Equal, Prosperous World for All* (New Haven, CT: Yale University Press, 2019).
2. Hans Rosling, *Factfulness: 10 Reasons We're Wrong About the World—and Why Things Are Better Than You Think* (New York: Flatiron, 2018), 52.
3. Deirdre McCloskey, *Bourgeois Equality: How Ideas, Not Capital or Institutions, Enriched Our World* (Chicago: University of Chicago Press, 2017), xiii.
4. Fred Turner, *From Counterculture to Cyberculture: Stewart Brand, the Whole Earth Network, and the Rise of Digital Utopianism* (Chicago: University of Chicago Press, 2008), vii.
5. Bob Dylan, vocalist, "Brownsville Girl," composed by Bob Dylan and Sam Shepard, track 6 on *Knocked Out Loaded*, Columbia Records, 1986.
6. Al Ramadan, Dave Peterson, Christopher Lochhead, and Kevin Maney, *Play Bigger: How Pirates, Dreamers, and Innovators Create and Dominate Markets* (New York: Harper Business, 2016), 3–4.
7. Robert D. Hof, "How Google Fuels Its Idea Factory," *Bloomberg BusinessWeek*, April 28, 2008, https://www.bloomberg.com/news/articles/2008-04-28/how-google-fuels-its-idea-factory.
8. Robert Greifeld, *Market Mover: Lessons from a Decade of Change at Nasdaq* (New York: Grand Central, 2019), 242–43.
9. Carlota Perez, "An Opportunity for Ethical Capitalism That Comes Once in a Century," United Nations Conference on Trade and Development, https://unctad.org/en/pages/newsdetails.aspx?OriginalVersionID=2077.
10. John Chambers with Diane Brady, *Connecting the Dots: Lessons for Leadership in a Startup World* (New York: Hachette, 2018), 41.
11. Claire Cain Miller, "Arthur Rock, Legendary V.C., Invested with Bernard Madoff," *BITS* (blog), *New York Times*, February 5, 2009, https://bits.blogs.nytimes.com/2009/02/05/arthur-rock-legendary-vc-invested-with-bernard-madoff/.
12. Arthur Koestler, *The Act of Creation* (1964; London: Hutchinson, 1976), 96.
13. Ray Dalio, "Billionaire Ray Dalio on His Big Bet That Failed: 'I Went Broke and Had to Borrow $4,000 from My Dad,'" Make It, CNBC, December 4, 2019, https://www.cnbc.com/2019/12/04/billionaire-ray-dalio-was-once-broke-and-borrowed-money-from-his-dad-to-pay-family-bills.html.

14. Steven Johnson, *Where Good Ideas Come From: The Natural History of Innovation* (New York: Penguin, 2010), 31.
15. "The Adjacent Possible: A Talk with Stuart A. Kauffman," Edge, November 9, 2003, https://www.edge.org/conversation/stuart_a_kauffman-the-adjacent-possible.

CHAPTER 6: THINK LONG TERM

1. Gary Hamel, quoted in Seth Kahan, "Time for Management 2.0," *Fast Company*, October 6, 2009, http://www.fastcompany.com/blog/seth-kahan/leading-change/hamel-hypercritical-change-points-radical-changes-required-management.
2. Jay Coen Gilbert and Alexander McCobin, "How to Build and Protect Your Purpose-Driven Business," Medium, November 12, 2018, https://bthechange.com/how-to-build-and-protect-your-purpose-driven-business-a2bc51557180.
3. Simon Sinek, *The Infinite Game* (New York: Portfolio, 2019), 9.
4. Peter Diamandis, "What Does Exponential Growth Feel Like?," Diamandis Tech Blog, https://www.diamandis.com/blog/what-does-exponential-growth-feel-like.
5. Salim Ismail, "Adapting to the Changes of the New World," Elevate Tech Fest 2018, Toronto, https://www.youtube.com/watch?v=FuXeh0Ymnog.
6. Kevin Kelly, *What Technology Wants* (New York: Viking, 2010), 73.
7. *William Gibson: No Maps for These Territories,* directed by Mark Neale, Mark Neale Productions, 2000.
8. Pierre Teilhard de Chardin, *The Future of Man* (1959; New York: Image Books/Doubleday, 2004), 186.
9. Attributed to Twain, in Alan Goldman, *Mark Twain and Philosophy* (Lanham, MD: Rowman & Littlefield, 2017), 127.
10. Philip Tetlock, *Superforecasting: The Art and Science of Prediction* (New York: Broadway Books, 2016), 32.
11. Attributed to Napoleon Bonaparte, in Jules Bertaut, *Napoleon in His Own Words,* trans. Herbert Edward Law and Charles Lincoln Rhodes (Chicago: A.C. McClurg, 1916), 52.
12. Kai Weiss, "The Importance of Entrepreneurs: An Interview with Deirdre McCloskey," Austrian Economics Center, n.d., https://www.austriancenter.com/importance-entrepreneurs-mccloskey/.
13. See Steven Pinker, *Enlightenment Now: The Case for Reason, Science, Humanism, and Progress* (New York: Penguin, 2018).
14. Phil Lebeau, "Relax, Experts Say It's At Least a Decade Before You Can Buy a Self-Driving Vehicle," CNBC, July 30, 2019, https://www.cnbc.com/2019/07/29/experts-say-its-at-least-a-decade-before-you-can-buy-a-self-driving-car.html.

CHAPTER 7: CONSTANTLY EVOLVE THE TEAM

1. *Jerry McGuire,* directed by Cameron Crowe (TriStar Pictures, 1996).
2. Marcel Schwantes, "Warren Buffett Says Look for This 1 Trait If You Want to Hire the Best People," *Inc.*, August 26, 2019, https://www.inc.com/marcel-schwantes/warren-buffett-says-look-for-this-1-trait-if-you-want-to-hire-best-people.html.
3. Larry Page and Sergey Brin, "2004 Founders' IPO Letter: 'An Owner's Manual' for Google's Shareholders," Alphabet Investor Relations, https://abc.xyz/investor/founders-letters/2004-ipo-letter/.
4. Gregg Thompson, *The Master Coach: Leading with Character, Building Connections, and Engaging in Extraordinary Conversations* (New York: SelectBooks, 2017), 34–35.
5. Dan Schawbel, "Denise Morrison: How She Became the First Woman CEO at Campbell Soup Company," Forbes, November 6, 2017, https://www.forbes.com/sites/danschawbel/2017/11

/06/denise-morrison-how-she-became-the-first-woman-ceo-at-campbell-soup-company/#3529be286be4.

6. Rand Stagen, "You're Doing It Wrong . . . How Not to Give Feedback," July 27, 2018, https://stagen.com/youre-doing-it-wrong-how-not-to-give-feedback/.
7. Linda Berens, "Typologies," Linda Berens Institute, n.d., https://lindaberens.com/typologies/.
8. Berens, "Typologies."

CHAPTER 8: REGULARLY REVITALIZE

1. "The Kiril Sokoloff Interviews: Stanley F. Druckenmiller," Real Vision, September 28, 2018, https://www.realvision.com/shows/the-kiril-sokoloff-interviews/videos/the-kiril-sokoloff-interviews-stanley-f-druckenmiller.
2. Dee Hock, "The Art of Chaordic Leadership," *Leader to Leader* no. 15 (Winter 2000), 20–26, http://www.griequity.com/resources/integraltech/GRIBusinessModel/chaordism/hock.html.
3. "Do American Workers Need a Vacation? New CareerBuilder Data Shows Majority Are Burned Out at Work, While Some Are Highly Stressed or Both," CareerBuilder, May 23, 2017, http://press.careerbuilder.com/2017-05-23-Do-American-Workers-Need-a-Vacation-New-CareerBuilder-Data-Shows-Majority-Are-Burned-Out-at-Work-While-Some-Are-Highly-Stressed-or-Both.
4. Eric Garton, "Burnout Is a Problem with the Company, Not the Person," *Harvard Business Review*, April 6, 2017, https://hbr.org/2017/04/employee-burnout-is-a-problem-with-the-company-not-the-person.
5. Leslie Kwoh, "When the CEO Burns Out," *Wall Street Journal*, May 7, 2013, https://www.wsj.com/articles/SB10001424127887323687604578469124008524696.
6. Richard Feloni, "The Founder of the B Corp Movement Celebrated by Companies Like Danone and Patagonia Explains How Overcoming Cancer Taught Him a Lesson That's Made Him a Better Leader," *Business Insider*, November 20, 2019, https://www.businessinsider.com/b-lab-cofounder-jay-coen-gilbert-shares-best-productivity-advice-2019-11.
7. Matthew Walker, *Why We Sleep: Unlocking the Power of Sleep and Dreams* (New York: Simon & Schuster, 2017), 8.
8. Walker, *Why We Sleep*, 8.
9. Rasmus Hougaard and Jacqueline Carter, "Senior Executives Get More Sleep Than Everyone Else," *Harvard Business Review*, February 28, 2018, https://hbr.org/2018/02/senior-executives-get-more-sleep-than-everyone-else.
10. Walker, *Why We Sleep*.
11. Andrei Codrescu, *An Involuntary Genius in America's Shoes (And What Happened Afterwards)* (Boston: David R. Godine, 2001), 130.
12. David Katz, "Diets, Doubts, and Doughnuts: Are We TRULY Clueless?" *Huffington Post*, August 13, 2016, http://www.huffingtonpost.com/entry/diets-doubts-and-doughnuts-are-we-truly-clueless_us_57af2fe9e4b0ae60ff029f0d.
13. Michael Pollan, *Food Rules: An Eater's Manual* (New York: Penguin, 2009), xv.
14. Dan Buettner, *The Blue Zones: Lessons for Living Longer from the People Who've Lived the Longest* (Washington, DC: National Geographic, 2010).
15. Nisargadatta Maharaj, *I Am That* (Bangalore: Chetana, 1973), 15.
16. Steven Johnson, *Where Good Ideas Come From: The Natural History of Innovation* (New York: Penguin, 2010), 172.
17. John Muir, *Our National Parks* (Boston and New York: Houghton, Mifflin, 1901), 56.
18. Florence Williams, "This Is Your Brain on Nature," *National Geographic*, January 2016, https://www.nationalgeographic.com/magazine/2016/01/call-to-wild/.
19. Kevin McSpadden, "You Now Have a Shorter Attention Span than a Goldfish," *Time*, May 14, 2015, https://time.com/3858309/attention-spans-goldfish/.

20. Adrian F. Ward, Kristen Duke, Ayelet Gneezy, and Maarten W. Bos, "Brain Drain: The Mere Presence of One's Own Smartphone Reduces Available Cognitive Capacity," *Journal of the Association for Consumer Research* 2, no. 2 (April 2017), https://www.journals.uchicago.edu/doi/abs/10.1086/691462.
21. Alison Coleman, "Six Business Leaders Share Their Digital Detox Strategies," *Forbes*, November 27, 2018, https://www.forbes.com/sites/alisoncoleman/2018/11/27/six-business-leaders-share-their-digital-detox-strategies/#46ee6ebf1456.

CHAPTER 9: CONTINUOUSLY LEARN AND GROW

1. *Autobiography of Benjamin Franklin* (1791; New York: Henry Holt, 1916).
2. Elizabeth Debold, "Epistemology, Fourth Order Consciousness, and the Subject-Object Relationship," interview with Robert Kegan, *What Is Enlightenment* 22 (Fall/Winter 2002), 149.
3. Charlie Munger at the 2003 Berkshire Hathaway Annual Meeting, quoted in Barton Biggs, *Hedgehogging* (2006; Hoboken, NJ: John Wiley & Sons, 2011), 198.
4. Peter Hartlaub, "SF Scientist Tells You How to 'Hack Your Brain' on Science Channel," *San Francisco Chronicle*, September 17, 2014, https://www.sfgate.com/tv/article/SF-scientist-tells-you-how-to-hack-your-brain-5762523.php.
5. David Epstein, *Range: Why Generalists Triumph in a Specialized World* (New York: Riverhead, 2019), 45.
6. Epstein, *Range*, 277.
7. Prasad Kaipa and Navi Radjou, *From Smart to Wise: Acting and Leading with Wisdom* (San Francisco: Jossey-Bass, 2013), 12.
8. Barrett C. Brown, "The Future of Leadership for Conscious Capitalism," MetaIntegral Associates, https://www.apheno.com/articles.
9. Andrew Marantz, "Silicon Valley's Crisis of Conscience: Where Big Tech Goes to Ask Deep Questions," *New Yorker*, August 19, 2019, https://www.newyorker.com/magazine/2019/08/26/silicon-valleys-crisis-of-conscience.
10. Howard Gardner, "An Education for the Future: The Foundation of Science and Values," paper presented to the Symposium of the Royal Palace Foundation, Amsterdam, March 14, 2001, in *The Development and Education of the Mind: The Selected Works of Howard Gardner* (Abingdon, UK: Routledge, 2006), 227.
11. Jimmy Aki, "Billionaire Charlie Munger Destroys Elon Musk's Hyperinflated Sense of IQ," CNN, February 28, 2019, https://www.ccn.com/charlie-munger-rips-elon-musk-high-iq.
12. Quoted in Erin Gabriel, "Understanding Emotional Intelligence and Its Effects on Your life," CNN, July 26, 2018, https://www.cnn.com/2018/04/11/health/improve-emotional-intelligence/index.html.
13. Daniel Goleman, *Social Intelligence: The New Science of Human Relationships* (New York: Bantam, 2006), 5.
14. Stephen Covey, *The 8th Habit: From Effectiveness to Greatness* (New York: Free Press, 2004), 53.
15. Albert Schweitzer, in a speech to the students of Silcoates School, Wakefield (along with "a number of boys and girls from Ackworth School"), on "The Meaning of Ideals in Life," at approximately 3:40 p.m. on 3 December 1935, "Visit of Dr. Albert Schweitzer" (as translated from the French of the address by Dr. Schweitzer's interpreter), *The Silcoatian*, New Series No. 25 (December, 1935): 784–85 (781–86 with 771–72; "Things in General").

APPENDIX

1. These rough estimates are based on data from the World Values Survey and other social science research. See, e.g., Ronald Inglehart, *Cultural Evolution: People's Motivations Are Changing, and Reshaping the World* (Cambridge, UK: Cambridge University Press, 2018); Ronald

Inglehart, ed., *Human Values and Social Change* (New York: Brill, 2003); Christian Welzel, *Freedom Rising: Human Empowerment and the Quest for Emancipation* (Cambridge, UK: Cambridge University Press, 2013); Paul Ray and Sherry Anderson, *The Cultural Creatives: How 50 Million People Are Changing the World* (New York: Harmony, 2000). See also Robert Kegan, *The Evolving Self: Problem and Process in Human Development* (Cambridge, MA: Harvard University Press, 1982); M. Commons, F. A. Richards, and C. Armon, eds., *Beyond Formal Operations*, vol. 1: *Late Adolescent and Adult Cognitive Development* (New York: Praeger, 1984); Don Beck and Chris Cowan, *Spiral Dynamics* (New York: Blackwell, 1995); Jenny Wade, *Changes of Mind: A Holonomic Theory of the Evolution of Consciousness* (Albany, NY: SUNY Press, 1996); and Jeremy Rifkin, *The Empathic Civilization* (New York: Tarcher Putnam, 2009).

2. Although the word integral is often associated specifically with the work of American philosopher Ken Wilber, the field of integral philosophy is much larger than Wilber's philosophy alone. Integral philosophy focuses on the structures and larger meanings behind the evolutionary development of humanity. This philosophy of evolution began with G. W. F. Hegel but it is not a strictly Hegelian philosophy. Other notable philosophers who have attempted to understand the evolution of consciousness and culture, and have thus contributed to integral philosophy, include Henri Bergson, Alfred North Whitehead, Pierre Teilhard de Chardin, Sri Aurobindo, Jean Gebser, and Jürgen Habermas. For more on the integral worldview and the philosophy behind it, see Steve McIntosh, *Integral Consciousness and the Future of Evolution* (St. Paul, MN: Paragon House, 2007), and *Developmental Politics: How America Can Grow into a Better Version of Itself* (St. Paul, MN: Paragon House, 2020).

INDEX

abundance, spirit of, 38
activist investors, 131, 133
"adjacent possible" concept, 125–26
adult development, 205–7
affirmation bubbles, 121
agents of change, 17, 69–70
Agile project management, 117
Agrawal, Miki, 123–24
Agrawal, Radha, 124
Airbnb, 109
Albertsons, 94
Alpert, Richard (Ram Dass), 220
Alzheimer's disease, 189
Amara, Roy, 150
Amara's law, 150–51
Amazon
  customer-centric ethic at, 20, 34, 96
  mentorship program of, 172
  and organizational design, 118
  Prime program of, 96, 97
  skill training offered at, 159
  success of, 144
  and Whole Foods, 42, 72, 81, 92–99
  and Wilke, 65
Amma, 44
Amrion, x
animals, interacting with, 198
animal welfare
  businesses as agents of change in arena of, 17
  and Friedrich's Good Food Institute, 122
  and Mackey's leadership at Whole Foods, 71–74
Apple, 111, 118, 122
appreciation, 25, 41–43
Aristotle, 177, 206
arrogance, 120
Asprey, Dave, 191
AT&T, 146
attention
  effect of technology on, 200
  and mental energy, 186
  power of, 40
Aurobindo, Sri, 214
authenticity, 61–63, 166–67
authority, 66

B Corps (Benefit Corporation), 11–12, 133, 182–83
Beatles, 22–23
beginner's mind, 208–9
Be Here Now (Ram Dass), 220
benchmarks, 170
Benioff, Marc, 193
Bennis, Warren, 34
Berens, Linda, 178, 179
Bergson, Henri, 203
Berkshire Hathaway, 93–94
Beyond Meat, 17
Bezos, Jeff, 20, 94, 104, 155
Bickford Senior Living centers, 49–50
bidets, 124
Big Five personality traits, 178
Big Sur coast, 213
B Lab, 133
Black Friday, 14
Blakely, Sara, 155
Blanchard, Ken, 34, 43
blood pressure, 189, 193
Bluepoint Leadership Development, 172
Blue Zones, 192
Bohr, Niels, 23
Boston Celtics, 110
Branson, Richard, 7–8
Braungart, Michael, 9
Bridgewater Associates, 120–21
Brin, Sergey, 155
Brown, Barrett, 213
"Brownsville Girl" (Dylan), 106
Buechel, Jason, 167
Buffett, Warren
  on buying companies at a fair price, 98
  on importance of integrity in hiring decisions, 162
  on trust in dealmaking, 85
  and Whole Foods, 93–94
burnout, 182
business categories, rapid changes in, 143

Campbell, Bill, 171
Campbell, Joseph, 103
Camp Campbell, 173
capitalism, 102. *See also* Conscious Capitalism movement
caring, practicing, 43–44
Carse, James, 135
challenge/support polarity, 23, 164–65
Chambers, John, 113–14
character, 162
charisma, hiring for, 161
Chase Bank, 98

Chautauqua movement, 206
Chick-fil-A, 223
Chipotle, 132
Chouinard, Yvon, 5
chronic pain, 193
Cisco Systems, 113–14
Civil Rights Movement, 91–92
Civil War, American, 4, 20
coaching
developing a culture of, 171–72
executive, 209, 218
Codrescu, Andrei, 191
collaboration
balancing autonomy with, 119
and competition, 108
and creativity, 108–9
and cultivating a conspiratorial element, 108–9
and emotional intelligence, 162
and organizational design, 116–17, 119
command-and-control organizational design, 116
communication
and cultivating a conspiratorial element, 109
and organizational design, 116
role of, in win-win-win mindset, 86
community building, 176–77
Community Giving Days, 98
community model of business, 31–32
compassion, 44–46
compensation, 55–56, 160–61
competition and competitors
and business metaphors, 27–30, 31
and cooperation, 22–23, 108
and innovation, 31, 107–8
and market transitions, 113
in natural foods industry, 108
concentration, 186
conflict-oriented metaphors for business, 26–31
Confucius, 206
conscious (term), xvi
Conscious Capitalism (Mackey and Sisodia), xiv, xv, 15
Conscious Capitalism movement
and higher purpose of an organization, 12
and ideal/real polarity, 19
importance of love in, 51
and negative perceptions of business, 12
and Shaich, 131
and shareholder activism, 133
and stakeholders, 31, 51–52
value creation and innovation in, 103
conspiratorial element in corporations, cultivation of, 108–9
Container Store, 33
continuous improvement, 31
convergence of technologies, 143–45
Cook, Tim, 43–44
cooperation and competition, 22–23, 108
counterculture movement, 214
courage, 63–65
Covey, Stephen
on role of trust in organizations, 66
and servant leadership, 33
on spiritual intelligence, 225
on win/win ethic, 85, 86
Covid-19 pandemic, 138
"Cowboy Capitalism," 108
creativity
encouraged by competition, 23
and importance of rest, 182
and mental energy, 186
and organizational design, 117
in seeking mutually-beneficial solutions, 89–90
cultural intelligence, 223–24
culture of organizations
created by founders, 167
and cultural benchmarking, 170
and role of cultural fit in hiring, 163
curiosity, 186, 197

daily routine, strategy for jump-starting, 142–43
Dalio, Ray, 120–21, 193
Darwin, Charles, 198
Darwinian-evolution metaphor for business, 27–28, 33
Das, Joyeeta, 200–201
Data.world, 177
Davis, Don, 63–64, 65, 66
Daybreaker, 124
decision making
considering stakeholders in, 52
and cultivating depth, 211–12
impact of higher purpose on, 19
importance of innovation in, 118
role of rest in, 181, 183
and subject-object relationship, 217
Declaration of Independence, U.S., 92
defense/offense polarity, 23
Deliberately Developmental Organizations, 224
Dell, Michael, 155
dementia, 189
depth, cultivation of, 211–12
developmental thinking, 141
Diamandis, Peter, 108
digital fasting, 199–201
disease, role of sleep in, 189
Disney, Walt, 5
disruptors and disruptions
creating/supporting a culture of, 112
and forecasting strategies, 146
and maintaining optimism, 148
paying attention to, 112, 113–14
societal impact of, 123
diversity, 223
Dixon, Mark, 174–75
Dorsey, Jack, 193
dot-com boom/bust, x–xi
Driversselect, 157
Druckenmiller, Stanley, 181–82
Drucker, Peter, 34
Dweck, Carol, 10
Dylan, Bob, 106

Easterbrook, Gregg, 149
Edison, Thomas, 104, 105–6
Einstein, Albert, 138

emotional energy, 186
emotional intelligence, 162, 219–23
Emotional Intelligence: Why It Can Matter More than IQ (Goleman), 220
empowerment of employees, 35
energy management, 183–87. *See also* revitalization
Energy Project, 183, 185
Enneagram, 178
Eno, Brian, 105
environmental impacts, 54–56
Epstein, David, 210
Esalen Institute, 213–14, 216
evolution metaphor for business, 27–28, 33
executive coaching, 209
exercise, critical importance of, 192–93
Expedia, 87–88
experimentation, 117
expertise, 210
exponential thinking, 137–43
Exponential Transformation (Ismail), 139–40

Facebook, 114
Factfulness (Rosling), 104
Farber, Steve, 26
feedback skills, developing, 170–71
feminine hygiene products, 123–24
Fifth Discipline, The (Senge), 99, 224
Finite and Infinite Games (Carse), 135
finite/infinite mindsets, 135
Flanagan, Glenda, 167
Florida Ice & Farm Company (FIFCO), 53–57, 69–70
focus, 186
Ford, 59–60
Ford, Bill, 193
forecasting strategies, 145–47
forgiveness, 46–47
Founding Fathers, American, 105
Frames of Mind (Gardner), 218
Franklin, Benjamin, 203–5
Freeman, Ed, 14–15, 51, 108
Friedrich, Bruce, 71, 122
From Counterculture to Cyberculture (Turner), 105

Gaiam, xi
Gallo, A. C., 167
game metaphors for business, 28–30
Game of Thrones (television series), 30
Game Plans (Keidel), 28
game theory, 86
Gardner, Howard, 218–19
Gardner, Tom, 170
Gartner's Hype Cycle, 150–51
Gates, Bill, 104, 155, 197–98
Geek Squad, 159
generalists, advantages of, 209–10
generosity, 38–39
genius, collective form of, 105
George, Bill, 59
Gettysburg Address, Lincoln's, 3–4
Gibson, William, 141
Gift Council, 112
Gilbert, Jay Coen, 133, 182–83
goal setting for employees, 169, 170
goals of businesses, 14–15
Golden Rule, 84
Golden State Warriors, 110
Goleman, Daniel, 220
Good Food Institute, 122
Goodwin, Doris Kearns, 11
Google
  and Bay Area ecosystem, 111
  "Don't be evil" mission statement of, 68
  intrinsic value behind work of, 13
  and organizational design, 118
  research on internal teams, 168–69
  and self-driving cars, 141–42
  sexist memo incident at, 223
  superiority of product of, 114
gratitude, 39–41
Great Idea Hunt practice of Motley Fool, 115
Greenleaf, Robert, 34
Greifeld, Bob, 112
Gretzky, Wayne, 113
grounding activities, 198
groupthink, 23
Grove, Andrew, 28, 115
growing and learning continuously, 203–27
  and adult development, 205–7
  and advantages of generalists, 209–10
  and analytical intelligence, 218–19
  and building a learning organization, 224
  and cultivating depth, 211–12
  and emotional intelligence, 219–23
  Franklin's commitment to, 203–5
  inner work of, 212–15
  lifelong learning, 203–5, 207–9
  and neuroplasticity, 208
  and spiritual growth, 224–27
  and subject-object relationship, 216–18

Hall, Steve, 157
happiness of team members, 165
Harvard Business Review, 182, 189
Harvard Medical School, 182
Hastings, Reed, 143, 155
help, requests for, 168
heros, finding inspiration in, 10–11
hero's journey, 103
hierarchical structure of business organizations
  balancing empowerment with, 119
  and command-and-control approach, 116
  efforts to minimize, 118
  and quasi-military "chain of command," 26
  and servant leadership, 34
  slow pace of, 116
  at Whole Foods, 118
higher purpose, pursuit of, 4, 7, 187, 226–27. *See also* purpose
Hill, Napoleon, 205
Hippocrates, 177
hiring internal vs. external candidates, 157
hobbies, 197–98
Hock, Dee, 182
Holacracy, 118
Home Depot, 34
honesty, 58–60
honor, 60–61

hope, 148–49
Hotels.com, 87–88
Houston Rockets, 110
HP, 111
Hsieh, Tony, 118
Huffington, Arianna, 201
Human Genome Project, 140
humanity and business, xvii
human potential movement, 206
humility
  competitive advantage of, 119–21
  self-reflection required for, 147
Hurt, Brett, 177
Hype Cycle, 150–51

Iceland's boom-and-bust, 128–30, 135
idealism, balancing pragmatism with, 15–20
immune function, role of sleep in, 189
impactful work, value of, 168
Impossible Foods, 17
individual/group polarity, 23
inequality, 102
Infinite Game, The (Sinek), 135
infinite mindsets, 135
ING Financial Group, 18
inherited orthodoxies, 215
innovation, 101–26
  and "adjacent possible" concept, 125–26
  and competition, 31, 107–8
  creating/supporting a culture of, 104
  and cultivating a conspiratorial element, 108–9
  and disruptors, 112, 113–14, 123
  ecosystems that support, 105–6, 110–11
  found in borders/boundaries of business ecosystems, 110–12
  humility's competitive advantage in, 119–21
  incentives that support, 106–7
  and infinite mindsets, 135
  and organizational design, 116–19
  and point of view of organizations, 109–10
  recognizing, 113–15
  reflecting on tradition of, 104
  in unexpected industries, 123–25
  and value creation, 102–3, 121–23
insomnia, 193
institutionalization, 111
Integral Life Practice (Wilber, Patten, Leonard, and Morelli), 75
integrity
  and agents of change, 69–70
  and authenticity, 61–63
  and courage, 63–65
  expanding concepts of, 67–68
  and hiring considerations, 162
  and honesty, 58–60
  and honor, 60–61
  meaning of, 57–58
  and Mendiola's work at FIFCO, 53–57
  and personal growth, 215
  reconciling personal and organizational, 70–74
  and self-righteousness, 74
  and spiritual growth, 227
  and trustworthiness, 66–68

Intel, 111, 115
intelligence
  analytical intelligence, 218–19
  cultural intelligence, 223–24
  emotional intelligence, 162, 219–23
  multiple intelligence theory, 218–19
  social intelligence, 222–23
  spiritual intelligence, 225
intention, power of, 94–95, 215
internal combustion engine, 144
internet, 144
intrinsic good, 13–14
iPhones, 113, 144
Ismail, Salim, 139–40

JANA Partners, 79–81, 93, 97, 131
jazz music, 110
Jefferson, Thomas, 58
Jerry Maguire (film), 160
job reviews, 169–70
Jobs, Steve, 104, 115, 155
Johnson, Barry, 23
Johnson, Steven, 125, 197
Journal of Consumer Research, 200
Journey to the East (Hesse), 34
Jump Associates, 142

Kaipa, Prasad, 212
Katz, David, 192
Kauffman, Stuart, 125, 126
Kegan, Robert, 206, 213, 216–17, 224
Keidel, Robert, 28
Keirsey Temperament Sorter (KTS), 178
Kelly, Kevin, 141
Kennedy, John F., 21
Keyser, Jonathan, 35–37
King, Martin Luther, Jr., 91–92
Knight, Phil, 7, 8
Koestler, Arthur, 117
Kroc, Ray, 103
Kurzweil, Ray, 140

L.A. Lakers, 110
Lamott, Anne, 181
Law of Doomsaying, 149
"law of the lid," xv
Lawrence, D. H., 39
leadership development, 157, 171
leadership vacuums, xii
leading by example, 166–67
lean manufacturing, 117
learning. *See* growing and learning continuously
learning organizations, 224
Lennon, John, 22–23
Leonard, Adam, 216, 217
liberty/equality polarity, 23
lifelong learning, 203–5. *See also* growing and learning continuously
Lincoln, Abraham
  and connecting people to purpose, 4–5, 8, 19–20
  Gettysburg Address, 3–4
Loehr, Jim, 184
London's rock-and-roll scene, 105

longevity, 192
Long-Term Stock Exchange, 133
long-term thinking, 127–51
  awakening, 130–34
  balancing short/long term interests, 136
  and changing business categories, 143
  and changing course, 147
  and conducting pre-mortems, 134
  and convergence of technologies, 143–45
  and exponential thinking, 137–43
  and finite/infinite mindsets, 135
  and forecasting strategies, 145–47
  and hope/hype cycle in technology, 149–51
  making room for, 132
  and optimism, 148–49
  as subversive choice, 131
  and succession planning, 136
  and Tómasdóttir's leadership in Iceland, 127–30
  and win-win-win thinking, 82
love, 25–52
  and appreciation, 41–43
  and care, 43–44
  and community model of business, 31–32
  and compassion, 44–46
  and conflict-oriented metaphors for business, 26–31, 33
  Eby's demonstration of, 48–50
  and forgiveness, 46–47
  and generosity, 38–39
  and gratitude, 39–41
  and new mental maps/metaphors for business, 31–33
  and servant leadership, 33–37, 39
  as source of strength, 47–48
  and spiritual growth, 227
Lovesac, 8–10
loyalty, 221

Ma, Jack, 155
MacDonald, Alan, 173
Mackey, Bill, 172–73
Manbeck, Keith, 167
Marcus Aurelius, 206
Market Mover (Greifeld), 112
market-oriented enterprises, 15–16
market transitions, 113
Marriott, 33
Master Coach, The (Thompson), 171
mastermind groups, 205
Maxwell, John, xv
McCartney, Paul, 22–23
McCloskey, Deirdre, 101, 102, 148
McCobin, Alexander, 82
McDonough, William, 9
McIntosh, Steve, xvi
McKinsey and Co., 146
meaningful work, value of, 168
meditation, 193–96
memory, 186
Mendiola, Ramón, 53–57, 69–70
mental energy, 186
mentorship
  for leadership development, 209
  programs for, 172–73
Merzenich, Michael, 208
metaphors for business, 26–33
Microsoft, 54, 118, 122, 144
millennial generation, 124
mindfulness
  of leaders of teams, 166
  of organization's purpose, 20
  and practicing compassion, 45–46
Mindset (Dweck), 10
mistakes, making, 168
modeling leadership, 106–7
Moment on Earth, A (Easterbrook), 149
Moore, Gordon, 115, 138
Moore's law, 138
Morrison, Denise, 173
motivation, role of purpose in, 15
Motley Fool, 115, 165, 170
movement, critical importance of, 192–93
Muir, John, 5, 199
Mulally, Alan, 59–60
multiple intelligence theory, 218–19
Munger, Charlie, 98, 207, 219
Murphy, Michael, 213–14, 215, 220
Musk, Elon, 104, 155
mutual-benefit mindset, 88–90
mutual improvement club of Franklin, 204, 205
Myers-Briggs Type Indicator, 178

Napoleon III, Emperor, 148
NASA, 21
Nasdaq, 112
National Public Radio (NPR), 18
nature, recharging in, 199
Nature Fix, The (Williams), 199
NBA basketball, evolution of playing styles in, 110
negative perceptions of business
  Conscious Capitalism's refutation of, 12
  of greed of businesspeople, 22
  and higher purpose of organizations, 22
  and short-term approach of businesses, 135
  and win-lose paradigm, 84
negativity, releasing, 186, 187–88
Nelson, Shawn David, 8–10
Nestlé, 173
Netflix, 118, 143
neuroplasticity, 208
Nike, 7, 18
ninety-minute work cycles, 185, 186
Nisargadatta, Maharaj, 196
nonprofit organizations
  and balance of pragmatism with idealism, 18
  and market-oriented approach, 17
Nordstrom, 35
nourishment, 190–92
Noyce, Robert, 115

Oblisk, Sonya Gafsi, 167
One Minute Manager (Blanchard), 43
open-mindedness, 208–9
optimism, 148–49
ordinary work, generating higher purpose from, 21
organizational design, 116–19
overreactions, 75

Page, Larry, 155
Panera, 131–33, 134
Papanek, Victor, 9
Paris, France, 105
Parlee, Bert, 23
Patagonia, 5
Patnaik, Dev, 142
Patterson, Tom, 201
Patton (film), 27
peer support groups, 205, 218
PepsiCo, 127
Perez, Carlota, 113
performance reviews, 169–70
personal computers, 144–45
personal growth. *See* growing and learning continuously
personality types, 177–79
personnel decisions, 157–60. *See also* teams and work environment
PETA, 122
Phipps, Carter, xvi
Phoenix Suns, 110
phones
  average time spent on, 200
  and digital fasting, 199–201
  exponential market growth in, 146
  iPhones, 113, 144
  platforms for, 145
physical energy, 186
physical exercise, importance of, 192–93
platforms, 143–45
Plato, 177
Play Bigger (Ramadan, Peterson, Lochhead, and Maney), 109
point of view of organizations, 109–10
polarity theory, 22–24
political polarization, 90–91
Pollan, Michael, 192
positive energy, 187
positive/positive polarity, 23
postmodern values, 223–24
poverty
  falling rates of, 84, 101–2
  and Mendiola's FIFCO, 69–70
  and negative perceptions of business, 84
pragmatism, balancing idealism with, 15–20
pre-mortems, conducting, 134
Price, Dick, 214
productivity patterns, ninety-minute increments in, 185
professional development, supporting, 169
profits
  purpose powered by, 11–15
  and value creation, 102–3
purpose, 3–24
  and balancing pragmatism with idealism, 15–20
  and businesses as agents of change, 17
  championing of, 13, 17
  communicating/demonstrating, 20
  connecting people to, 4–5
  determining the best expression of, 7
  discerning the higher purpose of an organization, 12–13
  as gradual/lifelong practice, 10
  and heros, 10–11
  and intrinsic good, 13–14
  maintaining mindfulness of, 20
  and negotiating the challenge/support polarity, 165
  and Nelson's Lovesac, 8–10
  of ordinary work, 21
  and personal growth, 215
  and polarity theory, 22–24
  profits powered by, 11–15
  revelation of, 5–8
  and spiritual energy, 187
  as a spiritual path, 226–27
  and stakeholder participation, 21–22
  and value creation, 13, 14, 15, 18, 32
Purpose Institute, 6

questioning, work cultures that support, 168

Radjou, Navi, 212
Ram Dass, 220
Range: Why Generalists Triumph in a Specialized World (Epstein), 210
Rauch, Doug, 108
reading, 207
realism, market, 18–20
reciprocal altruism, 84
REI, 13–14
respect, mutual, 85
rest, 182–83, 184, 185
reviews, 169–70
revitalization, 181–201
  role of digital fasting in, 199–201
  role of energy management in, 183–87
  role of grounding activities in, 198
  role of hobbies in, 197–98
  role of meditation in, 193–96
  role of nature in, 199
  role of nourishment in, 190–92
  role of rest in, 182–83, 184, 185
  role of sleep in, 188–90
  role of vacations in, 196–97
Reykjavik University, 128
ridesharing apps, 145
Ries, Eric, 133
risk taking, work cultures that support, 168
Ritz-Carlton, 34
Robb, Walter, 167, 198
Robertson, Brian, 118
Rock, Arthur, 114–15
Romantic poets of nineteenth century England, 105
Rosling, Hans, 104
Rosner, Cheryl, 87–88

Safer Way grocery store, 16
safety, psychological, 168–69
Saint Exupéry, Antoine de, 21
Salesforce, 109
Sanchez, Gisela, 53–54
Sanders, Henry Russell, 29
San Francisco, California, 110–11, 114
"scenius" term, 105
Schmidt, Eric, 111
Schwartz, Tony, 183–87

Schweitzer, Albert, 226
screen time, 200. *See also* phones
Seattle Seahawks, 193
secrecy, 61
self-driving cars, 141–42, 150
self improvement. *See* growing and learning continuously
self-knowledge/reflection
and emotional intelligence, 220, 221–22
and good judgement, 147
and humility, 147
importance of, in leaders, 62–63, 167
and shadow work, 62, 74–76
self-righteousness, 74
Senge, Peter, 34, 99, 224
September 11, 2001, terrorist attacks, 87
service
leadership as journey of, xv–xvi
as path to happiness, 226
servant leadership, 33–37, 39
7 Habits of Highly Effective People (Covey), 85
shadow work, 62, 74–76
Shaich, Ron, 131–33, 134, 176
shareholder activists, 98, 131, 133
Shark Tank (television series), 28
shark-tank business metaphor, 28
short-term thinking
and Iceland's boom-and-bust, 128–30
and investors' expectations, 130–31
and JANA Partners' campaign against Whole Foods, 81
shoshin (beginner's mind), 208–9
Sierra Club, 5
Silicon Valley, 105
Simmons, Russell, 193
simplicity/complexity polarity, 23
Sinek, Simon, 135
Sisodia, Raj, xiv
Sixteen Personality Factors (16PF), 179
sleep, value of, 188–90
Smedes, Lewis B., 46
social impacts, 54–56
social intelligence, 222–23
social justice, 223
Southwest Airlines, 33, 35, 165
Speigleberg, Frederic, 213–14
Spence, Roy, 6
spiritual energy, 187
spiritual growth, 224–27
sports metaphors for business, 28–30
Stagen, Rand, 171, 173–74
Stagen Leadership Academy, 171, 216
stakeholders
and B Corps, 133
and community model of business, 32
integration of, 51–52
participation of, 21–22
and purpose of corporations, xiv
two groups of, 51–52
and value creation, 122–23
and win-win-win thinking, 83
Starbucks, 33, 132, 223
Stern, Robin, 221
Street, John, 108–9
strength, love as source of, 47–48
stress, 182
structure/flexibility polarity, 23
subject-object relationship, 216–17
succession planning, 136
Sud, Jim, 167
Superforecasting (Tetlock), 147
sustainability, 223
systems thinking, 99–100

Team of Rivals (Goodwin), 11
teams and work environment, 155–79
chemistry of, 156
and coaching culture, 171–72
and community building, 176–77
and compensation, 160–61
cultivating environment of safety and trust in, 168–69
and happiness of team members, 165
and hiring considerations, 161–63
and hiring internal vs. external candidates, 157–59
and leadership training opportunities, 157
and leading by example, 166–67
and mentorship programs, 172–73
mindfulness of leaders of, 166
negotiating the challenge/support polarity in, 164–65
and personality types, 177–79
and providing clear goals/feedback, 169–71
and public recognition of leaders, 155–56
and self-awareness of leaders, 167
and terminating employees, 176
underperformers on, 169–70, 173–76, 176n
technology
addiction to, 201
and Amara's law, 150–51
convergence of, 143–45
and digital fasting, 199–201
exponential growth in, 139, 148–49
Hype Cycle in, 150–51
and Moore's law, 138
opportunities provided by, 148–49
See also phones
TED, 18
Teilhard de Chardin, Pierre, 144
terminating employees, 176
Tesla, 18
Tetlock, Philip, 147
Think Week of Bill Gates, 197–98
Thinx, 124
Thompson, Gregg, 171–72
3Com, 122
360 reviews, 169–70
tit-for-tat strategies, 86
Tómasdóttir, Halla, 127–30
town halls, 67
Trader Joe's, 34, 108
training, investing in, 159
transcendentalists, 206
transparency
and authenticity, 61
role of, in win-win-win mindset, 86
standard for, 59
and trustworthiness, 67
in wages, 161

transportation industry, 145
travel industry, 87–88
Trillion Dollar Coach (Schmidt, Rosenberg, and Eagle), 171
triple bottom line framework, 11–12, 53–54
Truman, Harry, 207
trust
  dynamics of, 85–86
  and emotional intelligence, 221
  and integrity, 66–68
Turner, Fred, 105
Tushy, 124
Twain, Mark, 147
Tyson, Mike, 146

underperformers, managing, 169–70, 173–76, 176n
Unilever, 18
Upcycle: Beyond Sustainability—Designing for Abundance, The (McDonough and Braungart), 9
urban environments, 110

vacations, 196–97
vacuums in leadership, xii
value creation
  and benefiting people, 14
  discerning intrinsic good at heart of, 13–14
  and innovation, 102–3, 121–23
  and long-term thinking, 129–30
  and profits, 102–3
  and purpose of organizations, 13, 14, 15, 32
  purpose statements reflecting, 18
value systems, 223–24
Varieties of Meditative Experience, The (Goleman), 220
videotaping, coaching with, 216–18
Vipassana, 195
vulnerability, work cultures that support, 168

Walker, Matthew, 189
Walsh, Roger, 79
war metaphor for business, 26–27, 33
wealth, 101, 102
Weiner, Jeff, 193
Welch, Jack, 113
Where Good Ideas Come From (Johnson), 125, 197
whistleblowers, 68
Whitman, Meg, 155
Whole Foods
  and Amazon, 42, 72, 81, 92–99
  and animal rights activists, 70–74
  annual sales of, xiv
  closure of poorly performing stores, 88–89
  competition encouraged in, 107
  competitors of, 108
  and cultural fit in hiring decisions, 163
  Dixon's career path in, 174–75
  and expressions of appreciation, 25, 41–43
  hiring practices at, 159
  incentivizing healthy behaviors at, 190
  innovation of, 103
  intrinsic good behind value proposition of, 13
  JANA Partners' campaign against, 79–81, 93, 97, 131
  leadership development in, 171
  long-term focus of, 131
  and Mackey's passion for food, 5
  Mackey's role as CEO at, ix–xiv
  and Mackey's strengths/weaknesses, 167
  market-oriented approach of, 15–16
  and organizational design, 117–18
  origins of, 15–16
  and perception of potential market, 114
  point of view of, 109
  purpose statement of, 18
WholePeople.com, x–xi, 144
Whole Planet Foundation, 98
Why We Sleep (Walker), 189
Wilber, Ken, 216
Wilke, Jeff, 63–65
Williams, Florence, 199
win-lose paradigm
  and JANA Partners, 93
  and metaphors for business, 29
  and negative perceptions of business, 135
  as prevalent mindset, 32, 84, 91
  and self-sacrifice, 85
  and zero-sum mentality, 89–90
win-win paradigm, 82–83
win-win-win, 79–100
  and Civil Rights Movement, 91–92
  communication's role in, 86
  as ethical strategy, 83–84
  and game metaphors, 29
  and Hotels.com launch, 87–88
  as job of leadership to create, 32
  and mutual-benefit mindset, 88–90
  and power of intention, 94–95
  stakeholders as beneficiaries of, 83
  and systems thinking, 99–100
  and trust, 85–86
  and Whole Foods' merger with Amazon, 79–81, 92–99
wisdom, 210, 211–12
Wojcicki, Anne, 155
workaholics, 189–90
work environment. *See* teams and work environment
Wozniak, Steve, 115

Xerox PARC, 121
X Prize Foundation, 108

youth, idolization of, 212

Zappos
  and balance of pragmatism with idealism, 19
  customer-centric ethic at, 34
  and organizational design, 118
  purpose statement of, 18
zero-sum mentality, 89–90
Zuckerberg, Mark, 155